Masters of the Sabar

In the series **African Soundscapes**

edited by Gregory Barz

Masters of the Sabar

Wolof Griot Percussionists of Senegal

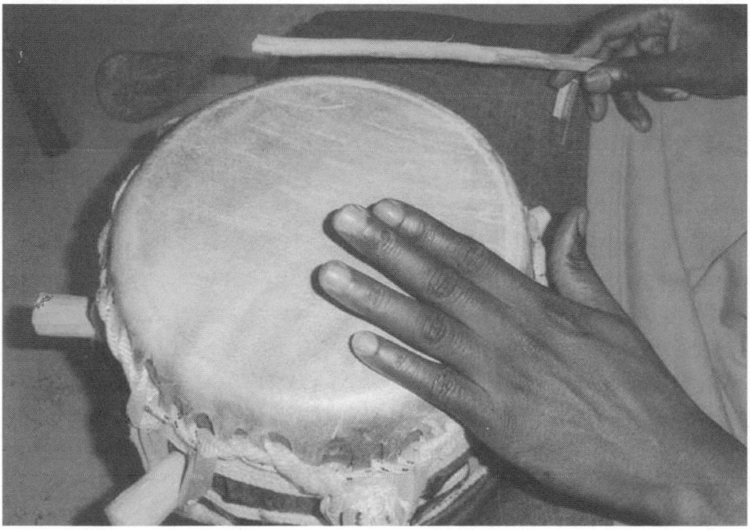

Patricia Tang

TEMPLE UNIVERSITY PRESS
Philadelphia

In memory of Serigne Cheikh Oumy Mbacké

For my parents, with love

Temple University Press
1601 North Broad Street
Philadelphia PA 19122
www.temple.edu/tempress

Published 2007
Printed in the United States of America

♾ The paper used in this publication meets the requirements of the American National Standard for Information Sciences—Permanence of Paper for Printed Library Materials, ANSI Z39.48-1992

Library of Congress Cataloging-in-Publication Data

Tang, Patricia, 1972–
Masters of the sabar : Wolof griot percussionists of Senegal / Patricia Tang.
p. cm. — (African soundscapes)
Includes bibliographical references (p.), discography (p.), and index.
ISBN-13: 978-1-59213-419-9 ISBN-10: 1-59213-419-X (cloth : alk. paper)
ISBN-13: 978-1-59213-420-5 ISBN-10: 1-59213-420-3 (pbk. : alk. paper)
1. Wolof (African people)—Senegal—Music—History and criticism. 2. Wolof (African people)—Senegal—Social life and customs. 3. Percussion ensembles—Senegal—History and criticism. 4. Music—Social aspects—Senegal. 5. Griots—Senegal. I. Title.
ML3760.T365 2007
786.9'1629632140663—dc22 2006020196

2 4 6 8 9 7 5 3 1

Contents

Illustrations and Musical Transcriptions

Contents of Accompanying Audio Compact Disc

All tracks (except tracks 22 and 25) were performed by Lamine Touré and recorded by Notable Productions (notable.com) in 2006. Track 22 was performed by Karim Mbaye and Group Rimbax in Dakar on February 22, 1998 (field recording by Patricia Tang), and track 25 was performed by Thio Mbaye and Group Rimbax in Dakar on April 10, 1998 (field recording by Patricia Tang).

Guide to Pronunciation and Orthography

I FOLLOW THE WOLOF ORTHOGRAPHY used in Munro (1997). The Wolof alphabet most often includes the following letters and letter combinations: *a, aa, à, b, c, d, e, ee, é, éé, ë, f, g, i, ii, j, k, l, m, mb, n, nd, ng, nj, ñ, o, oo, ó, óó, p, q, r, s, t, u, uu, w, x, y.*

The double consonant sounds (*mb, nd, ng, nj*) should be pronounced as such, without adding a vowel at the beginning of the word. For example, "Mbaye" should NOT be pronounced "Em-baye."

Some Wolof words that have been written in French have retained their French spellings. For example, the nightclub named "Thiossane" (pronounced cho-saan) will be spelled as such, instead of as "cosaan." Likewise, many Senegalese names retain their French spellings; for example, "Diop" is spelled as such, instead of as "Joop." In general, the spelling "Thi" followed by a vowel should be pronounced like a hard "ch," and "Di" followed by a vowel should be pronounced as "J."

Some common pronunciations include the following:

c (*ceebu jën*)	as in the "ch" in cheese
é (*géwël*)	as in the "e" in get
ë (*géwël*)	as in the "u" in hull"
x (*xorom*)	as in the "h" in horrible

Because Wolof orthography has yet to be standardized, I have generally chosen spellings most commonly used.

Acknowledgments

THIS BOOK WOULD not have been possible without the generous support I have received from family, friends, teachers, colleagues, and institutions throughout the research and writing process. I am deeply grateful to all for their encouragement, inspiration, and support.

I would like to thank Martin Obeng for introducing me to African drumming during my undergraduate years at Brown University. I thank all of my teachers at Brown University including Carol Babiracki, who fostered my initial interest in ethnomusicology, and then remained a mentor throughout my graduate years. I also studied with Michelle Kisliuk; she and Gregory Barz, Tim Cooley, Katherine Hagedorn, Sue Hurley-Glowa and Kathy McKinley all helped inspire me to continue my studies in ethnomusicology. I also thank David Locke, Godwin Agbeli, and members of the Agbekor Society for supporting my continued interest in African drumming after I left Brown.

I owe special thanks to Kay Shelemay who has been and always will be an extraordinary advisor, mentor and friend; her critical eye, patience and encouragement saw the initial manuscript through from start to finish. I also thank Emmanuel Akyeampong, Carol Babiracki, David Locke, Kofi Agawu, Beverley Diamond, J. Lorand Matory, Eric Charry, Matthew Lavoie, and Sarah Morelli for their helpful comments on the manuscript at various stages. I am deeply grateful to Gregory Barz and Leigh Swigart for their detailed comments on my initial manuscript, which led to substantial revisions. This book's strengths are largely due to these people's keen observations and criticisms; its weaknesses are solely my responsibility. I thank Will Hammell and Janet Francendese, who helped this project come into full fruition.

Research in Senegal was made possible by several Harvard University fellowships; a Whiting Fellowship supported the writing of my initial manuscript, and grants from the Dean's Fund at the Massachusetts Institute of Technology helped to support follow-up research in Senegal as well as book production costs.

I am grateful to my Wolof instructors, Michael Gomez and Fallou Gueye, and also to Abdoulaye Sall, for being my first Senegalese contact and whose family and friends hosted me during my initial trip to Senegal in 1996.

In Senegal, there are countless people who showed me teranga (hospitality) during my various stays, and I am grateful to all. It would be impossible to name all those in Senegal who have contributed to this book in some way. But of these people, I especially thank Papa Abdou Diop, my big brother, dear friend, and invaluable research assistant all in one. I am truly indebted to Abdou for teaching me how to live independently and thrive in Dakar. I am also grateful to Alioune Mbaye Nder et le Setsima Group, Mamadou Konté and the staff at Africa Fête, Ousmane Sène and the staff at WARC/CROA, and Serigne Cheikh Oumy Mbacké. I have shared my time in Senegal with fellow researchers and friends from the US, including Ben Herson, Timothy Mangin, Erin Augis, Ellen Foley, Jessica Morales-Libove, Robert Bellinger, Leo Villalón, Fiona McLaughlin, Leigh Swigart, and George Joseph. And, of course, my deepest gratitude goes to the Mbaye family, especially Lamine Touré, for so generously sharing with me their knowledge and love of the sabar tradition.

Back at home, the support of many dear friends has been instrumental in helping me through this endeavor. In particular, I would like to thank Sarah Morelli, Gail Barrington, and Maggie Moebius. Thanks also go to Jeff Yemin, Lara Pellegrinelli, Noriko Toda, David Kaminsky, Raúl Romero, Stephanie Treloar, Roe-Min Kok, Laura D'Onofrio, and Lahat Gueye. I owe special thanks to Eric Sommers and the Sommers family for their love and support. I am also grateful to my colleagues at MIT, including Ellen Harris, George Ruckert, Evan Ziporyn, Brian Robison, and Charles Shadle. I also thank Kristin Blank, Clarise Snyder, John Lyons, and Priscilla Cobb for their help and support.

I owe many thanks to Michael Lewis for his unfailing patience in assisting me with musical transcriptions; thanks also go to Marc Gidal, Sarah Morelli, and Aaron Girard for research assistance, and to Anna Bershteyn for editorial assistance. I thank Dan Cantor of Notable Productions and Ouzin Ndoye of Studio 2000 for production help for the accompanying CD on both sides of the ocean.

I have learned so much from the members of Rimbax International, my first sabar drum ensemble at Harvard, and the members of Rambax MIT, the ensemble I now codirect with Lamine Touré. These students challenge me to think about sabar in new ways. I thank all past and present Rambaxers for their support, and especially thank Susan Martonosi, Sasha Devore, Mélissa Edoh, Kimani Lumsden, Michael Lewis, and Akili Jamal Haynes. I also thank the members of Group Saloum who are a musical inspiration to me, and share my love of Senegalese music.

Finally, I express my deepest thanks to my family—Shirley Tang, Ting-wei Tang, Steven Tang, Joanne Tang, Rachael Tang, and Heather Tang—whose love and support for everything I do extends far beyond this book.

Introduction

GRIOTS ARE BEST KNOWN as artisans of the spoken word. Serving as oral historians, genealogists, storytellers, and praise-singers, griots have played a significant role in cultures throughout West Africa for over seven centuries. This study examines the role of Wolof griots in contemporary Senegalese culture. Unlike griots from other ethnic groups who are known for their verbal artistry, Wolof griots (*géwël*) are unique in that they are masters of the sabar drum. In Senegal, sabar drumming appears in everyday events ranging from life cycle ceremonies to sporting events, political meetings, and the popular music scene.

A closely guarded tradition, sabar drumming has been passed down for centuries from one generation of *géwël* family percussionists to the next. Traditionally, rhythmic phrases (or *bàkks*) played on the sabar were derived from spoken word, allowing the drums themselves to "speak" through rhythmic representations of verbal utterances. In recent times, there has been a shift toward creating new *bàkks* that are no longer based on spoken word but are rhythmically more complex, highlighting the virtuosity and musical skill of the percussionist. This development suggests that Wolof griots should not be seen as verbal artists but rather as percussionists, for it is their skill as drummers that has allowed them to perpetuate and enhance their role in Senegalese society.

This book focuses on several generations of percussionists within one *géwël* family, the Mbaye family. By examining their changing musical repertories, performance contexts, and creative processes, I explore the way *géwël* percussionists have used the sabar drum to adapt to changing social realities. Through the sabar drums and the rhythms associated with them, the hereditary knowledge of Wolof *géwël* is largely responsible for the continued empowerment of griots in Senegal and beyond.

The griot phenomenon is found in many societies throughout West Africa. Written descriptions of griots date back to 1352, when the North African traveler Ibn Battuta described his encounters with griots at the court of Mali. In the times of ancient empires, griots served as attendants to kings and nobility. Vital to the royal courts, the griots were often considered the kings' closest advisors, responsible for knowing the genealogies and histories of their wealthy and powerful patrons. Through their music and praise-singing, the griots both perpetuated the history and upheld the status of the kings and nobles who, in turn, generously compensated the griots for their services.

Seven centuries later, griots continue to play an important role in West African cultures. The amount of recent literature on griots is impressive, though the majority is written from anthropological or historical points of view, emphasizing the verbal texts of epics recounted by griots, such as the famous epic of Sundiata Keita, ruler of the Mali Empire.

Within the field of ethnomusicology, the most notable research on griots is that of Roderic Knight and Eric Charry. Knight (1973) was the first to carry out extensive musical research on a griot tradition in his pioneering study of Mandinka griots, or *jaliya*, and their instrument, the *kora* (a twenty-one-stringed bridged harp-lute). More recently, Charry (2000) has written a broader, comprehensive study on Mande music as a whole. In both works the griot is portrayed as singer and player of the *kora*, *balafon, koni*, and guitar. The *kora* in particular serves as the instrumental icon and symbol of griots to those outside of Africa, in part due to its increased exposure and growing popularity in the West.

Because little research has been done on the musical traditions of non-Mande griots, what is known about the Mande is often assumed to be true of other ethnic groups, at times resulting in false generalizations. This is especially inaccurate in the case of drummers, who in Mande culture, are not of griot origin. Because Mande griots are not drummers and Mande drummers are not griots, there is a widespread notion that the phrase "griot percussionist" is an oxymoron. This study seeks to correct this misconception by examining a group that plays a vital role in Senegalese music and culture today: Wolof griot percussionists, masters of the sabar drum. In contrast to the Mande, the Wolof ethnic group includes percussionists who are exclusively of griot lineage, with the sabar as their primary instrument.

Before delving into the subject of Wolof griot percussionists, one must situate them geographically and historically within a Senegalese context, as well as examine the complexities of Wolof social structure. The Republic of Senegal is located on the westernmost tip of the African continent (see Figure I.1). It is bordered on the north by Mauritania, on the east by Mali, on the south by Guinea and Guinea-Bissau, and on the west by the northern Atlantic Ocean. Senegal all but surrounds The Gambia, with the exception of The Gambia's western coastline. With a total land area of 76,000 miles, Senegal is just slightly smaller than South Dakota. The country can be described as having four distinct ecological regions: a maritime zone, along the coast from Dakar to Saint

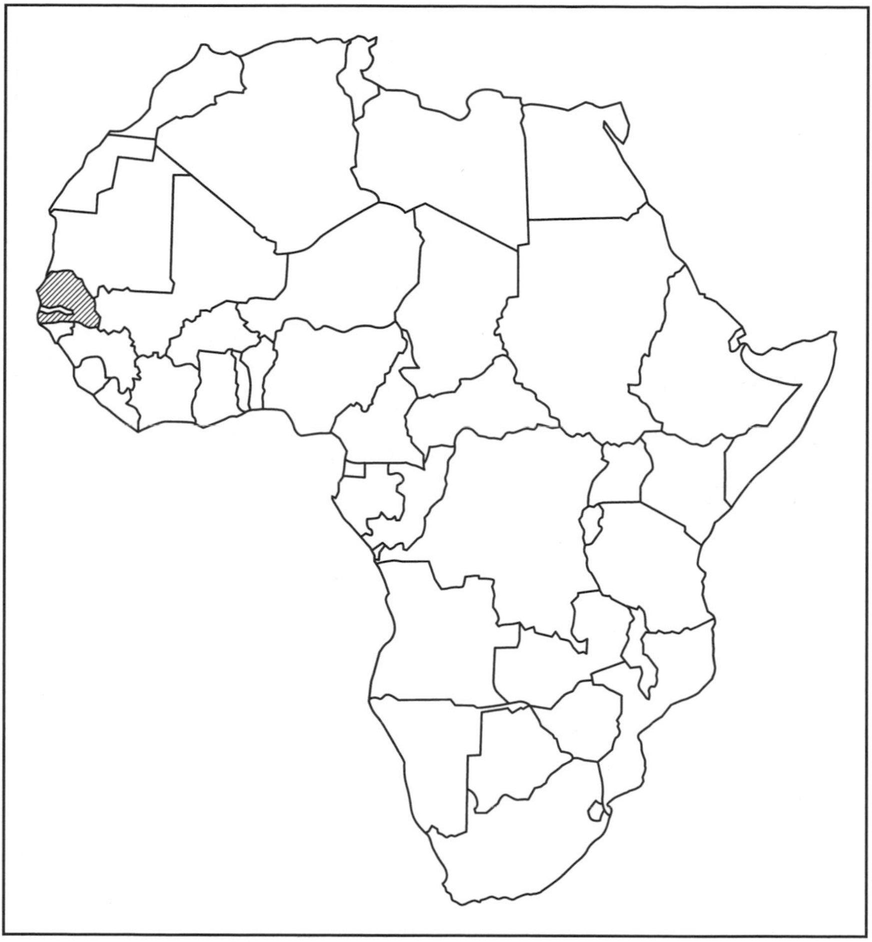

FIGURE I.1. Map of Africa

Louis; a mangrove region from the Petit Côte to the Saloum estuary; the Sahelian savannah or peanut zone; and finally, the semidesert region to the east (Leymarie 1978, 36). Senegal's terrain consists of mostly low, rolling plains, rising to foothills in the southeast. The climate is generally tropical and hot, but varies from the coast to inland, with increased heat and humidity away from the coast. The rainy season lasts from July through October, followed by a dry season marked by a dusty harmattan wind, with hot days and cooler nights.

Much of Senegalese history has resulted from the country's unique geographic position (see Figure I.2). Due to its proximity to North Africa, Senegal was involved in the trans-Saharan trade and was exposed to Islam as early as the first millennium. Its position on the Atlantic made it one of the first West

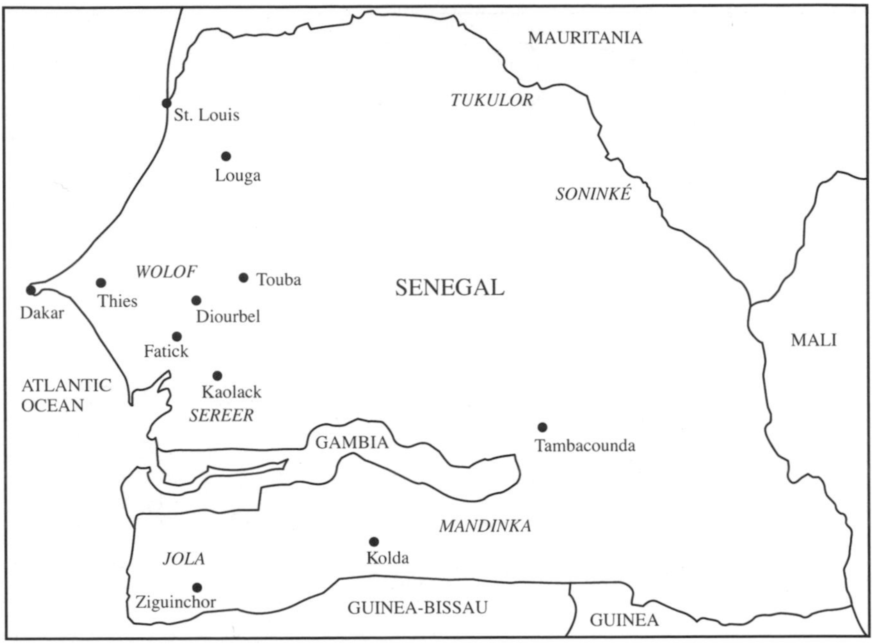

FIGURE I.2. Map of Senegal (with cities and major ethnic groups)

African areas to develop contact with Europe, as it soon became a major outpost of the slave trade. Dakar, its capital, remains a perfect example of the result of these various influences, boasting traditional Wolof culture, strong Islamic influences, and, of course, remnants of the French colonial period.

There are two common explanations for the origin of the name "Senegal." The first is that it comes from the term "*Zenaga*," referring to a Berber people who occupied the northern Senegambian region in ancient times. The second, more popular explanation is that it comes from the Wolof, "*suñu gal,*" which means "our pirogue," in reference to the numerous fishing boats used by the Wolof people when the Europeans first encountered them.

The population of Senegal is just over 11 million (July 2005 est.), with nearly half the population aged fourteen and under. Over one million people reside in Dakar (Dec. 2004 est.), the capital. The primary industries of Senegal are now agriculture (peanuts), fishing, chemicals (such as phosphates), and tourism. Peanuts have long been the most important agricultural product in Senegal, with millet a close second. Rice and fish are the primary diet on the coastal areas, whereas millet is more common inland.

Precolonial Senegal consisted of chiefdoms patterned on the Sudanic state model, in which a dominant ruling lineage established its hegemony over others through conquest (Gellar 1995, 2). One of Senegal's earliest precolonial states was the kingdom of Tekrur at the end of the first millennium. During the thirteenth century, Tekrur became part of the Mali Empire. Meanwhile, to the west, Njaajaan Njaay formed the Jolof Empire, which remained strong through the sixteenth century.

The first Europeans to come in contact with the Senegambia region were the Portuguese, who arrived in 1444. They would fuel the Atlantic slave trade over the next few centuries, increasing European contact. Following the Portuguese came the Dutch, British, and finally the French. By the eighteenth century, the English and French had essentially pushed out the Portuguese and Dutch, the English establishing themselves along the Gambia River and the French along the Senegal River area. Senegal's key position in the Atlantic slave trade intensified through the seventeenth and eighteenth centuries. Senegal served as a point of exportation, with Gorée Island as a holding pen for slaves from throughout West and Central Africa awaiting shipment to the New World.[1]

During the nineteenth century, slave trade was officially abolished. Gum arabic became the major trade item, but was soon surpassed by the peanut trade, which rose in the mid 1800s and remains the most important export to this day.

The French colonial conquest of the Senegambian region began around 1850. Initially, numerous traditional leaders fought against the French, including religious leader El-Hadji Omar Tall and other traditional leaders such as Lat Dior of Kayor and and Alboury Ndiaye of Jolof. By the turn of the century, the French had established a colonial government. With many traditional and religious leaders killed or deported, the Senegalese turned to the leaders of the two most influential Senegalese brotherhoods: Cheikh Amadou Bamba, founder of the Mouridiya brotherhood, and Malik Sy, of the Tijaniya brotherhood. These religious leaders held considerable political and economic power, controlling the groundnut economy. This, combined with their anticolonial sentiment, gained them an enormous following, thus strengthening the role of Islam in the country.

Dakar (and at one point, Saint Louis) was the capital of French West Africa, giving Senegal supreme status over France's other West African colonies. Senegal was also the only colony where the French applied assimilationist ideals, granting those born in the *communes* of Dakar, Gorée, Rufisque, and Saint Louis full French citizenship rights in Senegal, with greater political and educational privileges than those who were not born in these particular communes.[2]

Senegal gained its independence in 1960, with the famous poet Léopold Sédar Senghor as its first president. Senghor was succeeded by Abdou Diouf in 1980. Although Senegal has a multiparty democracy, the country had been ruled by the PS (Parti Socialiste) since independence. In 2000, however, political rival Abdoulaye Wade of the PDS (Parti Démocratique Sénégalais) was voted into power, thus ending forty years of one-party rule and beginning a new era for Senegal. This monumental change in power has been heralded worldwide as an example of fair and peaceful elections, now all too rare in Africa.

Since independence, Senegal has shown great support for the arts and expressive culture. Following the lead of other West African countries, President Senghor (who as a poet had a natural affinity for the arts) formed a national ballet. Based at the Daniel Sorano National Theater, the ballet became just one of many government-supported musical, dramatic and dance ensembles, all active to this day. At the turn of the twenty-first century, the National Ballet of Senegal remains one of the best-known African dance companies and tours internationally with great success. This governmental support is indicative of a broader Senegalese sentiment that recognizes and celebrates music and the arts, not only as an integral part of the culture, but also as one of the country's greatest assets. Likewise, the continued proliferation of Wolof griot percussionists stems from this public recognition of the importance of music in Senegalese culture.

The Wolof are the dominant ethnic group in Senegal, constituting 43.3 percent of the country's population (July 1999 est.).[3] Other major ethnic groups in Senegal include the Peul, Serer, Soninke, Diola, Mandinka, and Lebou. The Wolof language is spoken and understood by nearly 80 percent of the population, making it the lingua franca of Senegal.[4] About 1 percent of the Senegalese population is of European or Lebanese origin; these people reside primarily in urban areas such as Dakar, where the Lebanese control a large number of downtown businesses, such as *butiks* (corner shops), supermarkets, electronics stores, and fabric stores.

The Wolof inhabit most of the northern, central, and coastal parts of Senegal, with highest concentrations in the cities of Dakar, Saint Louis, Thies and Rufisque. Specifically, the Wolof have occupied the Waalo, Kayor, Jolof, Baol, and Sine-Saloum regions. In this book, I will focus on people of Wolof origin based in urban areas, as my field research was primarily based in the capital city of Dakar from 1997 to 2005.

The origins of the Wolof and their neighboring ethnic groups are unknown. However, we do know what early civilizations were active in the area now inhabited by the Wolof. Tekrur was one of the oldest precolonial African states, founded near the Middle Senegal river valley during the first millennium. Tekrur flourished from the trans-Saharan trade between North and West Africa. When Tekrur's Toucouleur[5] ruler, War Jabi, converted to Islam in the eleventh century, Islamic influence began to spread through the area, precipitating the Almoravid movement. By the thirteenth century, Tekrur had become a vassal state to the powerful Mali Empire that had expanded from the east, led by Sundiata Keita and his Mandinka people.[6]

Around the same time, the Wolof people came together under the ruler Njaajaan Njaay, the legendary ruler of the Jolof Empire who united the Jolof, Waalo, Cayor and Baol kingdoms, eventually absorbing the Serer kingdoms of Sine and Saloum as well. The Jolof empire flourished through the fifteenth century until its decline and eventual collapse around 1550, when Jolof, Cayor, Baol, Waalo, Sine, and Saloum became separate independent states.

A legend surrounds the first Wolof leader, Njaajaan Njaay. It is said that some children from neighboring villages in Waalo were fishing in the river. When it came time to go home, the children began to quarrel over the fish they had caught. Suddenly, a man rose from the water, divided the fish between the children, and then disappeared back into the water. The children were so amazed that they went home and told their parents about this apparition. The villagers, wanting to see the water spirit again, told the children to feign another quarrel over the fish. Sure enough, the man came from the water again, but this time, the people took him captive and begged him to stay with them. When word of this mystical being reached the Serer ruler of Sine, he exclaimed, "Njaajaan Njaay [an expression of astonishment]!" and the man became known as Njaajaan Njaay thereafter. The ruler of Sine declared that this man of the water should become the ruler of all Wolof people. This is the origin of Njaajaan Njaay, the first Wolof ruler.[7]

Because of their prolonged contact with neighboring ethnic groups, the Wolof themselves can be seen as a hybrid ethnic group made up of multiple ethnicities. In fact, there is a common saying in Senegal that "there are no Wolof people; Wolof is just a language." In the introduction to his study on the Wolof of Senegambia (1967), David Gamble states up front, "It is not a simple matter to generalize about the Wolof. Their culture now spans an enormous range. . . . Neighboring peoples . . . have all had some influence on the culture of neighbouring Wolof areas. . . . The variability in Wolof culture means that almost every statement made about them needs to be accompanied by a label as to time and place" (1967, vii).[8]

Today, this hybridity is further enhanced in large urban areas such as Dakar, which attracts a diversity of people drawn to cities for employment opportunities. After residing in the city, many people from different ethnic origins end up speaking mostly Wolof, whereas they might have spoken another native language in their home villages. This "Wolofization" of the urban area further disguises the multitude of ethnic origins of Senegalese people. Thus, there are many people who consider themselves Wolof, but upon further inquiry, they will reveal that their ancestors are from different regions and ethnic groups.

The Wolof language belongs to the West Atlantic branch of the Niger-Kordofanian language family (Munro 1997, iii). Little is known about the origins of the Wolof language, although most scholars date it back to the thirteenth century, with the birth of the Jolof Empire under Njaajaan Njaay (Leymarie

1978, 44). Over time, Wolof has absorbed numerous words from Arabic, French, and even English. In urban areas such as Dakar, numerous foreign (though mostly French) words are interspersed throughout the Wolof vocabulary, creating a form of Wolof creole.[9] However, the Wolof of more rural areas remains closer to "*Wolofu piir*," or "pure/authentic Wolof."

French, the official language of Senegal, predominates in educational institutions, governance, international commerce, and most texts (such as street and store signs). Indeed, most Senegalese are unaccustomed to written Wolof, and only recently have Wolof publications (most notably comic strips) become more common.[10] The overwhelming majority of printed material in Senegal remains in French, from newspapers to literature. However, Wolof is the preferred spoken language, and in the streets of Dakar, it is the language one will hear the most often. Although those who have attended school are fluent in French, a large number of Senegalese do not know French very well, especially those of the older generation and those who reside outside of Dakar.[11] Radio and television broadcasts are in French or Wolof, with Wolof gaining increased airtime. RTS (Radio Télévision Sénégal), the national radio and television station, now airs the evening news in French, Wolof, and occasionally other local languages.

My subject area deals with Wolof griots in urban Senegal, namely Dakar. By "Wolof" I am distinguishing people who identify themselves as Wolof and consider Wolof their maternal language, even though they may have some ethnic intermixing in their ancestral family lines. However, "Wolof" will be considered distinct from those other neighboring ethnic groups such as Serer, Lebou, Peul, Soninke, Diola, and Mandinka.

Islam has been present in Senegal since as early as the tenth century, when it was introduced by North Africans during the trans-Saharan trade. However, it was primarily the *jihads* (Muslim holy wars) throughout the nineteenth century that firmly established Islam in Senegal. At the turn of the twentieth century, less than 50 percent of the Senegalese population adhered to the Islamic faith (Gellar 1995, 111); a century later, over 92 percent are Muslim.

In Senegal, a path of Sunni Islam called Sufism is practiced. The Senegalese worship mystical orders called Sufi brotherhoods (*tariqa*), headed by religious leaders or *marabouts*, who act as spiritual advisors and to whom adherence and veneration will lead to *Àjjana* (heaven/paradise). There are four main brotherhoods: Quadiriya, Layène, Tidjaniya, and Mouridiya, with the overwhelming majority being Mouride and Tidjan. The Quadiriya sect traces its origins to the eleventh century in Baghdad, though the modern Senegalese Quadiri brotherhood was founded by Abu Naam Kunta in Cayor around 1809 (Clark and Phillips 1994, 223). The Layènes are a small sect seated in Yoff (near Dakar), founded by Seydina Limamou Laye (1856–1919). The Senegalese branch of the Tidjani movement (originally founded in Morocco in the late eighteenth century) was led by El Hadji Omar Tall (c. 1795–1864), a Toucouleur religious leader from the Futa Toro region, who launched a series of holy wars in the 1850s. After Omar Tall, El Hadji Malick Sy (1855–1922) became the primary Tidjan leader, moving the seat to Tivaouane. Cheikh Amadou Bamba (1853–1927) founded the Mouridiya movement, an offshoot of Quadiriya. The Mourides have built the country's largest mosque at their religious center, Touba, where Bamba is now buried. Every year, hundreds of thousands of Mourides flock to Touba in a *magal* (pilgrimage) to celebrate Bamba's return from exile in Gabon in 1907. The Mourides are known for their enormous success at groundnut farming and commercial (trade, import, export) activities, and they have developed important political power as a result.[12] Finally, it is worth mentioning a subsect of the Mourides called the Baye Falls. The Baye Falls are followers of Cheikh Ibra Fall, who was a disciple of Amadou Bamba, and his closest compatriot. Baye Falls are exempt from the Muslim rules of praying and fasting, and instead they devote their lives to hard physical labor in the name of their religious leader, following the example of Cheikh Ibra Fall. They are also characterized by their dreadlocks, patchwork clothing, and affinity for smoking marijuana.[13]

Religious affiliations can follow certain ethnic divisions as well. For example, although 5 percent of the Senegalese population is Christian (of whom most are Catholic), few Christians are of Wolof origin. Rather, Senegalese Christians are primarily from the Serer and Diola ethnic groups, who were more receptive to missionary contact (in the mostly Serer Petit Côte region and the Diola Casamance). There are similar divides within the Sufi brotherhoods. For example, the Layène brotherhood consists almost exclusively of the Lebou people, with roots in the Cap Vert region. Both the Mouride and Tidjani brotherhoods are mostly Wolof, though the Mouride brotherhood in particular is considered a Wolof brotherhood, with roots in the Cayor, Jolof, and Baol regions.

Music plays a role in Senegal's diverse religious movements, both Christian and Muslim. For example, the monastery of Keur Moussa, fifty kilometers east of Dakar, has become a tourist attraction, with Sunday services that combine the melodious sounds of Gregorian chant with *kora*, *balafon* (West African xylophone), and drums.[14]

The large *tabala* drum, which originated in Mauritania, has become an important part of Wolof Quadiriya religious practice. Among the Mourides, the singing and chanting of the *khassayid* (religious verses written by Cheikh Amadou Bamba) is an activity of central importance to the faith. Within the Baye Fall subsect exist the vibrant *xiin* drums, which the Baye Falls play while walking the streets daily and begging for alms. And in popular music, the impact of Islam (especially Mouridism) is most evident in song lyrics praising Muslim leaders.[15] Indeed, the topic of music and Islam in Senegal is too broad to be properly addressed here, though it remains a rich topic that I hope will be pursued by future scholars. In the meanwhile, since the overwhelming majority of Wolof griots are Muslims, it is important to at least be aware of this religious context for the purposes of this study.

In the Wolof social hierarchy, there are three main levels: the *géer* ("uncasted" or nobles); the *jaam*, (slaves); and the *ñeeño* (endogamous "casted" groups).[16] The *ñeeño* are further divided into subgroups depending on occupation, and include the griots (*géwël*), woodworkers, leatherworkers, blacksmiths, and weavers.

Since the country's independence from France in 1960, the caste system in Senegal has been officially abolished. Nonetheless, caste still plays an important role in one's personal identity, choice of occupation, and marriage. Although some born griots take up other occupations, the *géwël* institution is very much alive in modern-day Senegal. Wolof griots' primary means of musical expression is through singing and drumming; however, similarly to the way the *kora* is a symbol of Mande *jaliya*, the sabar is the instrument par excellence of Wolof *géwël.*

Sabar

The sabar is a single-headed drum played with one hand and one stick. Carved from the trunk of a mahogany tree, the sabar has a goatskin head held in place by seven pegs. The drums themselves vary in height, size, and shape; each height has its own particular name, but they can be referred to both individually and collectively as "sabar." The sabar ensemble usually consists of six to twelve drummers playing numerous parts that come together to create complex polyrhythms. The accompaniment parts include the *mbalax* (basic accompaniment), *tulli*, and *talmbat* (two bass drum parts). These accompaniments create the fabric upon which the lead drummer solos and the rest of the ensemble plays rhythms and *bàkks*. Some *bàkks* are derived from a tradition of rhythmically declaimed spoken word, called *taasu*; other *bàkks* are purely musical compositions that emphasize rhythmic style and creativity. In all cases, the *bàkks* are precomposed musical phrases that signify a specific *géwël* family's identity.

Sabars are an integral part of life cycle ceremonies (baptisms, weddings, and circumcisions), Muslim holiday celebrations, political meetings, and wrestling matches. "*Sabar*"[17] is also the general term for a neighborhood dance event with live drumming. Sabar drumming is inextricably linked to dance, and the *sabar* dance event is the most ubiquitous form of entertainment in Senegal.

The 1970s saw the rise of mbalax, the Senegalese genre of popular music made famous by singer Youssou N'Dour.[18] Sabar drums quickly became an integral part of the mbalax band lineup, providing the rhythmic backbone for this distinctly Senegalese sound. The prominence of sabar in mbalax music thrust *géwël* percussionists into the national and international limelight, thus raising the status of griot percussionists to new heights.

This book draws upon two years of fieldwork in Senegal carried out over a period of nine years (an uninterrupted year 1997–1998, followed by shorter, subsequent trips in 1998–2005). My field research involved ethnographic interviews, participant-observation and documentation of musical events, and collection and analysis of audio, audiovisual, and printed source materials. I also undertook intensive hands-on study of sabar, learning to play through individual lessons, group lessons, and frequent observation of sabar events in Senegal. My involvement allowed me to learn drumming techniques and the musical repertory: both standard dance rhythms and *bàkks*, longer musical phrases created by members of the Mbaye family. The latter are of particular significance because they act as specific markers of the family's identity and creativity, both through representations of spoken word, and more recently through purely musical compositions.

Chapter 1 discusses the fieldwork process and explores the multiple identities that I assumed and that were ascribed to me by others. I describe my fieldwork methodology and relationship to the field at the outset in order to provide the reader with a context for the rest of the book. In Chapter 2, I address the history of the sabar drum, drawing from both written and oral sources, which indicate that the sabar likely dates back to the fourteenth century. I then discuss the sabar ensemble itself, the different drums in the ensemble, their physical makeup, and aesthetics of sound.

Chapter 3 discusses the complex issue of caste in Wolof social structure. After assessing recent scholarship on this subject, I suggest a new model for situating Wolof *géwël* within caste structures. After establishing Wolof *géwël* as more than caste, including lineage and community as well, I focus on one family as the primary unit of study in Chapter 4. The life histories of three generations of Wolof griot percussionists in the Mbaye family are presented: those of Macheikh Mbaye, Thio Mbaye, and Lamine Touré. By focusing on these three musicians, I show how the role of Wolof griots has changed over time and how popular music has greatly impacted the modern *géwël*, his occupational activities, and his status.

Chapter 5 covers the traditional sabar repertory. In this chapter, I introduce the concepts of *rythme* (short dance rhythm) and *bàkk* (longer musical phrase) and then provide detailed explanations and musical transcriptions of the standard dance repertory of *rythmes*, as well as examples from the Mbaye family repertory of *bàkks*. I highlight the history of the *bàkk,* from its original representation of spoken word to its current, more virtuosic purpose.

Chapter 6 examines the various contexts in which sabar is played. These contexts include neighborhood dance events, women's association gatherings, weddings, baptisms, political meetings, wrestling matches, Muslim holidays, and nightclubs. The sabar's role in each of these contexts is unique, and this chapter will explore its multiple meanings.

The final chapter examines the role of sabar in the Senegalese popular music genre, mbalax, from its birth in the 1970s to its current status in the global music scene at the turn of the century. As the rhythmic backbone of mbalax music, sabar has tied mbalax to its traditional Wolof roots while propelling it to the international pop music scene, with singers such as Youssou N'Dour at the forefront. The career of percussionist Lamine Touré and his role as percussionist with Nder et le Setsima Group will be examined in detail, looking at the importation of traditional Mbaye family *bàkks* in popular songs.

As the first complete study of sabar drumming and drummers, this book creates an important space for Wolof griots in a previously Mande-oriented field of scholarship. By examining the transmission of this drumming tradition, it not only looks at the *géwël* family as the center for production and reproduction of sabar knowledge, but also at how its historical traditions have influenced contemporary performance practice. As Wolof social structure and caste systems have had to adjust to a rapidly changing social and musical environment, *géwël* have managed to adapt and transform their music and identities to modern times and tastes. Through this case study of one *géwël* percussionist family, this book will explore the ways in which contemporary griots perpetuate and develop their art, showing the vitality of a centuries-old tradition that continues to enrich the modern soundscape.

1

You Will Be Griot in Another Way

THE ETHNOMUSICOLOGIST'S STORY

> Look . . . that's why I told you one day, at Monaco Beach, I said, you are griot—you, Patricia. You said, no! I am not griot; I'm a tubaab[1]! I said, you're griot! Because me, I was born into a griot family, so I am griot. But you will be griot in another way. Because . . . if you love the sabar, huh? You learn to play it, you know how to play it, you play like griots . . . you are griot! So now, Patricia, you are griot. Because you play sabar, and you know how to play. So, you're griot! Write it down. You are griot. Write it down and write that I told you you're griot because I have the right to tell you that you are griot.
>
> —Lamine Touré (4/29/98)

RECENT ETHNOMUSICOLOGICAL SCHOLARSHIP has recognized the merits of critically discussing fieldwork issues as well as incorporating these issues into ethnographic writing itself. As ethnomusicologists are both informed and shaped by their fieldwork, an immediate exposition of this experience will give the reader a more honest understanding of the rest of the information presented in this book. In a study that deals extensively with the subject's identity—Wolof identity, griot identity, and family identity—I believe that the researcher's identity should be demystified upfront.

Why Senegal?

My love of West African music began in 1991, when I joined the Ghanaian Drumming Ensemble at Brown University (led by master drummer Martin Obeng). This piqued my interest in ethnomusicology as a field of study, and after majoring in music at Brown, I decided to continue my studies in ethnomusicology in the Ph.D. program at Harvard.

Interested in West African music in general, I entered graduate school without a specific idea of what my dissertation topic would be. Because many scholars had worked in Ghana, I wanted to do fieldwork in a place less studied. As I began to research possibilities, I noticed a marked lack of American ethnomusicological scholarship on the music of Francophone West Africa. Having long been a fan of Senegalese popular music, and intrigued by what I had read about West African griot traditions, I went to Senegal in August 1996 for a month-long preliminary research trip. A Senegalese friend residing in Boston recommended his friend in Dakar to be my host. This man was Papa Abdou Diop, who would later become my invaluable research assistant and close friend. The Diop family showed me true Senegalese *teranga* (the Wolof term for 'hospitality', in which Senegalese take great pride) and helped me immensely in this month-long trip as I attempted to get a feel for Senegalese culture and music. During this time, I established initial contacts with several griot singers in the popular music scene, including the then up-and-coming mbalax sensation Alioune Mbaye Nder et le Setsima Group. When I returned to Senegal in September 1997 for my year-long stay, I was interested in mbalax as a popular music genre and wished to better understand the role of the traditional sabar drums in mbalax bands, so I decided to learn about sabar first-hand by taking lessons with one of the percussionists in Setsima Group. After a *soirée* in mid-October, my research assistant (Abdou Diop) approached one of the drummers, Lamine Touré, explained to him that I was here in Senegal to do research on griots, and asked if he would be interested in teaching me how to play sabar. Lamine agreed and told us to come see him at his house in HLM5—a big griot house near the corner of the police station—"Just ask anyone; you won't miss it."

We found Lamine and discussed the specifics. He explained that the famous percussionist Thio Mbaye was his uncle and that he came from an important family of griot percussionists, originally from Kaolack. We discussed the terms of our agreement (fees and a lesson schedule). That was the beginning of my quest to learn about sabar.

Going regularly to the house for drumming lessons, I established a close friendship with Lamine and others in the family. During our lessons, members of the extended family would stop by to listen and even to give some playing tips. The head of the household, Macheikh Mbaye, remained respectfully distant, though his face appeared in the window from time to time, nodding with approval at my progress.

As I spent an increasing amount of time at the house, eating meals there and lingering for afternoon tea (the primary social occasion in Senegalese culture), I gradually became more like a part of the family. As the family came to like, accept, and respect me, they aided me with my research. Along with my sabar lessons, I began interviewing family members, accompanying and videotaping the family sabar group in their various performance contexts, and generally learning what it was to be part of the family, "hanging out" in their household. Much of what I have learned about the family has come not from the formal interviews, but from informal discussions with various family members, during tea, or at other times.

As I got to know the family better, I became keenly aware of its rivalry with other families, as my friends would often critique the others' playing in various contexts. Although I was introduced to the famous drummer Doudou Ndiaye Rose early in my stay (he came to the baptism of one of the newborn babies in the family) and I had some initial contacts with members of the Faye family,[2] it was made clear to me that because I had already established a strong relationship with the Mbaye family, to pursue any sort of in-depth contact with a rival family would be unwise and perhaps even detrimental to my existing relationships. I was increasingly seen at public sabar events with the Mbaye family percussionists, filming and sometimes even drumming. Percussionists from other families knew of me as "Lamine Touré's student" or as part of "Thio Mbaye and company," and Thio would even say that I was an honorary member of Group Rimbax because I knew the repertory well and was capable of playing the parts.

By choosing to work with one family, I unwittingly closed off any serious possibility of working with the other two families. Given the importance of the Mbaye family in the sabar tradition, I feel satisfied with my decision. Moreover, the time constraints of my research would not have allowed me to work with many different people. My own sabar lessons, following Setsima Group around on weekends, interviewing family members, and keeping up with the family sabar group's weekly activities proved difficult as it was; to do so with another family in addition would have been impossible. The deep understanding that I gleaned could only have been achieved with the time and effort that I spent becoming a part of this family. In addition, my close relationship to the Mbayes led me to focus on the concept of family and to recognize the importance of family as a unit of study.

Learning Sabar

Géwël drummers learn to play sabar by growing up in a sabar environment. They are surrounded by the sounds of sabar from an early age, and eventually learn to play by observing their older siblings and other family members.

An ethnomusicologist from the United States, I obviously had not grown up in a "sabar environment" and in fact had no experience playing sabar before I arrived in Dakar in September 1997. (Although I had some background in Ghanaian Ewe drumming and Mande djembé drumming, the Wolof sabar tradition is very different.)

As I mentioned earlier, I undertook a year of intensive, formal lessons with Lamine Touré in order to learn how to play sabar. In addition to basic sabar-playing technique, we began to cover the entire sabar dance repertory of standard rhythms, as well as some *bàkk*s composed by members of the Mbaye family. Although I focused specifically on the *mbëng-mbëng* (a medium-sized sabar), Lamine often accompanied me on the *cól* (bass drum), so that I could hear how the different parts go together. In addition to acquiring the repertory, we worked on sound production as well as endurance.

For the first few months, my lessons took place at the family compound; as a result, other drummers would often stop by to listen and even give some advice. During the month of Ramadan (December–January 1997–98), we moved our lessons to a nearby beach (Monaco Plage), where we would have fewer interruptions from passers-by and likewise not bother the head of the household's afternoon naps. However, we would often bring one or two of Lamine's brothers or cousins to the beach, who would sometimes accompany us on another drum.

Our lessons occurred regularly, usually two to three times per week (but up to five times per week during the month of Ramadan, when Lamine had more free time) and were supposed to last one and one-half hours per lesson, though we often went overtime. I recorded key parts of our lessons and also wrote down transcriptions of vocal mnemonics of *rythmes* and *bàkk*s. Between lessons I listened to the tapes repeatedly and, with the aid of written transcriptions, tried to learn new material.

In February 1998, I began attending more and more sabar events, from rehearsals at Thio's house (for upcoming wrestling matches) to baptisms, wrestling matches, women's association meetings, *sabar*s, and *tànnibéers*. Whenever possible, I videotaped the events, but I attended many more sabar events than I videotaped. This repeated exposure was in a way similar to a *géwël*'s upbringing: I attended as many events as possible, observing carefully, sometimes tapping out rhythms on my lap, while occasionally being asked to fetch new drumsticks for the players. Eventually I was allowed to play occasionally at various events (though I am sure my abilities did not warrant such an opportunity by *géwël* standards—the fact that I was a *tubaab* had a lot more to do with it.)

Although my private lessons were necessary for gathering research materials and getting personal instruction, it was the repeated observation of sabar events that led me to a broader understanding of sabar playing, as I gained a first-hand taste of how a typical *géwël* would learn to play.

At the beginning of the year, Lamine Touré was always extremely encouraging during my private lessons, complimenting my playing and telling me how I was much better than other *tubaabs*. However, as I became a more serious player and improved (in my own eyes), he became more and more critical and less patient, at times insulting me. This was difficult for me to take at times and led to great frustration and tears on my part; however, this surface ill-treatment symbolized to me a greater respect, because he was no longer treating me as a *tubaab*, but as a family member. Lamine also became increasingly impatient when I would ask him to replay something to record on tape, or I would stop to write something down—he wanted me to learn by ear, as a *géwël* would—why use these Western aids?

One of the greatest insults, which I will never forget, occurred when once, exasperated with my playing, Lamine told me "you are playing like a *géer* (noble), not a *géwël*!!" This comment insulted me deeply, and its effect on me indicated that I had, in a sense, become a *géwël,* or was at least trying to play like a *géwël;* so to be told I played like a *géer* was a great insult (whereas in reality, I was neither *géwël* nor *géer*.)

Ways of Being *Géwël*

From the outset, I had no intention of trying to "become a *géwël*."[3] I wanted to learn as much as I could about the role of *géwël* percussionists in Senegalese culture, and although I wished to learn how to drum like a *géwël*, I had no pretenses of ever "becoming" a griot. When I first arrived to do my year of fieldwork in September 1997, I spent a lot of time with my research assistant, Papa Abdou Diop and his family, a *géer* family. As many *tubaabs* are given when they come to Senegal, I was given a Senegalese name, Astou Diop, making me a part of their family, but also inadvertently (or not so inadvertently!) making me *géer*, as Diop is unquestionably a *géer* name. As time went on, and I spent more and more time with the Mbaye family of *géwël* percussionists, I was given a new name, Xadi Seck, with Seck being of course a *géwël* surname. After I tried to lead a sort of double-life, responding to both names, my *géwël* name eventually stuck more than my *géer* name, to the dismay of my *géer* family, who chided me for "becoming griot." Although the chiding was playful, I sensed some disappointment, and when I chose to spend the holidays with my *géwël* family for research purposes, my *géer* family expressed some amount of disapproval. Thus I found it difficult to try to balance my relationship with my *géer* family—my first Senegalese host family—and my *géwël* family. Despite knowing that I could never become *géwël*, and not trying to be, *ngéwël* ('griotness') was something that I metaphorically aspired to as a sabar player. Insofar as "being *géwël*" meant being a good sabar player, this was an identity I could accept.

Matters Monetary

The association between griots and money is most obvious in the practice of tipping.[4] Ever since ancient times, the Wolof griot has been given money in return for praise-singing and drumming. When famous griot singers perform at the National Theater, there seems to be a constant flow of patrons filing up to the stage, pressing bills into the singers' hands. Likewise, at any typical sabar event, money is given to the drummers.

Tipping occurs when the *géwël* specifically ask for money (by shouting the names of some patrons, or otherwise embarrassing people into giving money before they resume playing). But more often, tipping is unsolicited and occurs when an audience member appreciates the playing. Tipping even occurs between griots, and often the *dirigeur* (lead drummer of the sabar ensemble) will tip another drummer who is playing exceptionally well, boosting the morale of the entire group.

At all of the sabar events I attended with the Mbaye family sabar troupe, Group Rimbax, I engaged in tipping as was socially and culturally appropriate. In some cases it was solicited, but more often unsolicited. With time, I began to truly understand the ease with which this exchange happens, and rather than specifically deciding when to give money, I began to do it naturally. Whenever a drummer played exceptionally well, it made me so happy and excited that almost without my thinking about it, money would flow from my fingertips into the drummers' mouths.[5] Often my pockets were emptied by the end of an event, and I soon learned not to bring too much money with me to such events, for it would inevitably disappear.

At my *tànnibéer*[6] (organized for me at the end of my stay, in which I would demonstrate what I had learned throughout the year), my drumming teacher, Lamine Touré, tipped me with 5,000 cfa (an unusually large amount for a tip at a sabar). Although I knew it had probably been preplanned, the gesture was much appreciated. It was the first time I had ever been tipped, and it made me play even better.[7]

Unfortunately, monetary considerations were not relegated to the practice of tipping. Regardless of my ascribed, metaphorical *géwël* identity, I was first and foremost a researcher, and I struggled with the usual concerns that any researcher has when going to a foreign place. Ethnomusicologists and anthropologists now recognize the complicated issues of fieldwork created by colonial legacy, power imbalance, etc. Before going into the field, I was acutely aware of these issues and prepared to be extra-sensitive.

No matter how often I was told I was part of the Mbaye family, there were some aspects of my relationship with them that I could not ignore. I was an American researcher with money visiting Senegal to learn about Wolof sabar.

With their help, I would gather enough materials and experience to earn my doctorate and eventually write a book. With my help, the importance of the sabar tradition and their family in Senegalese music and culture would become better known in the United States; in addition, I was also a plausible source of income. The benefits of the relationship were mutual.

Although I had accepted these facts, I was determined not to fall into such clearly defined imbalances between researcher and subject. I had read other accounts of a European researcher interviewing famous griots in Dakar and what the typical "going rate" was for an hour of someone's time (Panzacchi 1994, 206). On a practical level, because of my student budget, I did not have the means to pay griots large sums of money for interviews, and on an ethical level, I felt somehow uncomfortable about what seemed like too easy an exchange of money for information. However, the primary reason that I did not want to remunerate griots for interviews was that I did not want to establish a patron-client (*géer/géwël*) relationship with them. Nonetheless, monetary matters were inevitably complicated, and exceptions were often made.

Rather than interviewing many different griots and paying them for the interviews, I elected to focus on the Mbaye family. In this way, I was able to establish a relationship with the drummers in the family before embarking on formal, taped interviews. I refrained from proposing formal interviews until I had been in Senegal for several months. This seems to have paid off, because the majority of my interviews felt less formal and flowed well, as if a conversation between friends, which in many cases they really were. In addition, much of what I learned about Wolof *géwël* and their music came from informal discussions, which meant that I did not have to rely completely on formal interviews.

The formal interviews were conducted in different ways depending on the person interviewed. Interviews with Macheikh Mbaye, the head of the household, were conducted with the aid of my research assistant, Pap Abdou Diop. Because of his elder status, Macheikh Mbaye requested a monetary "gift" in return for his interviews, to which I agreed.[8] But in all other interviews (which I conducted with many other family members), money was never solicited, though in a few select cases (all with griots of the older generation, and at my research assistant's suggestion) I did slip a small, unsolicited monetary gift to a griot as a token of appreciation. Within the Mbaye family, I tried instead to show my appreciation through less direct forms of payment, such as inviting family members to my apartment for a meal, bringing them fruit or homemade juice, or even giving money to those in need for a specific purpose (such as a sick baby's medication or transportation for a visiting relative). Although I was happy to help my griot family financially, and did so on numerous occasions, I tried to do so in a way that was not directly linked to interviews, and thus would not thrust me into a patron-client relationship.

Aside from the interviews conducted with Macheikh Mbaye, which were entirely in Wolof, the other interviews I conducted were in a mixture of Wolof and French. Although I have a fairly strong command of the Wolof language, in order to be thorough, my research assistant and I painstakingly transcribed all interviews word for word in Wolof and French, and then translated them into English. In doing this, I feel confident that I have been as true as possible to the original interviews when I have included translated interview excerpts in this book.

The formal, taped interviews that I conducted with members of the Mbaye family were my primary source of information about the life histories and roles of griots in modern Senegalese culture. However, issues of musical aesthetics and style were better learned from observing and attending sabar events. The one exception was my work with Lamine Touré, with whom I spoke at length on musical issues.

Documenting Sabar

Rather than recording entire sabar lessons, I chose to tape record only selected portions. For example, if I learned a new *rythme* or portion of a *bàkk*, I would tape it so that I could listen to it and remember it later. My tapes of the lessons served the purpose of auditory learning aids more than ethnographic documentation.

In learning the sabar repertory, I tried to learn as my teachers did, by ear. On occasion, I wrote down the mnemonics of various *rythmes* and *bàkk*s as well. However, I never attempted to notate anything rhythmically *per se*, using Western musical notation or any other notation. In addition to my desire to learn "like a *géwël*" as much as possible, I also heeded my teacher's warning that if I tried to notate everything, I would spend too much time trying to write things down rather than just listening. Indeed, I found that after some initial attempts to notate rhythms, I became preoccupied with and distracted by notational difficulties. By letting go of transcription/notation in the learning process, I was able to focus better on learning, absorbing and retaining the sabar repertory.

In writing this book, for analytical purposes, I found it necessary to translate my knowledge of the sabar repertory into written musical notation. Interestingly, my conception of the music has changed after seeing the "music in my head" transformed into "music on paper." Indeed, my understanding of the music is closer to that of my teachers *because* I did not rely on notation during my original conception of the repertory. Thus, the repertory is now a part of my musical memory, and it exists in written form only as I attempt to translate this information for readers, using Western notation in conjunction with *géwël* vocal mnemonics. All musical transcriptions are my own; *géwël* do not traditionally use written notation, as theirs is an oral tradition.

My musical participant-observation involved the numerous events animated by the Mbaye family sabar group, Group Rimbax, led by Thio Mbaye. I attended group rehearsals as well as performances—at wrestling matches, neighborhood dance events, weddings, baptisms, and womens' association gatherings, to name a few. I videotaped a select number of events, though I attended many more than I videotaped. I did not videotape more in part due to permission issues; but also because my observation skills decreased when videotaping. Near the end of my stay, I was even asked to drum with Group Rimbax on occasion, which of course made it difficult to videotape. Nonetheless, the videotapes I did make have been valuable for a number of reasons. Most obviously, they documented the events which otherwise would not have been documented, and since I always gave a copy to the people filmed, this was a concrete gift with which they could remember that special event.

Also, it became a sort of ritual to come to my apartment afterward and watch the videotape with some of the drummers in the group, during which time they often critiqued their playing and made other helpful comments.[9] I also set up some more formal sessions with Lamine Touré, during which we analyzed entire sabar events from beginning to end, with him clarifying the otherwise chaotic events, as well as giving an explanation of the rhythms and the repertory.

All of the events I videotaped were events that occurred naturally (that is, none of the events were mounted for videotaping) and were completely unsolicited on my part. The only exception was an instructional video that we made for the purposes of breaking down the standard sabar repertory so that I could better understand (and later transcribe) the various parts. However, despite the events being unsolicited, some of the behavior during the events was obviously affected by the presence of the video camera, as well as the person behind the video camera.

While in the field, I also collected numerous commercially available cassette tapes and videos, and I taped both television and radio broadcasts concerning sabar and Wolof griot music culture. Because there is little academic writing on my topic, I made extensive use of newspapers and magazines, which often featured interviews with artists and musicians, and performance reviews. Before and after my field research, I of course consulted numerous written sources, including early accounts of griots in Senegal, as well as general literature pertaining to my research topic.

Researcher by Day, Violinist by Night

Another large part of my fieldwork experience that may not be as evident through the course of this book was my intense involvement with the activities of Alioune Mbaye Nder et le Setsima Group, the mbalax band for which Lamine Touré was percussionist from 1997–2001. I spent a significant amount of time with this band, seeing them perform on the average two to three times per week, and I toured the country (and later Europe and North America) with them. As this was another context in which Lamine Touré played sabar, the time spent with the band gave me great insight into the nuances of the role of sabar and the sabar repertory in the modern music scene as well as the percussionists' creative process on stage.

Although I began as an observer, I eventually gained a new role within Setsima Group as a performer, more specifically as a violinist. How did I end up playing violin with a mbalax band that normally would not include this instrument? The answer requires some background information.

A classically trained violinist since the age of six, I decided to bring my violin to Senegal simply because I knew I would miss it and did not want to go a year without playing. One day in late October 1997, I was listening to Nder's latest cassette, *Lenëen*, which had just been released and was at the top of the charts. One song, entitled "My Sister," had a slower tempo than most other mbalax songs, and I thought that violin could go nicely with it. Just fooling around, I took out my violin and figured out a simple violin part to accompany "My Sister." A few close friends heard me play and encouraged me to play it for Nder; Nder liked it, and before I knew it, I had my debut with Nder and his Setsima Group at the famous Thiossane nightclub. From time to time, I appeared as a guest performer, playing violin for that one song.

In July 1998, the group began rehearsing for a new cassette and asked me to join their rehearsals. This culminated in the cassette *Aladji*, which featured violin in two songs, including the title track. I began to perform regularly with Setsima through August 1998, eventually improvising in more songs so that I could better integrate into the group. At the end of my year in Senegal, I went to Paris with the group to play a concert at the Parc de la Villette; since then, I have played with the group during their North American and European tours 1999–2001, as well as during my follow-up trip to Senegal in August 1999.[10]

My role as violinist in Setsima Group greatly impacted how I was viewed by others and how I understood their music. On a broader scale, it thrust me into the public limelight, which had both positive and negative implications. More importantly, it established me as a musician in my own right, and the other musicians in the band respected me for this. I was no longer just an American researcher who was trying to learn sabar, clearly a novice and a student of

Lamine Touré; I was an accomplished violinist and equal member of the group. I enjoyed my status as a musician in the group and realized that not only did the other musicians have more respect for me, but also they became more willing to include me in discussions concerning musical matters, which were of great interest to me.

The other very important result of my playing violin with Setsima was that it gave me a completely new perspective on the group's music-making. The process of creativity and improvisation was much clearer when I was actively involved in it. Although I had previously attended many of the group's performances as a careful observer, being an active participant gave me a much greater insider's view and insight into the creative process.[11]

Although I was incorporated into Setsima Group as a musician, the reasons behind this were not purely of a musical nature, and I was aware of this. Nder and the other musicians liked my violin-playing; violinists were hard to come by in Senegal,[12] and they certainly liked the sound as part of their band. But I am not just a violinist; I am an Asian American female violinist who, to the Senegalese audience, was somewhat exotic. I was often introduced as Patricia, "the American," and references were made to building bridges and integrating cultures and the like. No doubt, Nder and his management felt that my presence would enhance their live presentations, and indeed the audience responded very positively.

The "reverse exoticization" that I experienced was mostly a result of my Asian ethnicity. An Asian American, I was born and raised in the United States, though my parents were born in Taiwan and emigrated to the U.S. years ago to pursue graduate studies and eventually settle here. Growing up in the States, I have always been aware of my Asian origin (mostly through language and food); however, because I have always lived in areas where there are many Asians, I have never been overly conscious of my ethnic origins and have thought of myself more as an American than anything else.

This changed when I arrived in Dakar. Going to Senegal, I knew that I would inevitably bring some sort of cultural baggage with me as an American researcher. However, few people even believed that I was really American because of my appearance, which apparently screamed of Asian-ness. My facial features and straight, black hair undoubtedly marked me as Asian to the Senegalese, evoking daily shouts of "*Arigato*!" "*Konnichiwa*!"[13] "Hee-haw,"[14] "Chinois!" and "Koréenne?" from random people in the streets. Initially shocked, I quickly became accustomed to this and soon realized that the comments were not derogatory, but usually made out of curiosity and friendly outgoingness (and the hope that I might be a tourist coming to buy their goods).

Despite the attention that my Asian-ness attracted, I think this unique status helped me in many ways. Not being French was the first advantage (hence I didn't have to worry so much about colonial baggage); but likewise, it seemed helpful not to look like a stereotypical American woman. Although this is a generalization, I often heard stories of "loose" European and American tourist women who come to the Senegambia in search of sexual encounters with African men.[15] Thus, despite my identity as a *tubaab*, my status as an Asian American woman seemed to make me a little less easily categorized, and thus, less likely to be stereotyped.[16]

Although it had a less obvious effect, gender also played a role in my complex identity in Senegal. Despite the fact that there are some female drummers, and drumming is not forbidden for women, men comprise the great majority of drummers. But because I was a *tubaab*, people didn't seem to care too much that I was a woman, because somehow I was more "neutral."[17] Occasionally I would notice that the men would always insist on carrying the drums (too heavy for me) or that Lamine would tell me that I didn't have the physical strength to play certain things or to help with mounting new drumheads (which was true); but there was nothing that prevented me from learning how to play sabar. However, since I found myself in the company of men for the most part (in both the family sabar group and Setsima Group), I sometimes began to feel a bit like a "marginal male" (Shelemay 1991, 42).

Conclusion

In this chapter, I have laid out my fieldwork methodologies and the motivations behind them, and given a sense of my fieldwork experience and the at times conflicting identities that were ascribed to me and that shaped my relationships with my Senegalese teachers and friends. Although some of the topics discussed are less relevant to the primary subject matter of this book *per se*, they nonetheless had an impact on my experience in Senegal, and I feel that it is important to share these experiences, which will no doubt help the reader have a more informed understanding of the rest of the book.

2

There Once Was a King Called Maysa Waaly Jon

SABAR HISTORY, INSTRUMENTS, ENSEMBLE, AND SOUND

I'm going to buy my goat skin
On my way back, I'll buy my razor blade
When I get back home
I'll put the skin in water
Until it's nice and wet
I'll shave the skin 'till it's nice and smooth
I'll mount my sabar
The next day it'll be dry

—Bada Seck, "Sabar Yi"[1]

DRUMMING HAS EXISTED among the Wolof of Senegal for many centuries. Oral accounts from present-day *géwël* trace the history of sabar drumming back to the rule of Maysa Waaly Jon during the fourteenth century. Written records from the seventeenth century describe ensembles of single-headed membranophones played with hand and stick in the contexts of war, traditional wrestling, and recreational dance. In this chapter, I will attempt to reconstruct the history of sabar drumming through an examination of both written and oral sources. After looking at possible histories of sabar, I will then turn to the modern sabar ensemble, with a focus on the construction of the instruments, their function as an ensemble, and aesthetics of sound.

Written Histories

The history of sabar has not been well documented. As with the history of griots in West Africa, we can trace the history of griot drumming back several centuries to the written accounts of early explorers, though it is likely that the origins date back much further. From the famous written records of North African explorer Ibn Battuta, we know that griots existed during the Malian

Empire in 1352, and from the preliminary evidence, it seems likely that they had existed long before, at least since the first millennium (Hale 1998, 79). Although drums are mentioned in written sources since the Ghana Empire in the eleventh century,[2] it is difficult to determine exactly when Wolof *géwël* began drumming, what types of drums they used, and when they adopted the drum now known as sabar.

In our quest for the historical origins of Wolof *géwël* drumming, it is helpful to locate any specific written references to drumming, to the Wolof, or to the Senegambian region. Some of the earliest references appear in the seventeenth century. In 1637, a Capuchin missionary by the name of Saint-Lô wrote his *Relation du voyage du Cap-Verd*, an account of his travels by ship from Rufisque, a town on the coast of Senegal thirty kilometers south of Dakar, southward to other trading centers, including Portudal in January and February 1635 (Hale 1998, 84). For Saint-Lô, griots were drummers, as he describes in the following passage:

> Everybody assembled at a large square to dance, having no other instruments than the drums that their guiriots struck rather roughly, maintaining nevertheless some rhythm. They chanted at the top of their lungs and repeated often the same thing. They have on their arms and knees little pieces of flat metal with lots of rings that they call casquabelles; they make a little sound like cymbals. (trans. Hale 1998, 85)

About a half-century later, a more detailed description of griots in Senegal was written by Michel Jajolet de La Courbe in his *Premier voyage du Sieur de La Courbe fait à la Coste d'Afrique en 1685*, which appeared in published form in 1913. A chief administrator for the *Compagnie du Sénégal*, La Courbe traveled up the Senegal River to trade with local chiefs in villages and in the process witnessed Wolof griots in many different performance contexts (Hale 1998, 86–87). These contexts included a wrestling match, at which the women "encouraged [the young men] and sang praises for the winners, marking the cadence by clapping their hands, after which they began to dance to the sound of several drums" (La Courbe 1913, 92–93). La Courbe also describes men working in the fields:

> All of this done to the sound and cadence of a furious music made by six guiriots with their drums and their voices; it was a pleasure to see them work as if they were possessed, and they would augment or diminish their work according to whether the drums were louder or softer. (1913, 51–52, trans. mine)

In a description of a circumcision ceremony, La Courbe writes,

> All of the griots, more than twenty in all, who had been occupied with the feast all night long, came with their drums to serenade us at dawn and went around our hut creating noise like the devil; I thought that giving them something would quiet them down, but instead they increased their efforts in thanks; this went on for about the whole eight hours that they had requested us to come and see the ceremony. (1913, 116, trans. mine)

Another excerpt from La Courbe describes a drum played by a hand and a stick, the same technique used in sabar drumming:

> The guiriots of the village did not fail to come and give us a symphony with their drums, all of which were made from a carved out tree trunk, some long, others much shorter, which they play with a hand and a stick with much precision. It is to the sound of these instruments that the young girls and boys, after having dinner, relax from their work and dance with all kinds of diabolical postures and contortions well into the night. (1913, 77–78, trans. Charry)

In 1686, a Flemish traveler's[3] description of the Jolof kingdom provided another account:

> The Tambours are well-received in the Courts of the Princes during their lifetime; they are the musicians of Kings and the great noblemen of the country, and they beat the march when the King goes to war. Otherwise, they are not permitted to enter into the King's antichamber [*sic*], and if one of the King's noblemen marries the daughter of a Tambour, or debauches his wife, he will immediately be forbidden to appear before the Prince. Their drums are made from a carved tree trunk, about four or five feet in length, with one side covered with goatskin and the other side open. (trans. Charry 1992, 325)

This is one of the earliest descriptions of the drum as having a goatskin head and an open bottom. All earlier accounts described drums carved from hollowed logs; however, it is possible that those drums also had animal skin heads, but were simply not described in such detail. Interestingly, in the above example, the griot is referred to as "Tambour," the French word for 'drum', making the griot and his drumming activities synonymous.

Another contemporary, Father Jean-Baptiste Gaby, describes the role of griots in a sporting event in the Senegambian region in 1689:

> Five or six of their Guiriots come to the central square of the village, dragging on their left side their drums with a leather strap. They begin to sing and beat the drums in order to get everyone to come; and having assembled them,

> the leader of the band of Guiriots announces that Frougar [a local holiday] will begin with a wrestling match.
>
> The symphony begins with seven or eight drums of different sizes, some large, some small. At the same time, men and boys who want to wrestle enter into the Frougar circle.

The wrestling match is followed by a dance:

> The girls step forward and into the square, two or three at a time, dressed in their most beautiful clothes; and no sooner arrived in the middle of the square than they dance in a violent manner, lowering successively their shoulders, raising their arms into the air, moving their jaws and lips, smiling, opening and closing their eyes until the Guiriots approach, who redouble their symphony the closer they get, adding throaty yells that animate the girls and make them walk and dance with great agility. The Guiriots, seeing that the girls are beginning to become very hot, return to their earlier rhythm of music in order to get the girls to stop. (1689, 43–46, trans. Hale 1998, 93)

In the above excerpt, the drums are described as hanging from the drummer's bodies on the left side, which is how sabar drums are worn during modern performance.

Another description of what seems to be a sabar drum or perhaps an ancestor of the sabar appears in 1695, by Sieur Le Maire:

> Even though they have no mind nor aptitude, they love praise so much that they have people called Guiriotz whose only occupation is to praise people. The Guiriotz carry around a kind of drum that is four or five feet long and made from a hollowed out tree trunk which is played either with the hands or with sticks. (1695, 120, trans. Charry 1992, 326)

Again, the use of both hands and sticks fits the description of sabar-playing (as opposed to other drumming traditions, such as the Mande *djembé*, which is played only with hands). The length of the drum is longer than any modern-day sabar, but this makes sense, as the shorter-sized sabar are a fairly recent invention (to be discussed below in Macheikh Mbaye's oral history of sabar).

About a century later, M. Lamiral offers a description of "Blacks" of Senegal and Gambia in 1789, including what appears to be a recreational dance comparable to a modern-day *sabar*:

> The boys and girls gather together in the middle of the village, they sit in a circle and in the middle are the musicians who entertain the party with dances and lascivious gestures. They pantomime all of the caresses and

> raptures of love, the griottes approach the onlookers and seem to provoke them into an amorous combat, the young girls accompany them with their voices and say things appropriate to the matter at hand: they all clap their hands in time and encourage the dancers by their clapping. At first the music starts slow, the dancers approach one another and back off, the rhythm doubles, the gestures become quicker; the musicians thunder and the movements of the dancers get faster and faster, their bodies take all sorts of shapes; they hold each other and push each other away: finally out of breath they fall into the arms of each other and the onlookers cover them with their pagnes [skirt cloths]; during this time the drums make such a racket that it is impossible to understand anything that is said. (1789, 266–67, trans. Charry 1992, 332)

Accounts of griots and their drum and dance activities continue through the nineteenth century, with descriptions such as this one by a colonial advisory council, Héricé, in 1847:

> The griots . . . from Cayor, Yolof, and Walo . . . live at the expense of the Senegalese population and extract from them almost by force the ill-merited rewards of their vile profession, which consists of playing the drum to amuse the youth, play-acting, with songs and dances, on street corners where they congregate. . . . It is all so indecent, so outrageous for public morality, that it is really astonishing that the police have not yet taken notice of such horrors. (Héricé 1847, 9, trans. Hale 1998, 110–11)

Taken as a whole, these accounts shed light on possible histories of the sabar. On a most basic level, they constitute evidence for the existence of drums used in the Senegal region, and by the Wolof people. These drums were carved from a tree trunk, had open bottoms and goatskin heads, and were played with a hand and a stick—all descriptions matching the construction of the modern-day sabar.

The drum ensembles varied from five or six drummers to as many as twenty. Again, this is a likely description of a sabar ensemble, which can be flexible in its size (as opposed to the *saoruba/tantango* ensemble, to be addressed later, which always consists of just three drummers). The drums themselves were often described as varying in size, as are those of the sabar ensemble, though there were several references to a drum four to five feet in length, which is longer than the longest of the modern sabars.

The contexts in which drumming was found are also very similar to those in present-day Senegal. There are some differences, of course; with the era of kings long gone, drummers no longer accompany their royal leaders to battle. But until recently, sabar drumming has been an important part of *kasak* (Wolof circumcision ceremonies), and to this day, it continues to be an integral part of traditional Senegalese wrestling, as well as the ubiquitous recreational dance, the *sabar* or *tànnibéer*. Overall, these written accounts substantiate the long history of drumming traditions in Senegal.

In addition, these documents serve as interesting windows to colonial attitudes of the seventeenth through nineteenth centuries. The descriptions of drums "creating noise like the devil" and of "indecent" and "outrageous" dancing in "all kinds of diabolical postures and contortions" reflect the negative attitude of the colonialists toward these leisure activities. I now turn to Wolof oral sources, which sharply contrast with these colonial accounts.

Oral Histories

Oral history is of particular importance in African studies, where historically, written documentation is sparse, and oral tradition has been a primary means of transmitting history.[4] As shown above, European written accounts provide vivid descriptions of various drumming events and are important both as historical documents and as reflections of European attitudes of that time. Just as the written documents reflect their authors' attitudes, however, oral accounts also reflect the interest of the people who produce them. Thus in examining Wolof oral sources, from an origin tale to a genealogical account of the history of sabar, we will see how oral history can serve to legitimize the present, perpetuating the importance of Wolof *géwël* today.

To begin, we will examine a Wolof griot origin tale recounted by Ahmadou Mapaté Diagne that inextricably ties the first griot and his griot functions to drumming:

> A long time ago, two brothers were sent by their mother to look for firewood. They fought over a branch that each wanted, and the elder unfortunately killed the younger. Not knowing what to do, he picked up the corpse and carried it toward home. At the moment he was about to enter his mother's house, he was spotted by his parents, who chased him away, saying, "Go wherever you want with this dead person; we don't need it, we have no idea what should be done with it."
>
> The brother killer sat down behind the house in the shade of a large tree. At mealtimes, he called and was brought his share. When the wind blew very hard, his voice was not loud enough. To remedy the situation, he obtained two sticks that he struck against each other.
>
> One night, one of his sticks was hollowed out by termites. The next day, the unhappy brother killer noticed that this stick was louder than the other. Profiting from this discovery, he obtained a hollow log on which he struck his two sticks to produce melodious sounds.

> On the seventh day of his exile, two crows who were fighting landed on his head. He stepped back without touching them. One had killed the other, and then scraped out a hole in the ground with his claws and buried the corpse.
>
> The brother killer imitated him—an event seen as the origin of burials—and returned to the house with the hollow tree trunk and the stick that he would never part with. The neighbors came to see them, asking him to make sounds from them, and gave him various items to reward him.
>
> Since then, they have forgotten his accidental crime and think only of his drumming. (Télémaque 1916, 277, trans. Hale 1998, 61)

This story shares with other origin tales the association with blood ties and the transgression of mores (in this case, fratricide). However, the role of the drum is remarkable in the brother killer's survival. When his voice failed, he was saved by the discovery of percussive instruments. Drumming not only helped the griot to survive, but it made people forget his sins. It attracted the attention of others, and it even brought him rewards. Thus, in this tale, the first griot relies on drumming. Notably, drumming is given more import than the griot's own voice, which has been seen by scholars as the primary vehicle of a griot's power as "the master of the word."

Although I did not obtain any such origin tales firsthand from the Wolof *géwël* whom I interviewed, I was given other clues as to the history of the sabar itself. My primary source of such information was the *géwël* Macheikh Mbaye.

According to Macheikh Mbaye, Wolof drumming has its roots in neighboring Serer and Soosé drumming traditions. In his words,

> The Wolof people learned to play the drum from the Serer, who took it from the Soosé. There was a king called Maysa Waaly Jon; he was the king of Kaabu. I think the historians know about Kaabu. And that king, Maysa Waaly Jon, went into exile, and came to settle in Saloum with his whole court and the griot and everybody surrounding him. His griot brought some percussions the Serer had never seen, and it is called *saoruba.* So the Serer imitated the *saoruba,* and shaped what we call now the *ndënd* . . . the Serer people, they cut it in half and then came up with other drums. And as time went on, people from Dakar just imitated drumming from the Serer people. The Serer people just saw the Soosé people playing and just imitated as I said earlier the *ndënd*, and they came up with a particular rhythm called *pitam.* From the Soosé people, drumming went to Sine, from Sine it went to Saloum, from Saloum it came to Dakar. (3/5/98)

Much in the way that *géwël* trace personal histories, here the history of the sabar is traced in a genealogical fashion. Interestingly, this history parallels

Macheikh Mbaye's own personal history; although he was born in Dakar, his family has links to the Sine Saloum region.[5] This oral account thus legitimizes Kaolack as the center and birthplace of sabar. Indeed, comments from other members of the Mbaye family frequently made reference to the importance of Kaolack in the sabar tradition, boasting that the best sabar players always come from Kaolack.

As was discussed earlier, the Wolof absorbed traditions from neighboring peoples, and it appears that Wolof sabar was no exception. Wolof sabar has possible Mande, Soosé, and Serer origins; however, once localized, the sabar became a specifically Wolof tradition, with its own drum names and musical repertory.

Macheikh Mbaye's explanation sheds light on the history of sabar in various ways. It dates the origins of Wolof sabar back to the time of Maysa Waaly Jon's rule in the mid-fourteenth century and suggests that the drumming tradition might have spread from Kaabu (present-day Guinée) to Sine, from Sine to Saloum, and eventually from Saloum to Dakar. We will now explore the roots of Wolof sabar in the Maysa Waaly Jon period and the subsequent regional spread of sabar to its present locations.[6]

Maysa Waaly Jon was a *gelwaar* (prince) who ruled in the Sine Saloum region sometime in the latter half of the fourteenth century (approximately 1350–1375) (Gravrand 1983, 355). Believed to be of either Mande or Soosé origin (or a mixture of both), Maysa Waaly Jon left Kaabu and came to settle in the Sine Saloum region, becoming the first in the succession of *gelwaar* who reigned for six centuries until Independence in 1960. Despite their status as foreigners, the *gelwaar* were well accepted, in part due to their political savvy but mostly because of their respect for and ability to integrate into Serer culture and customs. The *gelwaar* phenomenon likely began during the reign of Sundiata Keita or immediately afterward, around 1250–1260 (Gravrand 1983, 238). Eventually, the *gelwaar* dynasties were seen as Serer, though they were originally of Mande/Soosé origin.

According to Macheikh Mbaye, Maysa Waaly Jon brought drums with his entourage when he came to settle in the Sine Saloum region. Historians confirm the existence of wrestling matches and dances in Serer villages during the time of Maysa Waaly Jon, mentioning the presence of griots with their "Tam-Tam"[7] (Gravrand 1983, 300).

Because Maysa Waaly Jon was of Soosé/Mande origin, the Mande tradition could well be what was then passed on to the Serer and consequently the Wolof. To trace the history of Mande drumming is beyond the scope of this study; however, a look at the modern Mandinka drum ensemble could shed light on the origins of sabar.

The basic set of Mandinka drums, known as *tantango* or *saoruba* (based on the *saoruba* song), is a set of three open-bottomed, single-skin drums, two short and one long. The smallest drum is called *kutirindingo*, the second smallest is *kutiriba*, and the largest called *sabaro*. The two *kutiro* provide the foundation of the three-drum ensemble, playing interlocking parts, whereas the *sabaro* is the lead drum, which signals changes in the rhythms to other drummers, and interacts with the dancers (Knight 1974, 32). The basic shapes of the drums and the way their heads are mounted is very similar to the Wolof sabar, and indeed, the name of the lead *tantango* drum, *sabaro,* bears close resemblance to the Wolof term sabar; however, the *sabaro* drum is much longer and narrower than a typical sabar drum. The Mandinka drums are normally played with a stick and a hand, except when accompanying *saoruba* singing, when the *kutiro* accompaniments are played with just the hands (this is in contrast to the Wolof sabar, which is always played with a hand and a stick). Roderic Knight describes the Mandinka drum ensemble in detail:

> The shell is hewn from a single log of a deep red mahogany known as kembo, and the goatskin head is both pegged and laced. It is said that the laces, made from twisted strips of antelope hide, are a fairly recent addition. They are woven through vertical slits in the skin just below the lip of the drum and tied under each peg, greatly facilitating the adjustment of the drum head.
>
> All three drums are conical in shape, but the cone flares back out just above the base of the long drum and just below the center of the short drums, giving the latter the slightest suggestion of an hourglass shape. The internal shape parallels the outside. The two short drums stand approximately thirteen and seventeen inches in height, the larger instrument having a head nine to ten inches in diameter, with the smaller one approximately seven inches in diameter. The head of the long drum is also about seven inches in diameter, but its body is between twenty-six and twenty-eight inches long . . . the long drum always has a *binsango* 'beard' made of long strips of antelope hide hanging from the lacing around the head of the drum. A stick-and-hand technique is used on all the drums . . . and on the left wrist is tied a pair of jawungo, iron rattles in the shape of a rolled leaf, which accentuate the movements of that hand. (1974, 28)

The Mandinka *tantango* ensemble always uses three drums, whereas the Wolof sabar ensemble can vary in size, according to the nature of the performance event. The Mandinka ensemble performs in contexts similar to the Wolof: in the Casamance region (southern Senegal), the *saoruba* are performed at baptisms, circumcision ceremonies, weddings, traditional wrestling matches, religious festivals, and as general entertainment (Zanetti 1997, 23). Beyond this, little research has been done on Mandinka drumming.[8]

How, then, does the Mandinka *tantango/saoruba* tradition connect to sabar history? According to Macheikh Mbaye, drumming was brought to the Sine

Saloum region by Maysa Waaly Jon, who was of possible Mande origin; that would indicate that the Wolof drumming has its roots in Mande drumming traditions. However, it is difficult to know for sure which tradition came first. According to Eric Charry, the dissimilarity of eastern Mande drums[9] to Wolof drums and the "uncanny similarity of western Mande drums to those of the Wolof" would suggest a direct line of influence from the Wolof to the Mandinka (Charry 1992, 180). We may never know which came first, Wolof sabar or Mandinka *tantango/saoruba*. The Wolof term sabar, as well as the Mandinka terms *sabaro* and *saoruba* seem to have an etymological relationship, though I have not been able to substantiate which word came first. Regardless, what we do know by tracing either or both traditions back to the time of Maysa Waaly Jon is that the Wolof sabar tradition is an old one, dating back to the fourteenth century.

From Sine Saloum to Dakar: Sabar in the Twentieth Century

In an interview on August 12, 1999, Macheikh Mbaye went on to name the earliest sabar players in the Dakar region.

> The first one ever to start playing in Dakar was a man named Medoune Coumba Dieye. There were just two people who started for the first time to play sabar in Dakar; they were Serer. They came from Sine to Dakar to implement playing sabar. The one is called Medoune Coumba Dieye Faye and the other one, Latsuka Faye. There was a man called Xole Diagne who had a son called Medoune Xole, and he was playing, he was the generation of my father. From generation to generation, and you know the generation of my grandfather Ndiaye Rabb, like Medoune Xole and Sing Sing Faye, Vieux Sing's grandfather, they were like, after that generation, it went from generation to generation, from my great grandfather Ndiaye Rabb up to my generation, you know; it was like that. What I told you is just particularly related to Dakar, but at the same time Manee Mbaye, Thio Mbaye's grandfather was in Kaolack playing as well. My father was not the same generation as Samba Maissa Seck; though Samba Maissa Seck was playing at the time of my grandfather, Mane Diaw Mbaye, but then you know, my father found Samba Maissa Seck playing.

Macheikh Mbaye also explained that in the days of his forefathers, the sabar ensemble was smaller than it is today and did not have as many different sizes of drums.

My forefathers would not use as many drums as people do today. Today there are a whole lot of drums. Now people can use up to fifty drums, or ten or fifteen—people would not use that many in that era. My forefathers would only use two different types of drums—*ndënd* and sabar. In the late 1920s, my fathers would only use the *ndënd* and accompany it with the sabar. Do you know why they called it *ndënd*? Because *ndënd* has a bass-like sound; it is kind of rooted, which is why they call it *ndënd*. While the sabar is more kind of talkative; if you hear some drumming going on, from 150 meters away, you will only hear the sabar.

The *ndënd* is the bass, whereas the sabar is higher. That's why they call it sabar. *Bar* is something that is fast. . . . That's exactly how people used to play the drum in that era. But when my fathers came, they came out with a modification. And then came a smaller *lamb* (bass drum) they call the *gorong,* accompanied by two sabars. At that time they didn't have any *mbëng-mbëng*; it was not invented yet. So as time went on, they came up with another drum called *mbëng-mbëng*, which was inspired by the *saoruba* [from the Casamance]. The drummers living in Kaolack invented the *mbëng-mbëng*, and they got it from the Serer community. And the *mbëng-mbëng* is just a *saoruba* cut in half. If you cut a sabar in half, it resonates harder and goes like "mbung, mbung." The difference between a sabar and a *mbëng-mbëng* is like someone speaking naturally, and someone using a microphone with loudspeakers. The sabar sound is kind of high, but as the *mbëng-mbëng* is the sabar cut in half, it has a stronger resonance. When you play it, it goes like "boum." And that "boum" sound brought a special rhythm into the drumming; it brought a real flavor. And nowadays you can notice the *mbëng-mbëng* is basic, because everybody uses *mbëng-mbëng* in their crew/batterie. That's it. (8/12/99)

The Contemporary Sabar Ensemble

The modern-day sabar ensemble consists of drums of various sizes. All instruments are carved out of a trunk of the *dimb* tree (mahogany), at a thickness measuring about two centimeters. They are mounted with goatskins, which are attached to the wood by seven wooden pegs and an intricate system of string and lacing.

The drum ensemble as a whole, as well as the individual drums, can be called sabar. However, the drums also have more specific names, depending on their size and shape. The drums in the sabar ensemble can be divided roughly into two categories: those with open bottoms and those with closed bottoms. The open-bottom drums (*nder, mbëng-mbëng ball, mbëng-mbëng,* and *tungune*) are of various heights, but all have the same slight hourglass shape, with a narrow waist and a slight narrowing again at the top of the head (which is normally about nine inches in diameter). These drums differ from the closed-bottom drums (*lamb/ndënd/cól/talmbat*) in that the open-bottom drums have an extra system of lacing around the pegs. The closed-bottom drums are more egg-shaped. Like the open-bottom drums, their heads are approximately nine inches in diameter, and they have seven pegs and string wound around their heads, but lack the extra lacing system described above. (In Figure 2.1, see *cól* (left) and *mbëng-mbëng* (right); *Mbëng-mbëng* has an extra lacing system.)

One exception is the newly invented *gorong mbabas* (also known as *gorong yeguel*), which combines the lacing system of the open-bottom drums with that of the closed-bottom drums. (This new drum is used to varying degrees by different families; Doudou Ndiaye Rose, who invented the instrument, uses it much more frequently than members of the Mbaye family, for example.) Below is a more detailed description of the drums in the ensemble. (Figure 2.2 includes, from left to right: *tungune, mbëng-mbëng, gorong talmbat, cól, nder, cól, tungune*, and *mbëng-mbëng ball.*)

nder: the tallest open-bottom sabar has the narrowest waist as well (about 17 inches circumference). Height: about 42 inches tall. This drum is typically the lead drum in the ensemble (though not exclusively). A second *nder*, called the *mbalax nder*, often plays an accompanying part. The *nder* has the widest range of sound of all the sabars, from a very deep bass to a high-pitched slap.

mbëng-mbëng ball: the second-tallest open-bottom sabar. (*Ball* means 'to gush/spout out' in Wolof; its size is bigger than an *mbëng-mbëng*). Height: about 27 inches tall. Waist: about 21 inches in

FIGURE 2.1. Sabar drum lacings

FIGURE 2.2. Full sabar ensemble

circumference; base: about 25 inches in circumference. The loudest of the *rythme/bàkk* parts, it has a very strong bass sound.

mbëng-mbëng: the medium-sized open-bottom sabar. Height: about 22 to 24 inches tall. Waist: about 21 inches in circumference; base: about 25 inches in circumference. One designated *mbëng-mbëng* plays accompaniment (*mbalax*); the others play the *rythmes/bàkk*s with the rest of the ensemble.

tungune: the shortest open-bottom sabar. (*Tungune* means 'midget' in Wolof.) Height: about 17 inches tall. Waist: about 20 inches in circumference. Base: about 25 inches in circumference. Plays its own accompaniment part (*tungune*). The most recent addition to the *mbëng-mbëng* family, invented in the second half of the 20th century. Has the highest pitch of all accompaniments.

lamb: the closed-bottom bass drum. Height: about 27 inches tall. The bulge at the middle of the drum has about a 35-inch circumference, and the base has a 26-inch circumference. Has the lowest sound in the ensemble. Also known as *cól* and *ndënd.* This drum became known as *lamb* due to its use in wrestling matches (*làmb*).

talmbat (or *gorong talmbat*): another closed-bottom drum, but usually slightly smaller (narrower) than the *lamb*, with a higher ("tenor") sound. (A typical height might be about 25 inches tall.)

Talmbat also refers to the name of the accompaniment played on this drum, as opposed to the *tulli,* which is played on the *lamb/cól/ndënd.*

gorong yeguel/gorong mbabas: a new addition to the sabar ensemble. (*Yeguel* means 'to pull' in Wolof. Also named *gorong mbabas* because it was used as lead drum for the dance *mbabas*; however, this dance is no longer in vogue.) Said to be invented by Doudou Ndiaye Rose. This is a closed-bottom drum in the shape of a *lamb*, but the head is laced on like an open-bottom drum. The result is a uniquely bright, sharp sound, but with a slightly different tone quality than the *nder*. When used, this drum can lead the sabar ensemble.

Within the sabar ensemble, each drum plays a particular role. The ensemble is usually led by the *nder*; however, a second *nder* may be used to play an accompanying part, called the *mbalax nder.*[10] One designated *mbëng-mbëng* plays the *mbalax* accompaniment part, and the *tungune* plays its own part; the rest of the *mbëng-mbëng ball*s and *mbëng-mbëng*s can all play the *rythmes* and *bàkk*s (musical phrases). The two bass drums, *lamb* and *talmbat*, each have their own part. The *talmbat* plays an accompaniment (also called *talmbat*), whereas the *tulli* part is played on the *lamb*. In contrast to the *talmbat*, the *tulli* part involves a lot of soloing and improvisation, and is usually tuned to a lower pitch.

Construction, Maintenance, and Care

The construction of a sabar drum is the joint venture of a member of the *lawbe* (woodworker's) caste and the *géwël*. The *lawbe* fashion the basic shells of the sabar (as well as *djembé* shells and mortar and pestles). *Géwël yi* normally establish a relationship with a particular *lawbe* to whom they will go (sort of like a preferred customer) to buy the sabar shells. For example, Lamine Touré goes to the *lawbe* outside the nearby Kolobane market, where he usually buys sabar shells from Boy Niaga and Njawar, his two *lawbe* friends (see Figure 2.3).

The *géwël* will sometimes go to examine existing sabar shells or to make special orders. Because the shells are handmade, each one is individually crafted and is thus slightly different in size. The *géwël* knows from experience which shells to choose and might have a certain size in mind.

Sabar shells are carved from *dimb* wood, a type of mahogany. According to Macheikh Mbaye, people used to use *yiir* (mimosa) as well as *dimb* to make sabars, though now only *dimb* is used. *Dimb* is found in the forests of the Casamance, as well as in Saloum, and is preferred because of its strong, hard wood.

FIGURE 2.3. *Lawbe* (woodworkers) at Kolobane

After purchasing the shell, the *géwël* constructs the drum. If there are no holes for the pegs, he either drills the seven peg holes with an electric drill or uses the more traditional method of heating a metal rod until it is red hot and burning holes into the wood. The holes and pegs are an important part of the sabar because it is only when the pegs are pounded deeply into the holes that the right sound of the sabar will emerge. After the holes have been made, he sands the shell smooth and then treats the wood with palm oil and lets it dry.

Only select *géwël* are capable of mounting a drumhead well.[11] At one time, drumheads were made of either goatskin or gazelle skin, though now goatskin is what people use, being thicker and more resistant to rupture than gazelle or sheep skin. First, a *géwël* must purchase the goatskins. Choosing good goatskins comes with experience, as one must be able to inspect the skin closely for defects or too much fat. If chosen correctly, one goatskin can be used for two drums. After purchase, the skins are soaked in water and laboriously shaved.

For a *mbëng-mbëng*, three slits in the edge of the skin are made per peg, through which each peg is woven, attaching the skin to the wooden shell through each drilled hole. The pegs are made of one of three types of wood: apple tree, *kel* (*tiliacée*—a hard wood similar to oak), or *niim* (*méliacée*). As these holes are made, a helping hand must grasp the wet skin and stretch it tightly over the opening of the drum until all pegs, alternating from opposite sides of the drum, have been inserted. (For the *cól*, five slits should be made instead of three.)

Next, a long piece of string (*xir*) is wound around the skin, starting about midway between the top of the drum and the pegs. On the *cól*, small slits in the skin may be made to thread the initial ring of the string and hold it down, though doing so is not required. The beginning of the *xir* is secured by looping it around an initial eye tied in the string and winding it back. This string must be tightly wound around the top of the drum; when it reaches the pegs, it is wound beneath the pegs for at least four revolutions. A final knot secures the *xir*.

At this point, the excess goatskin can be trimmed off by pulling on the skin and cutting it with a knife just below the bottom ring of string. However, a small tab of skin should be left between each peg to tuck back up into the bottom rings of string, holding the string in place. (With the *cól*, this is the final step, as there is no intricate lacing on the *cól*.)

Next, a series of small slits must be cut halfway between the top of the head and the pegs. The slits should be approximately one centimeter from each other, with about six slits between each peg.

A thick string called *fer* (named for the beaded belt women wear under clothing—also called *jel-jeli* or *bin-bin*) is threaded through the holes by twisting one side of the thread over the other, using a v-shaped metal or wooden threader. This *fer* is wound around and then secured in the starting knot.

Next, strips of *mees* (wide nylon ribbon, much like that found in camping gear) are threaded through the slits in the skin in like fashion above the string. These are threaded between each peg, then looped around the bottom of each. (In Macheikh Mbaye's time, when *mees* didn't exist, they would use strips of cow skin.) When the skin is dry, the *mees* loops are tightened more securely, and the drum can be tightened and tuned until the head is extremely tight and has a bright, sharp sound. Finally, the dry head is shaved once again to get rid of the finest hairs. Packs of sticks are purchased and trimmed down to be used as drum sticks (made of *sideem* [jujube] or *daqar* [tamarind]). The sabar drum is now ready to be played.

Once a sabar is made, it can last a very long time if given proper care. Drumheads break frequently with use, and thus sabars are frequently reheaded; however, the wooden shells can last for decades. The *géwël* care for their sabars by oiling the insides with palm oil every few months to help prevent cracking. If a crack does occur, it can be filled with a mixture of glue and sawdust. A sabar shell is rendered useless only when a crack is so severe that it cannot be mended or no longer resonates properly.

Sabars are chosen individually for their shape, weight, size, and sound. Although a group of sabars is likely owned (and housed) by a *géwël* family, they are neither made nor treated as a set. A *géwël* family typically keeps at least six to eight sabars at a time so that there are enough to form a proper ensemble. However, drums are occasionally lent to relatives and friends, sometimes permanently. As a result, there is a constant flow of new instruments replacing old or missing ones.

Décor and Dedication: Visual Aesthetics

The sabar drums are usually decorated in some manner. Artwork can be carved, painted, or made from golden thumb tacks (*pinces*), on the outside of the drum. Artwork can range from simple bands carved around the base and middle of the drum to something as elaborate as a palm tree, map of Africa, or traditional African mask-style faces. Carving is more common than painting, and the use of *pinces* is perhaps the most common, most visible form of decoration, due to the color contrast. These *pinces* may be used to draw pictures such as the items mentioned above or to create other creative geometric patterns.

However, the most common form of decorations are names. The tradition of naming someone after someone else (*turando*) is an important practice in Wolof culture and something that is practiced to this day. A newborn baby is not given an arbitrary name but rather the name of a relative (often an aunt, uncle, or close family friend). Likewise, sabar drums are typically named after people. Having a sabar named in one's honor is an honor indeed, since the drum will likely be around for a long time, and once named, a drum will keep that name during its lifetime. When my drumming teacher Lamine Touré was in the process of writing my name on a new *cól*, Macheikh Mbaye told me that I should be honored because that drum would last for a long time, and thirty years from now, if a child saw the drum and asked who "Patricia" was, they would learn the story of Patricia the American woman who came to Senegal to learn about sabar.

Perhaps most importantly, by giving names to sabar drums as one would give names to newborn children, these names (and drums) become important markers of a family's identity. For example, when Lamine Touré made my set of sabars to bring back to the United States, I chose to name each sabar after a member of his family. My sabar drums are named after Thio Mbaye, Lamine Touré, Alassane "Alou" Djigo, Mustapha "Niass" Mbaye, Lendor Mbaye, Macheikh Mbaye Jr. and Talla Seck. Thus, any sabar player in the U.S. who sees my drums will know which sabar family taught me how to play sabar. In addition, these sabars will remain a form of dedication and remembrance, especially since one family member, Lendor Mbaye, has since passed away; his legacy will live on in the *cól,* which is named for him.[12]

The practice of giving names to sabar drums is not only a way of decorating the instruments, it also expresses the importance of family. By being named after family members, the sabars themselves become a continuation of family tradition and are vibrant markers of that family identity.

The Ensemble

The sabar ensemble varies in size and instruments, depending on the nature of the performance event, as well as the practical consideration of the availability of drummers and drums.

For a typical *sabar, tànnibéer*, or baptism, a full-fledged sabar ensemble will include ten to twelve players (for example, three or four *cól* and six to eight *mbëng-mbëng*-type drums; see Figure 2.4). *Sabar*s, *tànnibéers*, and baptisms are usually led by the *nder* drum. Wrestling matches have a similar ensemble, but the ensemble is led by a *cól* instead. (The use of a *cól* as lead drum has historical roots, to be explored in Chapter 6.) In any of these large ensembles, the drummers will sit or stand in a square horseshoe shape facing the audience circle, with the *cól* players sitting in the back, a row of *mbëng-mbëng* players on each side (standing with their *mbëng-mbëng*s strapped to them and hanging on the left side of their bodies), and the lead drummer in the front center. If playing an *nder*, the lead drummer may strap the *nder* to his shoulder (which allows him to be mobile, but is also physically taxing due to the weight of the drum); or he may prop the drum diagonally on a metal chair (the more common practice). When the *nder* is placed on a chair, the lead drummer begins by facing the other drummers, with his back to the audience; when the dancing begins, however, he will turn to face the dancers.

Smaller ensembles are often used for less important events, such as small afternoon *sabar*s organized by children/teenagers, or women's association gatherings (*tur*), which can have as few as three or four drummers.[13] The smaller ensemble lacks the full-bodied sound of the large ensemble, as there is usually just one person playing each part.

With the exception of wrestling matches, in which the lead drummer (*dirigeur*) interacts with the wrestler he is supporting, the main role of the lead drummer (usually on the *nder*) is to interact with the dancers. Although the lead drummer plays more solos, decides which *bàkk*s to play, and cues changes in the music, his primary purpose is to interact with the dancers. An experienced leader will adapt his music to the dancer, whether an energetic young woman with flirtatious moves, or a sophisticated elderly woman who dances with slower, more refined steps. Dancers are inspired by good playing, and, likewise, the lead drummer is inspired by good dancing. The inspiration is mutual.[14]

FIGURE 2.4. Row of *mbëng-mbëng* players at a *tànnibéer*

A typical Mbaye family sabar ensemble is led by the *nder*. However, at times one (or more) of the *cól* players might take turns leading with an ornate solo. For example, a dancer might provoke a *cól* player to solo for her. Sometimes it may appear that both the *nder* and the *cól* soloist are leading simultaneously. This flexibility of leadership is not seen as a usurpation of power, but is welcomed and adds vitality and variation to the event.

A more recently invented drum, the *gorong yeguel*, is also occasionally used to lead, though it is rarely used in the Mbaye family; I only saw one instance during my year of fieldwork. However, Doudou Ndiaye Rose and his family more commonly use the drum, as Rose invented the instrument.

When asked about his choice of lead drum, Thio Mbaye explains:

> For soloing, it depends on what you are most at ease playing. There is the *gorong mbabas*; there are lots of people who lead with that. But us, we lead with the *nder*. We can lead with the *gorong* too, but. . . . Pfft! It's like if you play with a Fender jazz guitar or a Takamine—they're all guitars in the end. They don't have the same sound, the *nder* and the *gorong mbabas*. But you can lead with either one. Also there is the *lamb*; there are rhythms that you lead with the *lamb*. For example, at wrestling matches. (5/23/98)

Tuning and Aesthetics

A sabar drum must be well-tuned in order to have a good sound (*bon son*). Ideally, the head is pulled extremely tight, allowing a wide range of pitches from bright, high tones to deep, resonant ones.[15] Although the bass tone of a sabar has a well-defined pitch, there is no particularly desired pitch for which *géwël* strive; rather, each instrument has its individual sound, and the best sound is attained when the skin is pulled tight, regardless of the actual pitch produced.

Repeated use, combined with climate changes, can cause a drumhead to loosen, lowering the pitch (*descendre*). Therefore, it is necessary to periodically tune a sabar. Tuning differs for open-bottom and closed-bottom sabars. The heads of open-bottom sabars are held tight by the *mees*, which is laced around the pegs. To tune these drums, one must remove the pegs and reinsert them. To remove a peg, one can hit it on the sides with a rock until it loosens and can be pulled out manually. Typically, the peg is then moistened with saliva, rolled around in some dirt for friction, then reinserted into the hole. It is then forcefully pounded back into the hole with a rock. If the drum is tuned too tightly, the skin can tear, so one must be careful to tune the sabar to the greatest tightness possible before it reaches the breaking point. Once a drum is tuned, it should stay tuned for a period of time.[16]

The closed-bottom drum (*cól*) can have more variation in pitch because there are no *mees* laces attaching the skin to the pegs. As a result, pegs can often be pulled out and pushed back in by hand with considerable ease. *Cól* players are constantly pulling out and pounding in their pegs in order to change the pitch and sound of the instrument. The aesthetic reasons behind this will be discussed below.

The tuning, sound, and tone quality of the different drums in the sabar ensemble and their relationship to each other are very important. Lamine Touré explains:

> You see, if you tune it, if you tune all the sounds, the *nder*'s sound will resonate a lot because it is the longest drum. The sabar that is the longest, that is the one who will have a lot of sound. Why do we lead with the *nder*? We chose it because it is long, and its sound is very different from the other sabars. And the sound resonates well too. So if you lead with that, everyone will know it's the leader . . . that is why people also choose the *gorong* to lead too; because the *gorong*, it's a *cól* which has been tuned until it goes "Kek!" So its sound is very unique as well. If you lead with it, everyone will know it's the *gorong* because of the unique sound. So the *nder*, too, why do we use it? Its sound comes out well. We tune the *nder* well, and we tune the *mbëng-mbëng* too . . . but the *mbëng-mbëng ball*, we don't tune too high.

> You need to tune it so that it has a nice bass . . . the bass sound is important. But the *mbëng-mbëng*, you need to tune well. The *tungune*, you tune well. The *mbalax nder* is tuned well too. And the *nder* too. (8/17/99)

Indeed, when tuned correctly, the *nder* will have both the highest-pitched and deepest, most resonant tones, allowing the sound of this lead drum to carry above the rest of the ensemble. The other open-bottom drums also need to be tuned tightly to maximize their sounds.

In contrast, the *cól* can be tuned to different pitches depending on the rhythms being played. Lamine explains why players often tune the *cól* up and down. The aesthetics of sound are expressed in his words:

> The *cól* that plays *tulli*[17] . . . there are rhythms for which you need to lower the sound. There are other rhythms for which you should tune it up. There are rhythms like *farwu jar*,[18] you need to lower the sound. If we play *ceebu jën*, one must tune up the *cól*, so that you can hear it clearly. So the *talmbat*, for *farwu jar*, it's the *cól* that will go down, the *talmbat* which will tune up. *Ceebu jën*, it's the *talmbat* which descends, and the *cól* which will come up. It's the *talmbat* which will be tuned up all of the time; it is a bit higher than the *cól*. They don't have the same sound. The *talmbat* is higher than the *cól*, the *tulli*. *Tulli* always has a more bass sound. But since the *talmbat* accompanies, if it had the same sound as *cól*, you wouldn't notice it. In *ndëc*, the *cól* is lower; the *talmbat* is higher. It's higher because it is the accompaniment. But there are many different ways, rhythms for the *talmbat*, where it is tuned down, like the rhythm *baar mbaye*, you must tune down the *talmbat*; you need to tune down the *cól* too, so that it can adopt the rhythm. For a well-tuned sabar, if you play *baar mbaye*, you need to lower the sound of the *cól* and the *talmbat*. . . . There are many griots who don't even know how to tune their sabars properly. Who just play "*jep, jep, jep,* let's go play!" But Thio, when he plays a sabar, he makes sure all of the sabars are well-tuned. That is why he has such a good group. Me, too, when I play, all my sabars are properly tuned. (8/17/99)

Lamine Touré also talks about his own experience learning the different parts/drums in the sabar ensemble:

> Not all griots learn in the same way. The way I learned, Kaolackois, griots, our family, we all learned the same way. . . . The way we learn, at the beginning, one must do *mbalax*. . . . What you will begin with, even if you are playing on tomato cans, you must do *mbalax*. Afterward, you change around. For example, if I played *mbalax*, when I was little, on the little tomato can sabars, Lendor would play *tulli*; afterward, when I got tired, I would give him *mbalax*, and I would do *tulli*—an exchange. We take turns. That's why we all know how to *mbalax*; we all know how to *tulli*; we all

> know how to *talmbat*; we all know *mbalax nder* because we took turns. . . . That's how I learned to lead (*diriger*) too—we took turns. But there are some griots who don't know how to lead; there are griots who don't even know how to *mbalax*. . . . That is not good. In Kaolack, all griots know how to *mbalax, talmbat,* and all the accompaniments because that's how we learned—it's a technique we have in order to be the best. (8/17/99)

Every percussionist has his favorite drum/part to play. For example, in Group Rimbax, Thio is normally the leader (on *nder*); Lamine always plays the *mbëng-mbëng*, as do Niass and Karim. Mbaye Samb, Khalifa Mbaye, and Mini Mbaye play *cól* (though Mini Mbaye occasionally plays the *mbalax nder*). Although they all know how to play the other instruments, each percussionist has his strength and generally sticks with that particular instrument.

Lamine Touré explains why he likes to play *mbalax* (*mbëng-mbëng*) the best:

> The most important part in sabar, the best part, is *mbalax*. *Mbalax* is the basis of the sabar . . . I love playing *mbalax*. I know how to *tulli* very well, but I love playing *mbalax* the most. *Mbalax* is the most important in sabar. . . . That's how you know if a percussionist is good or not: [from how they] *mbalax*, play *cól*, and lead (with *nder*). *Talmbat* is easy; everyone can learn *talmbat*. On the *cól*, you play many notes; on the *nder*, you play many notes too; *mbalax,* you play many rhythms. That's how it is. (8/17/99)

With roots in Mande, Soosé, and Serer drumming, the Wolof sabar tradition was likely born in the Sine Saloum region in the fourteenth century, under the rule of Maysa Waaly Jon. But were the rhythmic patterns also disseminated with the drums? To answer this question would require a large-scale, comparative study of Mande, Serer, and Wolof drumming repertories. While studies of Mande and Serer drumming are beyond the scope of this book, I will present the Wolof sabar repertory in considerable detail in Chapter 5. First, we must turn to the issue of caste in Wolof society.

3

The Griot Lineage—We Are One

WOLOF CASTE AND IDENTITY

> I'm talking about the griot lineage
> If you do anything griot-related
> Know what you're doing
> If you say anything griot-related
> Know what you're saying
> The griot lineage is rich
> The griot lineage, we are one
> I'm talking about the griot thing
> Griots, griots
>
> —Bada Seck, "Nguewel"[1]

A SYSTEM OF SOCIAL ORGANIZATION commonly known as *caste* is found in societies throughout West Africa. These societies are generally divided into three main categories, from highest to lowest: nobles/freeborn, *casted* or endogamous ranked specialist groups, and slaves (or their descendants). This social hierarchy was prevalent among numerous societies throughout West Africa, including the Soninke, Bambara, Malinke, Khassonke, Wolof, Tukulor, Senufo, Minianka, Dogon, Songhay, Fulani, Moorish, and Tuareg people (Tamari 1991, 221). Some of the earliest evidence of castes appears among the Malinke, Soninke, and Wolof, with evidence of Wolof castes dating at least as early as 1500. Within the Wolof, casted people have been estimated at just 10 to 20 percent of the population (Tamari 1991, 224).

Although I will be using the term caste to refer to these endogamous occupational specialist groups, for lack of a better term, one should be aware that the term caste used in reference to West African societies has been cause for considerable debate. Because the term caste originates in reference to Indic societies, its relevance to non-Indic societies is questionable. In his classic study, *Homo Hierarchicus*, Louis Dumont defines what he sees as the fundamentals of the caste system:

> The caste system divides the whole society into a large number of hereditary groups, distinguished from one another and connected together by

> three characteristics: *separation* in matters of marriage and contact . . . ; *division* of labor, each group having, in theory or by tradition, a profession from which their members can depart only within certain limits; and finally *hierarchy*, which ranks the groups as relatively superior or inferior to one another. (1970, 21)[2]

In addition, Dumont discusses ritual purity and impurity as another vital characteristic of the caste system. However, his critics have argued that the purity/impurity dichotomy is culturally specific to Indian societies and thus is not relevant to other societies, such as those in West Africa, rendering the caste concept useless for comparative purposes. Nevertheless, the other characteristics of separation (endogamy), division of labor (occupational specialization), and hierarchy are characteristics found in West African societies. Thus for the purposes of simplicity, I will use the term caste in reference to Wolof society, while being aware of the issues that accompany the use of this term.

Ways of categorizing the Wolof caste system vary according to different scholars. In the following section, I will discuss and analyze the work of Cornelia Panzacchi, Tal Tamari, Abdoulaye Bara-Diop, and Bonnie Wright. Familiarity with these recent scholarly works will provide some background on the complex issue of Wolof caste.

Wolof Caste: An Overview

Wolof society is most often described in terms of three main social groups. Cornelia Panzacchi divides Wolof social structure into these three groups. The highest ranking is *géer*, or noble/freeborn; the lowest rank is *jaam*, the slaves or descendants of slaves; and the middle rank includes the *ñeeño*, or casted groups (see Figure 3.1). The *géer* caste consisted of the freeborn, ranging from members of royal lineage to commoners. *Géer* were landowners and made their living through agriculture.

On the other end of the social hierarchy were the slaves. Slaves' rights varied; for example, domestic slaves could not be sold, and though they had to work for their masters, they were usually given land of their own to farm, and permission to marry and raise families. In contrast, trade slaves (captured in war) had no rights whatsoever. The warrior crown slaves (known as *ceddo*) were a special class of slaves, and those who showed exceptional military prowess could hold high-ranking positions, lead armies, and even own other slaves (Gellar 1995, 4). However, the slave caste as a whole remained at the bottom of the Wolof social order.

In the middle of the Wolof social hierarchy were the *ñeeño*. The *ñeeño* were freeborn, but unlike the *géer*, they did not control land distribution and thus

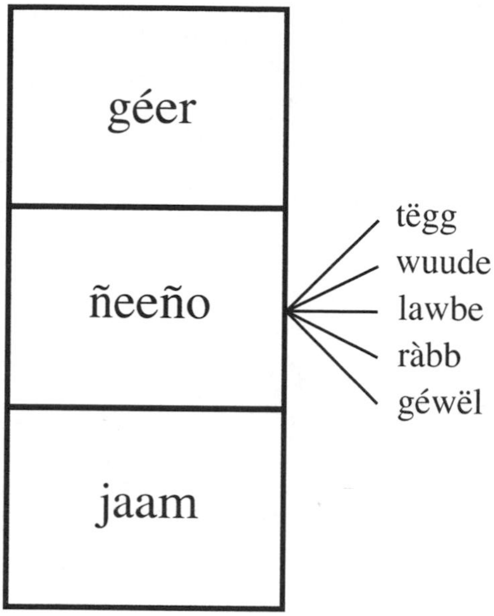

FIGURE 3.1. Panzacchi's interpretation of Wolof caste system

lacked political control. They were also forbidden to bear arms (Panzacchi 1994, 190). The broad *ñeeño* group can be divided into numerous subgroups according to occupational specialty: *tëgg* (blackmiths), *wuude* (leatherworkers), *lawbe* (woodworkers), *ràbb* (weavers), and *géwël* (griots). Within the *ñeeño* groups, the subgroups are sometimes ranked as well, with *géwël* usually ranking the lowest; however, there is considerable disagreement about this, so I will not place much import on such subrankings.

Tal Tamari also divides Wolof social structure into three main categories, but further subdivides the freemen and slave categories (see Figure 3.2). According to Tamari, the freemen (*jaambur*), generally designated as *gor*, have subcategories of *garmi* and *gellwaar* (royals), *dom i bor* (notables), and *baadoolo* (commoners). Within the *jaam* group, she creates the subgroups of *jam i garmi* and *jam i bor*.

In contrast to Panzacchi and Tamari, Abdoulaye Bara-Diop does not consider *jaam* a part of the caste system. Instead, Diop discusses Wolof society in terms of two separate organizations: castes and political orders. Within the caste system, there are just two categories, *géer* and *ñeeño*; *jaam* is considered part of the political order (see Figure 3.3).

Diop discusses the caste system with respect to division of labor. Instead of defining the *géer* as nobles or freemen, he defines them in terms of what they are not: artisans, members of professional occupational groups. That is, artisan

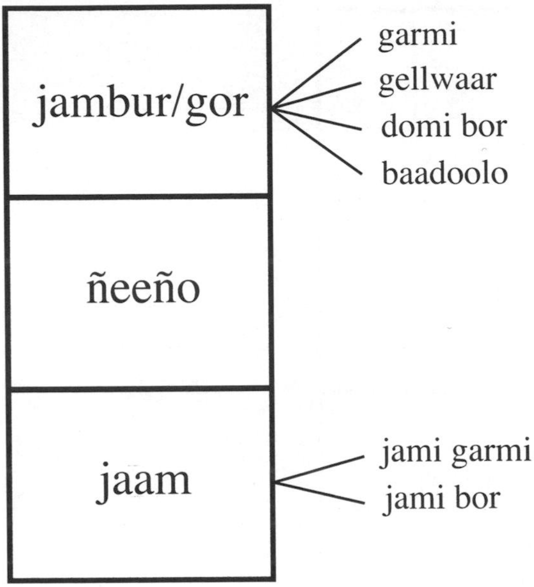

FIGURE 3.2. Tamari's interpretation of Wolof caste system

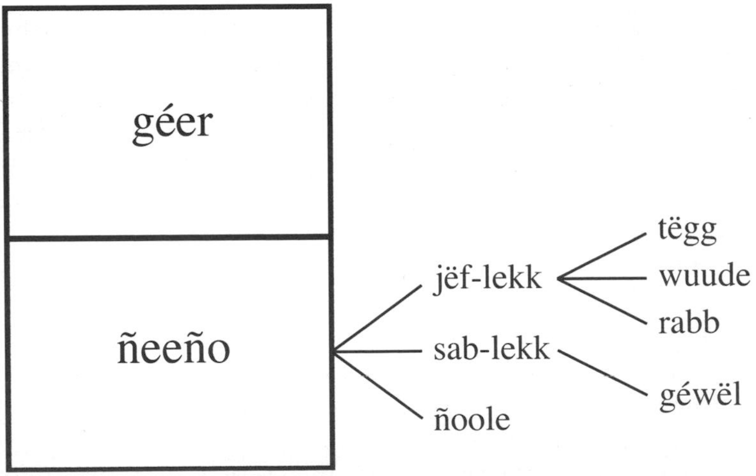

FIGURE 3.3. Diop's interpretation of Wolof caste system

work is forbidden to the *géer*. They may engage in any other activities, such as agriculture, fishing, etc., and are generally peasants. Ranking below the *géer* are the *ñeeño*, the artisans. The *ñeeño* can in turn be divided into three main subgroups: *jëf-lekk* (literally, those who make a living with their hands), *sab-lekk* (those who live from their singing, or "crowing"); and *ñoole* (a marginal group). The *jëf-lekk* includes *tëgg* (blacksmiths), *wuude* (leatherworkers), *seeñ* (coopers) and *ràbb* (weavers). The *sab-lekk* are the griots (*géwël*): artists, singers, musicians, oral historians, and praisers. Finally, the *ñoole* are the courtiers, servants, and buffoons.[3]

Diop then considers a separate system of political (and economic) orders (*ordres*), to describe Wolof society. In this system, there is no longer a *géer/ ñeeño* dichotomy, but rather a *gor (jambur)/jaam* (freemen/slave) dichotomy. This differs markedly from most other descriptions of Wolof caste systems, which group everything together (see Figure 3.4).

In Diop's *ordres*, the *gor* are also known as *jàmbur*, or freemen. Under the monarchy of the precolonial states, *jàmbur* meant 'notable.' Diop further divides the *gor/jambur* into the *garmi* and the *baadoolo*. The *garmi* were the nobles of the precolonial kingdoms, and their descendants; the *baadoolo* were peasants, commoners. Among the freeborn, the *baadoolo* were of lower status than the *garmi*. They often had to give their earnings to their kings and chiefs. They were not warriors and were thus often the victims of pillages from neighboring attacks. Similarly, within the slave group (*jaam*) were the *jaami-buur*, the royal slaves, and the *jaami-baadoolo*, the slaves of the commoners.

This system of political order was intricately linked to the precolonial states, or monarchic states, of Waalo, Jolof, Cayor, and Baol: as a whole, colonial and postcolonial events have greatly impacted the Wolof political order and caste system.

Because I am interested in caste as a function of division of labor rather than of political systems, I will follow Diop's categorizations and focus on the social hierarchy of castes, with his two main categories: the *géer* (freeborn, nobles) and *ñeeño* (endogamous artisan groups). However, these categories

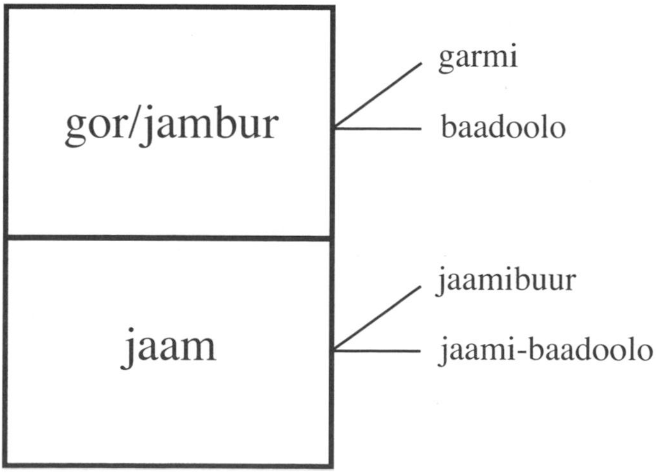

FIGURE 3.4. Diop's political order chart

should not be seen as fixed structures; they interact with each other and are subject to multiple interpretations. We will now turn to a discussion of present-day Wolof and how they perceive issues of caste and social order.

Caste in Contemporary Senegal

Although caste has been officially abolished since Independence, it remains an important marker of personal identity. Modern Dakar offers a mixture of opinions about caste. *Géer* are proud to be *géer* and often look down on *ñeeño*, especially *géwël*.[4] *Géer* might remark that *géwël* are loud, obnoxious, greedy, impolite, always asking for money, and are keepers of dirty homes. On the contrary the *géwël* whom I interviewed were all fiercely proud of being *géwël*. Aside from being proud of their function in society and of their skill at sabar drumming, they boasted about the virtues of *géwël*, some more serious and some more tongue-in-cheek: *géwël* cook better rice, *géwël* are better at bargaining for cloth at the market, and *géwël* are better lovers.[5] Interestingly, none of the above comments were ever made to me in the presence of another caste (*géer* in front of *géwël*, or *géwël* in front of *géer*).

One reason why caste is so conspicuous is that caste is revealed through one's surname, and people formally introduce themselves by surname. For example, names such as Mbaye, Mboup, Ngom, and Samb are typical *géwël* patronyms, whereas Diop, Fall, and Ndiaye are typical *géer* patronyms.

The tension between *géer* and *géwël* is evident in the continued practice of caste endogamy. To this day, marriage across caste boundaries is very rare. Even among *ñeeños,* people generally marry within their subgroup; however, if marrying outside of one's caste subgroup, it is still considered better for a *ñeeño* to marry another *ñeeño* than to marry a *géer*. In precolonial times, the exception was that a high-status *géer* or *garmi* man might sometimes take a *géwël* as a third or fourth wife "to bring happiness to the household" (Wright 1989, 48).

Caste subgroups are further complicated by the question of ethnicity. A notable example of this confusion is the *gawlo,* of Peul/Fulani/Toucouleur origin.[6] Although of non-Wolof origin, longtime presence in Wolof society has given the *gawlo* their own place in Wolof social structure. Most often considered a subset of *géwël*, the *gawlo* are best described as "the griots of the griots"—that is, the griots for the *géwël*. In former times, the *géwël* would accompany the kings and warriors to the battlefields, drumming and singing their praises and witnessing their courageous deeds so as to extol them later. The *géwël* were unarmed and risked their lives out on the battlefields just as the warriors did, so when the *géwël* returned from the battlefields, it was the *gawlo* who welcomed and provided entertainment for the *géwël*.

The *gawlo*, unlike *géwël*, were not percussionists; rather, they were singers who sometimes accompanied themselves with the *xalam* (plucked lute). However, in modern times, because both *gawlo* and *géwël* can be singers and hold a similar function in society, the two terms are often used interchangeably, and both are translated as 'griot'.[7] Here we have an example of a caste subcategory crossing ethnicities and becoming recognized as a new subcategory within the Wolof social system.

Even within the Wolof language, caste and ethnicity are not viewed as distinct categories. As Bonnie Wright points out in her article "The Power of Articulation," there is no single word in Wolof that means "caste" as opposed to "ethnic group." The questions "*Ban xeet nga?*" (What race/ethnic group are you?) and "*Gan gir nga?*" (What ethnicity/paternal line/family are you from?) can be answered with "I am griot," or "I am from Waalo," or "I am Wolof." In absolute literal terms, *xeet* refers to maternal lineage, whereas *gir* refers to either paternal lineage, family, or ethnicity; however, the ambiguity of the question is reflected in the various answers that can be given.

Another term that Wright does not mention, but that I found to have prevalent use among *géwël*, especially in reference to themselves, is the term *askan*, as in *askani géwël*.[8] In Munro's dictionary, *askan* is translated as "paternal lineage; family inheritance (according to one's last name)"; in Fal/Santos, it is translated as "origin, people, race." Thus again, lineage, family, and race/ethnicity are intertwined in reference to Wolof *géwël*.

For the purposes of this book, I propose a concept of *géwël* not as a strict subset of an immutable caste system, but rather in broader terms, encompassing lineage, family, ethnicity, and even community. Although any discussion of griots necessitates discussion of caste, I will also focus on the familial and social ties that bond *géwël* together and keep their identity strong to this day.

Modern Interpretations of Caste

The conventional view of the Wolof caste system as being hierarchical fails to give a complete understanding of the system, since the relationship between the different groups is equally important.[9] Wright argues this eloquently, stating that "the West African caste system, rather than being composed of hierarchically ranked groups, is really best understood as a set of groups differentiated by innate capacity or power sources" (1989, 2). I agree with Wright's view, since the relationship between *géer* and *géwël* is not simply one of superiority and inferiority: although the *géer* is of higher caste status, it is the *géwël* who upholds the *géer*'s status by praising him and telling him about the greatness of his ancestors, and so on. The *géwël* has tremendous power in speech, and if a *géer* is not seen as being sufficiently generous, the *géwël* has the power of publicly insulting or embarrassing the *géer*, thus lowering his/her status. Many *géwël* are very well respected for their abilities and have gained high personal status, despite the overall "lower" status of *ñeeño* as a whole.

In addition to the general relationship between *géer* and *géwël*, there is a special relationship called *géwëlu juddu*, or "griot by birth." Every *géer* family had a particular *géwël* family to which it was attached, continuing from generation to generation. Thus, although numerous *géwël* may appear at family gatherings and life cycle ceremonies, there is usually one *géwël* in particular who has a special tie to that *géer* and has intimate knowledge of his lineage, genealogy and ancestry. Indeed, the relationship between *géer* and *géwëlu-juddu* can be quite close, usually developing into a genuine bond of reciprocal friendship. (That is, not only with the *géer* giving and the *géwël* taking, but also with the *géwël* sometimes bestowing gifts upon his/her *géer*.)

As researchers reevaluate the *géer–géwël* relationship in modern times, the activities of *géwël* are likewise being reconsidered. In looking at people of griot origin in contemporary Senegal, Cornelia Panzacchi (1994, 92) divides people of griot origin in contemporary Senegal into three categories: (1) those who have decided to refrain from practicing their hereditary profession and have taken up some other occupation; (2) those who continue to perform, without innovation, the tasks and responsibilities handed down to them from their parents and grandparents in the traditional way; and (3) those who have managed to find or to create a new kind of occupation that still seems to fit the traditional griots' ethos, adapting the art of their ancestors to modern requirements and possibilities. Although Panzacchi notes that the categories "overlap and are not mutually exclusive,"(1994, 92) I would argue that most griots have had to adopt their skills and professions to changing times; thus, the griot who performs "traditionally . . . without innovation" is, in my opinion, nonexistent.

Panzacchi focuses on her third category, which includes griots as private detectives, griots as historians, griots in praise, business, and politics, and finally, griots in "showbiz." The griots who act as private detectives may do research on family origins and reputations of prospective marriage partners. The griot historians may lecture on history and popular wisdom, be hired for broadcast on RTS (the national radio and television station), or work with foreign scholars interested in learning oral histories. Griot praisers are ever present at family ceremonies (such as baptisms and marriages), and since Independence, politicians hire griots to sing, drum, and perform at political rallies. Finally, griots in "showbiz" include those who sing in the modern music arena, as well as those who drum and dance. However, Panzacchi focuses primarily on griot singers and considers their ability to recite genealogies as a large part of their continued success.

Panzacchi makes an important point, which is that "the difference between drumming, singing and history is not as great as it may seem to us outsiders, because in Wolof culture the three skills are based on a single common element: on genealogies" (1994, 203). She then discusses how genealogies can be conveyed through certain drum rhythms, or *bàkk*s, and how each family has its own *bàkk*. I will expand on this issue of *bàkk*s much more in Chapter 5 (on sabar repertories); but for the moment, it is sufficient to be aware of this link between drum rhythms and genealogies.

Among griots who continue to participate in "griot activities," there are those who make a living from their oratorical skills (as historians, or even politicians), and others who are singers and players of various instruments, of which the sabar drum is by far the most prominent.[10] These *géwël*, masters of the sabar drum, are the focus of this study, as they are perhaps the most prominent of all *géwël* today. Also known as *tëggkat* (literally, 'those who beat'), masters of the sabar drum are more often called just *géwël*. Thus, the term *géwël* can simply mean "sabar drummer." For example, when I asked if someone was a drummer (*percussionist*) or not, the answer would be, "Yes, he is *géwël*," rather than, "Yes, he can drum" ("*Waaw, mën na tëgg*"). This identity conflation between *géwël* and sabar drummer is an interesting one because it states the importance of the sabar drum in the contemporary *géwël* drummer's personal identity.

Master of the Word, Master of the Drum?

The griot has traditionally been thought of first and foremost for his oratorical skills, as singer, praiser, and keeper of oral history. As Senghor wrote, "*En Afrique noire, le griot, le troubadour, est souvent appelé 'Maître de la Parole'* [In Black Africa, the griot, the troubadour, is often called the Master of the Word.]" (1979, 105). Bonnie Wright discusses this association of the griot with orality in the context of a speech/action dichotomy, in which action is ideologically allocated to the *géer* and speech to the *géwël* (1989, 40). The *géwël* is the articulator of action—the one who "identifies" the other through speech, which is in a sense his action.

Likewise, Abdoulaye-Bara Diop identifies Wolof *géwël* with speech, categorizing them as *sab-lekk*, those who eat from singing (crowing) as opposed to the other *ñeeño, jëf-lekk*, those who eat by action. Here, instead of being contrasted with the *géer*, the *géwël* are contrasted with other *ñeeño*, who are seen as working through "action" rather than "speech." Again, the *géwël* are touted for their abilities in the oral domain.

What, then, of *géwël* percussionists, masters of the sabar drum? Do they not eat from action, from beating their drums? This is the point I would like

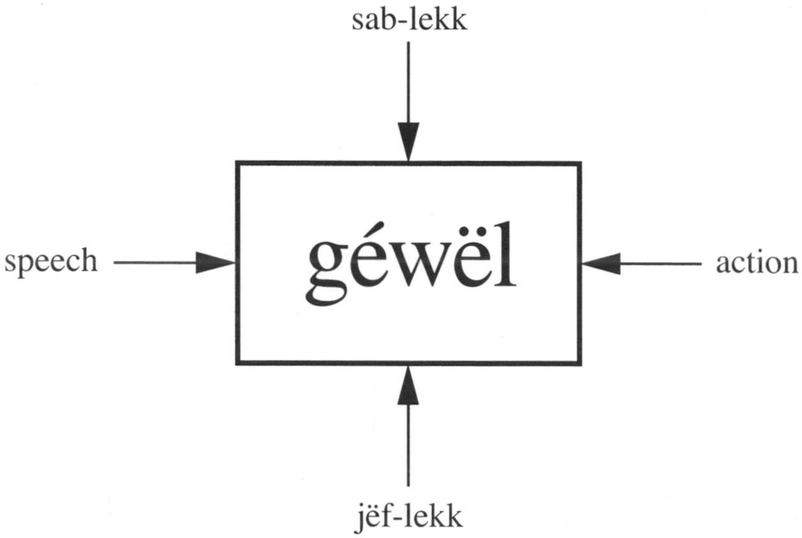

FIGURE 3.5. A new model for *géwël*

to clarify. In nearly all of the literature on West African griots, the griots are seen primarily as "masters of the word"—as singers, oral historians, those who make a living through their tongues. It is true that sabar drummers do also speak—many shout praises and are creators of *taasu*, the Wolof spoken word poetry. However, what I hope to show in this study is that the Wolof griot should not be seen primarily as a verbal artist, but as an *instrumentalist*, and it is his skill as a drummer that maintains and elevates his status. It is true that this status is in part due to the rhythmic representation of the spoken word (in *bàkk*s, which will be explored in greater detail in later chapters), but I will argue that drumming has become much more than just a representation of spoken word. The role of sabar drumming in Senegalese culture, from traditional events such as baptisms and neighborhood dance events to the modern music scene, where the sabar has become the hallmark of Senegalese popular music both at home and on the international market, has made the Wolof *géwël* something more than *sab-lekk*, he who eats through crowing. Indeed, the Wolof *géwël* percussionist makes his living through drumming, not speech. Through the sabar drums, Wolof *géwël* are able to transform and transcend the word (see Figure 3.5).

4

My Foreparents Used to Beat the Drums

WOLOF FAMILY, KINSHIP, AND MUSICAL GENEALOGY

> In Wolof in general, all those people named Mbaye, they are *géwël.* If you meet somebody named Mbaye, most of the time he will tell you that he is a *géwël.* . . . I myself, I am an Mbaye. . . . In our culture, the Wolof culture, my foreparents used to beat the drums. They used to be in front of the warriors; the king would just ride his horse, the warriors would follow with their guns, . . . but my foreparents would be in front of all of them, beating the drums, walking. . . . To be able to talk about the history of drumming, you have to be born in a family where everybody plays—your father, his father, his grandfather, up to five generations. Then you will be able to master the history of playing.
>
> —Macheikh Mbaye

IN THE PREVIOUS CHAPTER, I considered Wolof *géwël* not as a strict part of an immutable caste system, but as a broader category, encompassing family, lineage, ethnicity, and community. In this chapter, I turn to the family as a main unit of study.

The family is of central importance to Wolof *géwël*, fostering the production and reproduction of *géwël* knowledge. The family acts as learning environment, performance troupe, and creator of a unique sabar repertory. In this chapter, I will discuss the concept of family in general, then focus specifically on the Mbaye family, providing life histories from three generations. By examining the lives of these three musicians, I hope to show how the role of the Wolof *géwël* has changed over time, and how modern music has had an enormous impact on *géwël* percussionists and their status in Wolof society.

What Is "Family"? Kinship and Caste in an Urban Locale

In discussing "family," in the case of the Wolof, I mean the extended family—for among the Wolof, the important kinship unit is not the conjugal family but rather a much wider group of relatives. A household (*kër*) typically includes the eldest male as *borom-kër* (head of the household) and his first wife and children; but any number of other relatives may live there as well—siblings, nephews and nieces, grandchildren, and even fictive kin (with no actual blood ties). The frequency of divorce and children born out of wedlock further increases the number of dependents in a given family. Thus, the notion of family should not be rigidly defined, but rather has ever-shifting boundaries, allowing for exceptions to the strict rule of blood lines.

The importance of the extended family is reflected in the Wolof vocabulary. For example, the word *mbokk* meaning "relative," is derived from the root *bokk*, "to share."[1] The term *maam* is used for the class of grandparents and other ancestors; so no distinction is made between a grandfather and a grandfather's siblings. Likewise, for people of the same generation, the words *mag* (elder) and *rakk* (younger) would be used, depending on the person's age relative to the speaker; however, there is no distinction of whether this person is a brother, sister, or cousin. Thus, in a sense, every person in an older generation is a grandparent; likewise, every peer is a brother or sister. This lack of linguistic distinction promotes the inclusion of all relatives as "family."

In tracing kinship, the Wolof use a double descent or bilineal kinship structure. Although in former times, matrilineage was traditionally more important, the rapid spread of Islam in the late nineteenth century gave greater import to patrilineage. Thus, today, although families tend to be patrilocal and children are given the last names of their fathers, both lineages are considered important.

The Wolof believe that a person inherits from the mother's side blood (*dërët*), flesh (*soox*), character (*jiko*) and intelligence (*xel*) (Abdoulaye-Bara Diop 1981, 19). Certain serious illnesses such as leprosy are considered hereditary through the mother's side; likewise, witchcraft (*ndëmm*), the ability to kill and eat the souls of other human beings, is also inherited from the mother. From the father, one receives bones (*yax*), nerves (*siddit*), and courage (*fit*); supernatural vision (*nooxoor*) can also be inherited from one's father, but no other witchcraft powers may be inherited from him (Diop 1981, 20).

A child is thought to inherit more from his mother than from his father, as blood, flesh, character, and intelligence are arguably more important than bones, nerves, and courage. The ubiquitous explanation that Wolof *géwël* provide in reference to how they came to play sabar, "it's in my blood," reflects a matrilineal inheritance. Thus, although a young *géwël* most likely learns to play sabar from his father or other male relatives in his family, he is also able to inherit drumming from his mother's side.[2]

Family and kinship ties are further complicated when considering the issue of caste. Although there is a strong sense of distinguishing between different *géwël* families (which I will explore in depth in the course of this chapter), on another level, *géwël* sometimes consider each other "family," even if they are from different blood families. For example, *géwël* percussionist Lamine Touré explains:

> All the griots are the same. If you look closely, you will see that we [from different families] have different ways of playing, but if you want to generalize, we are all the same. For example, me and Macheikh Mbaye, we are not really from the same family; but when he was young, he played with my grandfather, and they became family. It's because of the sabar that we became family. (8/17/99)

Urban locale is another important factor in determining what constitutes family. With employment opportunities drawing increased migration from rural areas or even small cities into big cities, city dwellers often find themselves supporting large numbers of relatives, as migrants naturally seek kin to help ease the transition (Leymarie 1978, 92). In my primary case study, the Mbaye family, I will consider Macheikh Mbaye's household as an important family center for relatives coming from Kaolack to Dakar in hopes of pursuing careers as percussionists. Because the majority of mbalax (popular music) bands are based in Dakar, many young percussionists are drawn to Dakar in hope of starting a career in *musique*.[3] Whenever possible, these musicians permanently resettle in Dakar, renting their own rooms once they can afford to. However, the crucial transition period is often helped by Macheikh Mbaye, who not only provides food and shelter, but also serves as a mentor and connection for the newly arrived musicians.

Major Percussionist Families in Senegal

The perpetuation of the sabar tradition within family lines has led to the dominance of several specific *géwël* families in Dakar. Although there do exist other *géwël* who are active percussionists, sabar (in both traditional and popular music) is dominated almost exclusively by three extended *géwël* families. These are the families of Doudou Ndiaye Rose, internationally known percussionist of the older generation; Mbaye Dièye Faye (Youssou N'Dour's percussionist, whose family is commonly referred to as "Sing-Sing," named for one of their ancestors, Sing Sing Faye); and finally, the family of Thio Mbaye, also referred to as Mbayène.[4] At over fifty *sabar*s encountered in 1997–1998, by choice or by chance, when the drummers were not from the Mbaye family, they were either from Doudou Ndiaye Rose's family or the Sing-Sing family. An examination of the names of percussionists in all of the major popular music groups that perform regularly in Dakar (in 1998) yields the same result (see Table 4.1).

TABLE 4.1. Mbalax Percussionists

SINGER/GROUP	PERCUSSIONIST(S)	FAMILY
Youssou N'Dour/Super Etoile	Mbaye Dièye Faye	Sing-Sing
Thione Seck/Raam-Daan	Babacar Seck	Jeri-Jeri[5]
Omar Pène/Super Diamono	Pap Ndiaye	Mbayène
	Thio Mbaye (f)*	Mbayène
	Alassane Djigo (f)	Mbayène
	Aziz Seck (f)	Jeri-Jeri
Baaba Maal/Dandé Léñol	Bahkane Seck	Jeri-Jeri
	Bada Seck (f)	Jeri-Jeri
Alioune Mbaye Nder/Setsima	Lamine Touré	Mbayène
	Talla Seck	Jeri-Jeri
Lamine Faye/Lemzo Diamono	Moussa Traoré[6]	Sing-Sing

*(f) = former percussionist of the group.

More evidence of the prominence of these three *géwël* families can be seen during the annual Grande Nuit Diakarlo that takes place on April 4, the national holiday of Independence Day. Since 1995, this annual celebration has taken place at Dakar's Théâtre National Daniel Sorano. Termed the "*Regroupement des Tambours Majors de Dakar—Grand Nuit Diakarlo*" ("the reunion of master drummers of Dakar—the big night of debate/face-to-face"), the event is organized by all the major percussion families. In 1998, the Diakarlo was co-hosted by Macheikh Mbaye, Vieux Sing Faye, and Doudou Ndiaye Rose, representing the three main families. A celebration of the Senegalese tradition of sabar drumming, this Diakarlo was a lengthy concert of various famous singers (including Youssou N'Dour and Dial Mbaye) and *tassukat* (experts of Wolof oral poetry), interspersed with introductions and short speeches from the co-hosts and other famous griots. And to finish off in proper *géwël* style, the evening of course ended with a staged *tànnibéer* (evening *sabar*) led by Thio Mbaye and his group Rimbax, as women from the audience jumped up on stage to dance to the pulsating rhythms of the sabar drums. The annual Diakarlo, led by the three living patriarchs of the major sabar-playing *géwël* families, was and continues to be a vivid testimony to the importance of these families in present-day Senegalese culture.

Before launching into a more detailed discussion of my primary case study, the Mbaye family, I will provide an overview of the families of Doudou Ndiaye Rose (henceforth the Ndiaye family) and of Mbaye Dièye Faye (henceforth Sing-Sing).

The Ndiaye Family

Born Mamadou Ndiaye on July 28, 1930, Doudou Ndiaye Rose (who took his mother's name, Rose, as his last name, as is sometimes practiced) is perhaps the most world-renowned Senegalese percussionist. His international career began in 1960, when he met the famous jazz singer Josephine Baker in Dakar. His experiences touring and teaching around the world have led to collaborations with the Rolling Stones, Miles Davis, The Philharmonic Orchestra of the Netherlands, Salif Keita, Mory Kanté, and Julien Jouga (Panzacchi 1996, 195). He has recorded a CD entitled "Djabote," which is available from Real World Records (1994).

To this day, Doudou Ndiaye Rose continues to tour with his troupe of percussionists, The Doudou Ndiaye Rose Orchestra, which consists of over thirty members of his extended family. His family troupe has toured extensively throughout Africa, Europe, Japan, and North America. One particular subset of his troupe that has gained the most interest is the "Rosettes," his all-female troupe consisting of fourteen daughters and eight daughters-in-law.[7] With the Rosettes, Doudou Ndiaye Rose is credited with being the first to form and to promote a performance troupe of female percussionists.[8] In Dakar, Rose and his family are not very active in the mbalax scene, but can be found playing at baptisms, wedding celebrations, and *tànnibéer*s throughout the city.

The Sing-Sing Family

Mbaye Dièye Faye, also known as Babacar Faye, has enjoyed a long and successful career as Youssou N'Dour's percussionist. A close childhood friend of N'Dour's, he grew up with N'Dour, playing on the same neighborhood streets of the Medina quarter. They performed together in Ibra Kassé's Star Band in the 1970s. When the young Youssou N'Dour left the Star Band in 1977 to form his own group, Etoile de Dakar, which then became the Super Etoile de Dakar in 1979, he took Mbaye Dièye Faye with him (Cathcart 1989, 10). To this day, Mbaye Dièye Faye is not only Youssou's inseparable sidekick on stage, but he remains his extremely close friend as well. Indeed, the Super Etoile de Dakar stands apart from all other mbalax groups because of N'Dour's kindness and commitment to his musicians in a day and age when the cutthroat music business has made frequent changes in band members the norm.

In addition to his status as Youssou N'Dour's percussionist, Mbaye Dièye Faye leads his own group of sabar players (made up of brothers and cousins), known as Sing-Sing Rhythme.[9] Sing-Sing Rhythme (in its various forms) has toured Africa, Europe and North America. In Senegal, the group frequently performs at *soirées sénégalaises*, in addition to the usual *sabar*s, *tànnibéers*, baptisms, weddings, and wrestling matches. In recent years, following the lead of Thio Mbaye's pioneering cassette *Rimbax*, Mbaye Dièye Faye et le Sing-Sing Rhythme has released two cassettes: *Oupoukay* ('fan', named for a dance rage of the same name) and *Tink's Daye Bondé Biir Thiossane*. Both cassettes feature sabar drumming, with help from other musicians from Super Etoile.

The family sabar group is named after the family's famous ancestor, Sing Sing Faye. Unlike Doudou Ndiaye Rose's family, the Faye family is a griot family with a long history of sabar-playing. Originally from Sine but having since settled in the Cap Vert peninsula, the Faye family (originally of the Serer ethnic group, but eventually becoming Wolofized after settling in Dakar) has long been a prominent part of the music culture in the Dakar region. Thus ancestors Sing Sing Faye, Mousse Yess Faye, Biram Gueye, and Daouda Faye are credited with being some of the earliest great master drummers of the sabar tradition. The current patriarch of the family is now Vieux Sing Faye, a percussionist of the older generation and a contemporary of Macheikh Mbaye. However, Mbaye Dièye Faye remains the best known and most popular of the younger generation of his family, due to his association and longtime work with Youssou N'Dour.

Competition and Rivalry

As one might expect in a culture in which family pride is extremely important, there is a great deal of competition and rivalry among these three griot families: the Ndiayes, Fayes (Sing-Sing), and Mbayes. Although on one level all are griots and drummers and thus share that common bond, on another level there is a strong sense of loyalty to one's particular family, with all other families being seen as rivals. This feeling of rivalry manifests itself in a number of historical contexts, including drumming contests, political associations, wrestling competitions, fear of *maraboutic* practices, and today, the competitive nature of mbalax bands. Whether on a practical level, for money and patrons, or more broadly, for status and respect, competition among Wolof *géwël* was perhaps most obvious during the colonial era.

Drumming contests (*concours*) have historically been a part of Wolof culture.[10] These competitions flourished during the 1940s and 1950s in the colonial period, with winners being decorated and honored by colonial officials at events such as exposition fairs. In my interviews with *géwël*, I encountered many anecdotes about these competitions, which determined the best percussionist in a given region (such as Dakar or Kaolack). Such awards are great sources of pride and legitimacy for drummers, as shown when they speak of their ancestors, family members, or even themselves as having won such competitions. Although such *concours* were primarily a colonial practice and do not take place anymore, the competitive atmosphere remains in such events as the above-mentioned Diakarlo, the annual celebration of drummers. Although not a competition *per se*, the title of the event (which translates as "debate" or "face-to-face") invokes the atmosphere of friendly competition, with representatives from each of these three major families.

During the colonial period, the political parties also contributed greatly to fostering competition among drummers (and by extension, griot families). Political rallies, or "meetings," were elaborate performance events involving speechmaking, dancing, praise-singing, and, of course, drumming. The *géwël* drummers would play to announce the event, attracting spectators within earshot. Although rallies varied in size and function, their common features included *géwël* drumming and praise-singing, politicians rewarding the *géwël* with cash, and speeches given by politicians, with the highest-ranking politicians speaking last (Heath 1990, 213). Griot families played in support of particular political parties, lending an inherently competitive atmosphere to these musico-political events. Unlike *concours*, the sabar's presence at political meetings has continued beyond the colonial period and maintains its importance at the turn of the twenty-first century.[11]

In the world of sport, competition is a given. Thus, the strong association of drumming with traditional Senegalese wrestling is another major root of competition between drummers and drumming families. There is always a ferocious sense of rivalry, with each group playing its special *bàkk*s to support its wrestler.[12]

Competition and rivalry are also manifested in the spiritual realm, with the strong Wolof belief in *maraboutic* practices. Many griots fear that a rival can ask a *marabout* to create various *gris-gris* (mystical amulets) that would destroy the griot's ability to play. For example, the famous ancestor of the Mbaye family, Samba Maissa Seck, is remembered not only for his ability to play sabar, but for his mystical powers, for which he was greatly feared. Legend has it that if a *géwël* posed a competitive threat to Samba Maissa Seck, the latter would recite some mystic formulas into his drum sticks, and when the competitor began to play, either his drum skin would pop or he would suddenly wound his hand. Another family member, Maissa Mbaye (Macheikh Mbaye's younger brother) is said to have eventually given up drumming after falling sick due to the *gris-gris* of other griots who were jealous of his lucrative performances at wrestling matches.[13] Even during my fieldwork, some percussionists have confided in me their wishes to avoid disturbing or competing too fiercely with other percussionists for fear of mystical repercussions. Protective measures are constantly taken, with many percussionists wearing various *gris-gris* to protect their hands from evil harm.[14]

Competition between drummers is also evident in the mbalax music scene. In Dakar, where musicians such as Youssou N'Dour are held in higher esteem than even governmental officials, music is taken very seriously. During afternoon tea,[15] common topics of animated debate and discussion include the strengths and weaknesses of a new cassette release, any recent changes in personnel in a given musical group, and, of course, who is better (singer, percussionist, or other musician), X or Y. So for example, the question of "who is a better percussionist, Thio Mbaye or Mbaye Dièye Faye?" will invariably cause a passionate argument, with numerous supporters of both in each camp.[16]

Many of these insights on rivalry and competition arise from my own work with members of the Mbaye family. In my experience, members of one family will inevitably privately critique another family's drumming. These critiques cover the areas of playing style, hand technique, "stealing" and "copying" other family's *bàkk*s, innovation, simplicity or complexity of their own *bàkk*s, originality, and so on. Interestingly, the same critiques may be exchanged within the family. The nature of critique depends on which identity a given person is invoking. For example, in discussing his personal strengths and aspirations as a percussionist, a *géwël* may talk about how he is a better player than his cousin; in watching a *soirée sénégalaise* animated by a rival family, he may discuss how his family's playing style is more interesting and innovative than that of the rival family; and in the U.S., he will consider drummers from that same "rival" family back in Senegal to be his "brothers," as they share the *géwël* sabar tradition and inevitably bond to make a living in a new and foreign place.

On the broadest level, there remains a great deal of mutual respect among all *géwël* percussionists, since they share a tradition that binds them together, a highly guarded tradition that sets them apart from the rest of society. However, their most important alliance and trust remains within the family. This alliance can make it extremely difficult to carry out in-depth field research with more than one family. In Chapter 1, I explained how I came to work with the Mbaye family, and it is to the Mbayes that we will now turn.

Focus: The Mbaye Family

As I have mentioned earlier, their urban locale accounts for the Dakar Mbaye family's central role within their extended *géwël* family because family members from Kaolack resettle in Dakar in hopes of making a better living. Before launching into the biographical sketches of several key members of the Mbaye family, I will briefly describe the family's household environment. What is it like to live in the Mbaye family household?

The Residence: "*La Grande Maison*"

Since 1976, the Mbaye family has resided at Villa 2326 in HLM5 (a middle-class quarter next to the bustling HLM marketplace and one of the most densely populated neighborhoods in Dakar). Macheikh Mbaye, who will be introduced in greater detail below, is the head of the household. The house itself consists of a small courtyard area where family members socialize and greet visitors as they enter the compound. They share the courtyard with various animals, including pigeons, rabbits, and sheep. On top of the roof are more hutches of rabbits and chickens (see Figure 4.1).

At the entrance of the compound is an enclosed *salon* (living room), off of which is the master bedroom. Guests are normally received in the *salon*, and the head of the household is usually found there. The family television is also in the *salon*, so other family members (especially the children) sometimes congregate there to watch their favorite shows. However, the courtyard is the main congregating area, where the children play, the young adults gather to make tea each afternoon, and sabar drums are repaired and maintained.

In addition to a kitchen area and two bathrooms, there are seven other bedrooms in the compound, ranging from medium sized to quite small; and, of

FIGURE 4.1. Mbaye family residence: inside the courtyard

course, there is the "chambre de sabar," a small room where all of the sabar drums are kept (see Figure 4.2).

At any given time, there are at least fifteen to twenty people living in the house. By this I mean that many people actually sleep there—there are always many more people who come to visit, take meals, and spend most of their day there, myself included. For example, Lamine Touré makes enough money to live separately and thus rents a room down the street from the main household where he sleeps and keeps his personal belongings. Nevertheless, he takes his meals at the main household and can generally be found there throughout the day.

Other relatives, such as Thio Mbaye, have their own houses in different neighborhoods. Thio lives in HLM Grand Yoff with his wife, children, brothers and sisters. However, even Thio and his immediate family visit the main household on a regular basis, just as members of the main household sometimes go to visit Thio. The family is a very important part of the *géwël* community and Wolof culture as a whole.

FIGURE 4.2. "Chambre de sabar"

The atmosphere at the "grande maison" (as Lamine calls it) is typical of a *géwël* household—busy, active, and always with a certain element of chaos and disorder. Sounds of animated conversation, shouting matches, arguing, and children screaming and running around unattended mix with the occasional sheep baaing and chicken squawking to create a noisy and bustling soundscape. The noise level is only occasionally brought to a halt by the head of the household, usually when he is receiving guests, reading the newspaper, watching television, or trying to take a nap. Visitors constantly come and go, and during the afternoon especially, young adults gather for the daily ritual of *attaya* (Senegalese tea). As they sit around waiting for all three rounds of tea to brew, the young adults might discuss a range of topics, from the latest neighborhood gossip to their favorite mbalax groups, from politics to the recent bargain one got on a pair of used Sebago shoes.

The household is well known within the neighborhood as a house of *géwël*, so people routinely come to the house to procure the services of percussionists for a baptism, a women's association gathering (*tur*), or a *tànnibéer*. Many friends and acquaintances of the head of the household are also griots of his generation; likewise, young *géwël* of the extended family (such as Bahkane Seck, Bada Seck, or Talla Seck) pay an occasional visit. Without a doubt, villa 2326 at HLM5 is a true center of *géwël* activities, business, and socializing.

The Living Generations: Perspectives on Old and New

In the following section, I will present biographical sketches of three *géwël* percussionists in the Mbaye family, representing three different generations. The first, Macheikh Mbaye, is one of the few remaining "tambour-majors" (master drummers) from the older generation, with his career flourishing during the 1960s, in the early years of Independence. The second, Sitapha "Thio" Mbaye, is the current leader of the family sabar group, a major recording artist in the popular music scene. Thio is widely recognized as one of the best sabar players in Senegal. And finally, the third is Lamine Touré, an extremely talented percussionist of the younger generation.

By looking at several generations of percussionists within a single *géwël* family, I hope to capture a perspective that combines both the synchronic and diachronic: diachronic in that we are learning from the life histories recounted in these *géwël's* own words, spanning the 1930s to the present; synchronic in that these are portraits of three living people who are all currently active percussionists to varying degrees, expressing their thoughts and stories as they existed in the late 1990s. Judith Vander used a similar generational approach in her study of five Wind River Shoshone women whose ages spanned five decades, lending an important historical perspective to Wind River songs and musical experience (1988). I believe that if these generational perspectives within one particular family can be considered, additional insights can be gleaned about the role of the family in the life of every *géwël.*

Presenting Life Histories

In order to present these people's lives as honestly and vividly as possible, I have elected to include many lengthy interview excerpts and quotes as an integral part of this chapter. The purpose is to present these lives with "the richness of autobiography rather than the sketchiness of archival reconstruction" (Slobin 1989, 78),[17] and in so doing, give a sense of what it means to each person to be a *géwël* percussionist.

The use of life history as a window into African cultures can be seen in numerous important works, including Mary Smith's classic *Baba of Karo* (1981), Patricia Romero's *Life Histories of African Women* (1988), Mirza and Strobel's *Three Swahili Women* (1989), and Marjorie Shostak's *Nisa: The Life and Words of a !Kung Woman* (1983). Ethnomusicologists have also focused on the lives of individual musicians, with notable examples including the work of Mark Slobin (1989), Timothy Rice (1994), Simon Ottenberg (1996), and Maria Teresa Velez (1998). In keeping with this tradition, however, I fully acknowledge the complexities involved in presenting life histories. Despite my attempt to represent these people "in their own words," the end result is inevitably a collaborative product of both researcher and informant, since the interviews were initiated by me, reflecting my own interests and motives. Similarly, the final presentation of these interviews results from my editorial decisions.

These life histories with members of the Mbaye family were recorded only after I had already spent five months in Senegal and knew my interviewees quite well.[18] Although I had not specifically set out to collect life histories, the open-ended nature of my questions (with most interviews beginning with the question "tell me about yourself—your life, when you were young," and so on) led my interviewees to discuss their lives in great detail.

The interviews with Macheikh Mbaye were conducted in Wolof with the assistance of my research assistant, Papa Abdou Diop. Translations of these interviews were also done with Diop's assistance. I conducted the interviews with Thio Mbaye in French and prepared the translations myself, as I did other interviews in a mixture of French and Wolof (with occasional assistance from Diop). All interviews were transcribed verbatim in their native language before being translated in English, which is how they appear in this book. I have tried to maintain the continuity of the original interviews, keeping sections in chronological order and editing out as little as possible. Edited pieces are marked with brackets.

Three Life Histories: Macheikh Mbaye, Thio Mbaye, and Lamine Touré

Macheikh Mbaye

Macheikh Mbaye is the *borom-kër*, or head of the household, at HLM 5 villa no 2326. One of the best-known *tambour-majors* of the older generation, he had by 1997 officially retired, but still drummed on occasion (see Figure 4.3).

Managing the household is no easy task, as there are at least fifteen to twenty people living in the household at any given time, including several small children. Aside from providing food and shelter for his family, Macheikh has been instrumental in welcoming relatives interested in drumming. In this way, his household has served not only as a place to live but also as an important learning environment for promising young sabar players. The significance of this household's role in providing a learning center for sabar will become clear as we look at the life histories of family drummers in younger generations, namely Thio Mbaye and Lamine Touré.

FIGURE 4.3. Macheikh Mbaye

Macheikh Mbaye was born on October 21, 1932, in Dakar. Born into a *géwël* family of sabar drummers, Macheikh Mbaye is fiercely proud of his family history.

> My parents [Daouda Mbaye and Fatma Ndiaye] taught me everything I know. And they were taught by their parents, and their parents by their grandparents, and their grandparents by their great-grandparents, and so on and so forth. So . . . I am not a kind of *géwël* who just "learned to play." When I was born, my family was immersed in drumming. My father was born in a drumming environment, and my grandfather as well. My mother used to be the best dancer in Dakar . . . in her generation . . . and she was a very good singer as well. So I was born in a real *géwël* environment. (3/2/98)

During his teenage years, Macheikh Mbaye was raised by his maternal uncle, Modou Yacine Ndiaye, another accomplished drummer. At this time, Macheikh's own father was aging and was therefore not actively drumming. But in the mid-1940s, Modou Yacine Ndiaye was at the height of his drumming career, winning numerous awards throughout the country.

While living with his uncle, Macheikh Mbaye attended school, starting at the age of ten. However, his mind was elsewhere.

> When I went to school, I was not good at all because my entire mind was on the drums. I would live with the drums, all day; when I woke up, I saw the drums; when I got back from school, I saw the drums; I was surrounded by them all of the time. So I would just play, when I was a little kid. I would play and play, and as I grew up, I found myself becoming a pretty good drummer. Nobody ever taught me how to play; I mean, nobody just took my hand and showed me the way to play. I was simply surrounded by the drums, and I learned how to walk by bumping into the drums. When I was three, four, five years old, I was able to play. When I was eight, my uncle used to watch me playing, and he would cry. People would ask him why he was crying, and then he would say, "He is still a young boy, but what he is playing is beyond me! That's why I cry." This is what explains [why I have the right to] talk about this topic, because I inherited it. Drumming and singing is something you inherit; you don't study it. It's in the blood. (3/2/98)

In 1948, Modou Yacine Ndiaye passed away. By this time, at the age of sixteen, Macheikh Mbaye had become a talented drummer and began playing for political rallies organized for Léopold Sédar Senghor's party, Bloc Démocratique Sénégalaise (BDS). In 1952, Macheikh was supposed to join the army, but he was exempted after his medical examination. At this point, Macheikh's father told him it was time to make a career of drumming.

He told me, "You are nineteen, you have to play. You're a man now; you have to play. Because I used to play, your uncle who raised you used to play, so you have to play. You can play; you were born in a *géwël* family, so anyway, you have to play."

At that time, the cultural associations gathering all the women in town wanted me to play for them. But I was scared. My dad forced me to go play, and I remember the first sabar I ever played was organized by the BDS, in an area called Rue 17 angle 6. It was at Mbaye Diop Fari Mbaye's house, at nighttime. Everybody came to see that *tànnibéer*, and they were all amazed afterward because they thought I had been playing for a hundred years. That's incredible, some of them said! And that was the beginning of my story. I was playing, playing, playing in ceremonies such as weddings and baptisms . . . I was playing everywhere. There is not a street in Dakar I haven't played on. In those days, I was very popular. Everybody was calling me. I would go to Thies, to Saint Louis, to Casamance; I was playing everywhere. (3/2/98)

In 1958, a political party by the name of RDA (in Bamako, at the time of Modibo Keita, who would soon become the first president of Mali) sent a telegram to Macheikh Mbaye summoning him to go play in Mali for the Senegalese people living in Bamako. He took the train with his drumming crew and spent over two months in Mali. Upon his return in 1959, he was asked to join the newly created Ensemble Instrumental Traditionnel as the lead drummer.[19]

Soon after, the national ballet in Senegal (La Linguère)[20] was planning a European tour. Maurice Sonaar Senghor, the director of the Théâtre Nationale Daniel Sorano, asked Macheikh Mbaye to join the ballet as the lead drummer. This was the beginning of many touring seasons, which brought Macheikh all over the world, including to France, Germany, England, the United States, Brazil, Columbia, Panama, Argentina, Morocco, Algeria, and Tunisia.

In 1969, the national drama troupe was to go to Algeria to perform the theatric performance of *The Exile of Alboury in the Pan-African Festival*, an adaptation of the novel by Cheikh Ndao. Again, Macheikh Mbaye was invited. The troupe won the gold medal, and upon his return, on November 12, 1969, Macheikh Mbaye was awarded the *Chevalier de l'ordre du merite* by President Senghor, "for his services rendered to the Senegalese people by promoting their culture."

Soon after, Macheikh Mbaye stopped touring in order to care for his aging mother. When he left the Théâtre Nationale, the government gave him a job at SOTRAC (the national transportation system). He worked[21] at SOTRAC until retirement in 1987, but throughout this time, and up to the present, he continued drumming.

Aside from his own performing career, Macheikh Mbaye prides himself on his role as teacher, passing on his knowledge to the younger generations.

So the other people in my crew, I taught them how to play. Now, many of them have passed away, but some of them are still alive, though they are not playing anymore, such as Moussa Ngom, Ibou Ndiaye, Saa Louga, Mbalo Samb[22] . . . a lot of people. So when my children grew up, I decided to give them what I got from my parents. Now my son Khalifa is playing in [the ensemble of the] Théâtre National Daniel Sorano; Biran, my nephew, is playing; Moustapha Niass [my son] . . . I'm passing on to them everything I know. And now they are very good drummers. They take the drums that belong to me and play with them. I have a nephew, Pap Talla Ndiaye, now living in Holland, who is a great drummer. . . . I taught him how to play. There are many great drummers in Dakar whom I taught how to play; people like Boy Diouf, for example. He has his own crew. If you go to Pikine or Guediawaye,[23] there are many drummers out there who I taught how to play. Even if you go to Saint Louis, I have my impact on the drummers. What I learned from my father, and what my uncle taught me, I passed it on to the next generation. (3/2/98)

There is, however, one drummer in particular who was taken in by Macheikh Mbaye as a child and grew to become arguably the best sabar player in Senegal today. That drummer is Thio Mbaye. Although Thio is now an integral part of the family (see Figure 4.4), the story of their relationship goes back to sabars, not a blood relationship *per se*.[24] Macheikh Mbaye explained the story.[25]

The relationship that I have with Thio Mbaye actually goes back to his father, Massaer Mbaye. Massaer Mbaye and his wife, Agida Seck, are the parents of Thio Mbaye, and you know Massaer had a legacy as a drummer because his father, Mane Diaw Mbaye, was a great drummer. As I said before, Mane Diaw Mbaye, the father of Massaer Mbaye, was a great *tama* player . . . and then Massaer Mbaye got that legacy from his father Mane Diaw Mbaye and became one of the [greatest] drummers ever. He's well known throughout Senegal because he used to be a very good player, among the best players. So, Massaer Mbaye and I got acquainted back in 1951. At that time I was about eighteen or nineteen years old, and then that was the time President Senghor . . . through his party BDS, was running for the candidacy to the French Assembly . . . I was acquainted with Massaer Mbaye through that political campaign. At that time, I was very good at playing the drum. As I told you already, it's a legacy; you know; I did not learn it. It's a legacy because both my parents, my mother and my father, are descendants of griot families. So, this is a legacy I got from my parents. So in 1951, there was a large ceremony that took place here in Dakar in a neighborhood called Guel Tapée at someone's house. . . . At this time, all those percussionists from Kaolack and Dakar [were] invited. And for the sake of the campaign, it was a big event for all the drummers from Kaolack and Dakar,

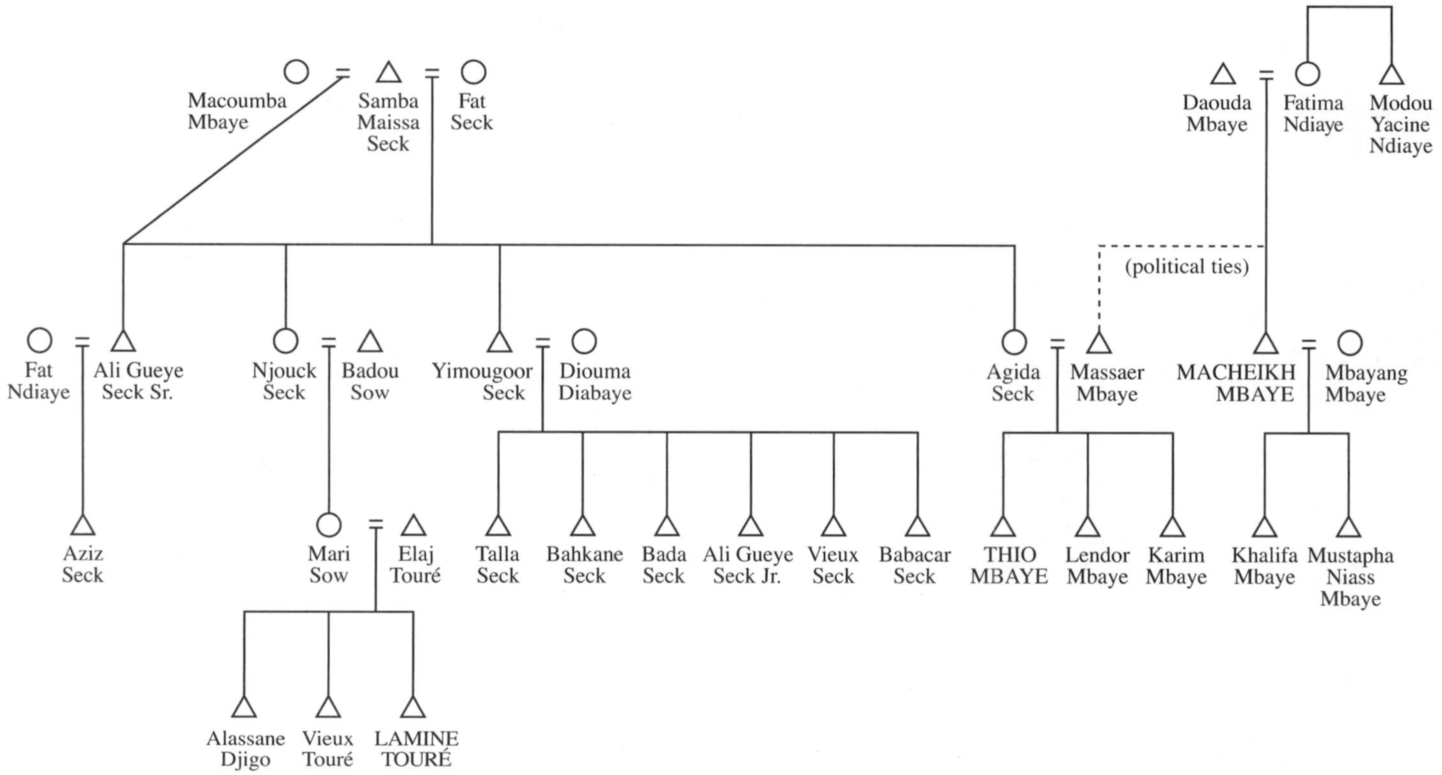

FIGURE 4.4. Family tree

to just compare the styles, or whatever—it was a big event. And at that time there was that guy called Sitapha; Thio was named after him because you know, Thio's real name is Sitapha. Thio is just like an artist's nickname or something. But his real name is Sitapha. The guy, Sitapha, the real one Thio was named after, used to be a *faux lion*,[26] actually, that's what we call *simbkat.* And there were just a few in Senegal, because we had one in Kaolack, one in Dakar, probably one in Thies and one in Saint Louis, and Sitapha was an excellent *faux lion.* At that time, the ceremony we call *simb* was very popular, and people liked it a lot; it's different from what you can see nowadays, because there's some kind of [theatrics] added to the ceremony nowadays, but in the former times, it was a real thing that people would just enjoy. At that time, Massaer Mbaye was invited for the sake of that ceremony, the political ceremony, and he came with his own *batterie* [drum ensemble], you know; all the guys just came at that time, Thio Mbaye wasn't even born yet, let alone Lamine and all those other guys. And I was young; I was about nineteen years old—very good at playing. And somehow, I came to know Massaer Mbaye. You know, before even coming to Dakar, Massaer Mbaye was told that there was a boy in Dakar who [was] very, very good at playing. That boy was named Macheikh Mbaye, and then he was playing with his uncle. . . . So, through the grapevine, Massaer Mbaye had already heard about me. So in any case, we got to know one another. Since my uncle . . . was playing for [the] BDS political party here in Dakar and Massaer Mbaye was playing for the BDS section in Kaolack, when they were invited, we got to get together, and you know at that time, Massaer Mbaye had heard about me. . . . So on that day, we finally met each other. So the delegation from Kaolack came Saturday morning at about nine o'clock here in Dakar, and it was like everybody, with their green flags—you know, we had women, young men, old men, like a big caravan coming back to Dakar, and it was a Saturday night, and the event was to take place in the evening. In the morning time, Massaer Mbaye was to perform, to play with his crew. And then I was not even there. And you know, my uncle could not play without me. No matter what, I had to be there for him to be able to play. At that time, I was the heart, what I can say was the heart of the *batterie*; if I was not there, then it was difficult for him to play, and the *batterie* would not be able to perform as well as it would if I were present. In the afternoon, I saw many sabars out there; I didn't even know Massaer Mbaye. I saw those guys; they had played already. But I saw the sabars, and we were supposed to play right afterward. I saw a nice drum with the Sine Saloum sign on it. It was a beautiful drum, and I asked to whom it belonged; and Massaer Mbaye told me that it was his drum. I started to play; he was so impressed . . . like being hit in the eyes. I impressed him so much that he nearly went crazy because he could not even imagine that a nineteen-year-old boy could play that well . . . In the afternoon the big event was to take place, the *faux lion* event we call *simb*, and then since Sitapha was the *faux lion* from Kaolack and Massaer Mbaye was the head drummer from

Kaolack, Massaer Mbaye had to play for Sitapha, and it was to take place in the afternoon. And Massaer Mbaye just asked my uncle if he could let me play for him, because he wanted me to have an impact on the playing style [of his group]. As you know, what I used to do for my uncle, which we call *tulli*, is some kind of the soul of the rhythm, because when playing, the one that is leading the *batterie* is like number one; and the second, next in line, is the one who is playing *tulli*, which is like the soul of the rhythm. To be a great player, you have to play the *tulli* because it's the basis of any rhythm. At that time, my uncle didn't want to let me play because he was like, "You don't know him, you can't play with him," and I told him that I could, and I begged him to let me play with them. But the *faux lion* was in a house, over there in the back, and he heard the playing in progress, he noticed that there was something different. When he came into the crowd, he saw me—he had not seen me before, and he was asking who I was. Sitapha was like a real *faux lion*; he was tall, strong, black, and very ugly. And when he came, people started running, and then Massaer Mbaye made way for him and he was right in front of me, looking at me, and this let me play better than I could ever play, because being in front of a *simb* is something very stimulating for me. Sitapha started to dance; he was dancing, falling down, dancing—after a while, he was just amazing. He stared at me. After a while, dancing for a while, you know, some people don't speak; so he asked the crowd who I was and everybody started to applaud. That day I was given so much money, people were so happy because of my playing, and that was the beginning of my relationship with Massaer Mbaye. You can say that between me and Massaer Mbaye, there was no blood relationship *per se*, but through the political campaign, we just got acquainted, and that was the beginning of a long lasting relationship of the two families. . . .

After that event, when Massaer returned to Kaolack, I decided to go to Kaolack to see him, and I told my mother about it. I had never been to Kaolack before, but ever since I played with Massaer Mbaye, I felt like he was the best player [I'd seen] in Dakar, you know; even my uncle wasn't his equal. So I decided to go to Kaolack in order to have a little of their flavor, like to suck their flavor, because I knew that those guys were playing so well and I felt like if I went to imitate and learn their playing style, maybe I could be a very extraordinary player. When I went to Kaolack, I found Massaer Mbaye playing, so first I was listening, and then after he invited me to play, and then people living in Kaolack were totally amazed because they could not imagine such a boy playing that well, and they kept asking who I was, and then Massaer would tell them that he has never been to Kaolack before, but if he plays that well, it's normal, because it's a legacy for him, because on his father's side, everybody's a player—his father, his grandfather, his great grandfather, and on his mother's side, likewise. So it was quite normal for him to play that well. Massaer would tell everybody in Kaolack that it was quite obvious that I played so well because my father was one of the—actually he was the greatest player ever—and then that's right, you know, as well as my uncle, the brother of my mother, who was a very good player—my uncle was named Modou Yacine Ndiaye. Along with his father, along with his father they were the best players ever.

At that time, Thio Mbaye was very young; he was about five or six years old; and some years later, Massaer came to see me and telling me that he was the father of Thio Mbaye and he wanted me to take care of his son. Massaer Mbaye told me that "Thio Mbaye must be a good player because I, Massaer, am a good player," and on Thio's mother's side, Agida Seck, his mother, came from a griot family where people played very well. So in any case, Thio was supposed to be a good player. But he wanted me to guide, to direct Thio Mbaye and give him a style, a particular style. He went on telling me that if Thio Mbaye stayed in Kaolack, he was going to be a good player, but [he would have better opportunities in Dakar]. So when he first told me that, I refused; I denied the offer. I could not just give lessons to anybody. The second time, Massaer Mbaye came to see me, with Thio's mother. And then when they reiterated the offer, then I could not refuse it, so I accepted Thio, so he came to stay with me, and he was playing *mbalax* for me, during all my playing. After playing *mbalax* for me, then he went on playing the *tulli* for me. And then, as time went on, he was actually the leader of the *batterie* because he was very good; he just got it as a legacy from his parents, too. Thio Mbaye was even not—I mean, people from Kaolack, when they came to Dakar, could not even recognize Thio Mbaye because he had changed a lot; I mean, he was so amazing, so much so that people from Kaolack could not recognize him. And there was something new in his playing. And then these other people from Kaolack followed the same steps, like Bada came right along, just staying in my house, in order to just have the same flavor Thio Mbaye had had. They all wanted to follow Thio's steps; after Thio Mbaye, Bada Seck came, and after Bada, Alassane Djigo came, and then long after, Lamine Touré came too—that was the story about my relationship with all the kids. (8/12/99)

Sitapha "Thio" Mbaye

Born to Massaer Mbaye and Agida Seck on September 18, 1959 in Kaolack, Sitapha "Thio" Mbaye was born into a family steeped in the griot drumming tradition (see Figure 4.5).

Above all, I was born in a griot family. My father and his father were both drummers. So I inherited it from my father. . . . You know, I already had rhythm in my blood. I was born into it, so it was part of me. When I was young, I watched my father playing, my uncles, my elder brothers . . . I watched how they played. And so at an early age, I taught my peers how to play the accompaniments, and I tried to play like my father, like my

FIGURE 4.5. Thio Mbaye

uncle, the brother of my father, because everyone in the family played sabar. So, I learned in this way; this is how I grew up. And as I grew up, I created my own style of playing. Yes. My own rhythm . . . I already played my fathers' rhythms; for example, if I played, and you listened, you would say it was my father playing, or my grandfather, or my uncles . . . I could already do this. But as I grew up, I tried to create Thio Mbaye. But it's a heritage, what I've inherited from my father. (5/23/98)

Thio traces the history of sabar drumming in his family through both his mother's and father's lineages.

My father's father was named Mane Diaw Biran Mbaye. My father's mother, her name was Ndeye Cheikh Mbaye. The father of my mother was Samba Maissa Seck; my mother's mother was Fat Seck. . . . When my parents were young, they [with their parents] came to settle in Kaolack.[27] And since they were the great drummers, the great griots, it's how my father, Massaer Mbaye, grew up in Kaolack until he became a great *tambour-major* in Kaolack. And my mother's elder brother too—my uncle. And his father . . . that's how they came to Kaolack.[28]

> So it was like that, the big family; and it was a big family because there was my mother's brother, big brothers and little brothers. . . . And the others played sabar, but they stopped playing early. . . . My father had a little brother who has since passed away, but he played sabar too. So, it was a big family of sabar players; griots, you know, in that time. And we were the greatest of that time period. The biggest in the continent, honestly. That's why I am part of this family; excuse me, because it's not modest. But it's a true story, because they say here in Senegal, according to the historians, on the radio, and . . . even you hear from time to time, they speak of my father, my uncle Ali Gueye Seck Sr., the father of Aziz Seck . . . yes. It's my mother's side. (5/23/98)

In Thio's family, the men were not the only percussionists.

> Even my mother, she played sabar . . . she was the first woman in Senegal to play sabar [at a large public event], with my father. . . . It was in Dakar at the Stadium Iba Mar Diop. [She played sabar] because she was a great dancer. You know, when you are a good dancer, you should play sabar, too, because in order to be a good dancer, you have to have a good ear. . . . My father, he played often. He played at circumcision ceremonies, *kasak*. From time to time, if there should have been six players, but there were only five, my mother would replace the sixth. . . . I wasn't born yet. Or if I were alive, I was just a few months old. I don't remember it. But the archives, other people, other griots talk about it, so I have learned the story. It's too bad that they never filmed this; there were no video cameras; otherwise it would be a wonderful souvenir. (5/23/98)

Despite his family's long history of percussionists, Thio was not initially encouraged to pursue sabar as a career. When Thio was young, his father sent him to school to train to become an electrician. Although a percussionist himself, Thio's father felt that it was difficult to earn a living as a percussionist and wanted his son to have other career opportunities. However, Thio's heart remained with the sabars. As he continued his studies, he continued his sabar playing as well. He finally confronted his father and expressed his desire to pursue a career as a percussionist.

Reluctantly, his father gave in and sent him to Dakar to be raised in the household of Macheikh Mbaye.

> My father did not want me to become a drummer. He wanted me to be somebody—a bureaucrat, or the head of a business or something like that, but not a percussionist, because in those days, being a percussionist was not as lucrative as it is now—there weren't many music groups, or ballets or

> whatever. But even at that age, I had visions for the future—and I believed in these visions. So finally I asked my father for permission to really play the drums. He wasn't happy, but I told him really, if you let me play, I will become a percussionist and earn lots of money from my art, and he responded, that's impossible. Because he only saw the *sabar*s that one organizes in the street, the little *sabar*s [which hardly earn any money]. . . . You cannot build a house from such money. But I told him, I have another objective. So he finally gave in and wished me luck. (5/23/98)

With his father's reluctant blessing, Thio moved to Dakar in 1971 to begin his career as a percussionist. In 1979, Thio joined the famous *Ballets d'Afrique Noir* under the direction of Mansour Guèye. The ballet was an important learning experience for Thio, allowing him to learn new styles of music. Thio toured around the world during his fifteen-year stay in the *Ballets d'Afrique Noir*.

Thio's main entry into the popular music scene came when he started playing with Ismael Lô in 1984 (when Ismael Lô left Super Diamono for a solo career). Thio played with Ismael Lô until Lô's group experienced a breakup in 1992, and in 1993, Thio returned to Super Diamono New-Look, now under the direction of Omar Pène. After a solid five years with Super Diamono, not to mention recording with nearly every well-known singer in Senegal from Youssou N'Dour to Coumba Gawlo and even Malian singer Salif Keita, Thio officially left Super Diamono to launch his own solo career in February 1998. Since then, he has toured with Cheikh Lô and is preparing for an upcoming tour with Africando.

Alongside his successful career in other singers' bands, Thio Mbaye became a pioneer in the Senegalese popular music scene by being the first percussionist to release a solo cassette in 1993. The title song "Rimbax" immediately rose to become the country's number one hit song, proving that a sabar-based cassette could win the support of the Senegalese public.

This sabar-based cassette, which won the support of the Senegalese public, helped to blur the boundaries between popular music and the traditional music Thio had been involved in. Throughout his professional career, while he was playing and recording with internationally known singers, Thio was also the leader of his family sabar group, Group Rimbax (namesake of the cassette). The family sabar group would perform (and continues to perform) at naming ceremonies, weddings, wrestling matches, neighborhood dance events, political rallies, and other occasions.

Within the family sabar group, one particular percussionist receives the highest praises from his uncle Thio and is considered second in command. That person is Lamine Touré.

Lamine Touré

Lamine Touré was born to Mari Sow and El Hadj Touré on September 13, 1973, in Kaolack (see Figure 4.6). Lamine's father, El Hadj Touré, was not a griot. However, Lamine traces his griot blood through his mother's lineage and explains that he was raised as a griot.[29] The importance of his griot identity is evident in Lamine's words.

> My father . . . was not a griot. It's my mother who's griot. My mother, all of her family, is griot. So I was born into a griot family; I was not born at my father's. I was born in my mother's house. She gave me a griot naming ceremony, I know griot things, I have the ways of a griot, they educated me as a griot. . . . My mother did this. So I became accustomed to playing. (4/28/98)

Growing up in Kaolack, Lamine's childhood years bear some similarities to those of his uncle, Thio Mbaye.

FIGURE 4.6. Lamine Touré

> When I was very small, I began to play when I was four years old, the pots, the little sabars. You know, the little sabars that we made. . . . When the tomatoes were finished, we would take the big tomato can and mount it with a skin, and we would play on that. . . . We would play, me with Lendor [Thio's brother]; I was the oldest, he was a few months younger, and I was four; we began playing in the doorway of the main household. We had an order. . . . Do you know why we played well? We were well organized. We were accustomed to going to big *sabar*s to watch, so we saw how important discipline was. We would say, "it's you who will lead today." The rest would follow. Another day, somebody else would lead. . . . We played all the time, in that big doorway. . . .
>
> When I slept, I would play [tapping] my stomach. After eating lunch, when I went to take a nap, I would play on my stomach because I liked playing. I learned like this. When I was all alone in my room, I would also speak *rythmes* and *bàkk*s with my mouth. (4/28/98)

Lamine's childhood years included a brief residence in Mali, which exposed him to drumming traditions other than sabar, namely *djembé*.

> I went to Mali for several years with my mother (she was doing commerce there). When I was in Mali . . . you know, in Mali, they play *djembé*. So I asked my mom for one, and she bought me a little *djembé*. . . . After one year, I began to speak Bambara better, and I even began to forget Wolof. I started to follow my interest in *djembé*. The Bambaras organize something like *sabar*s, but there, they play *djembé*s instead. It's like a *tàanibéer* of *djembé*s. So I went to watch these events, and I liked them, and got used to them. This is how I began playing *djembé*. Whenever I went to watch an event, I would return home, then try to play [what I had learned]. After school, when the kids got out, I would go to school to play for the other kids. Nobody wanted to leave; when I played, all the other kids would stay with me to listen. (4/28/98)

When Lamine returned to Kaolack at the age of seven, he brought back with him his *djembé* skills, which he eagerly showed his friends. Although his friends were impressed, Lamine returned to find that they had advanced with their sabar playing in his absence and were now playing sabars made from old mortars.[30] It took him several months to readjust to playing sabar, to speak Wolof again, and to get reacquainted with his friends.

Lamine's return to Kaolack also meant he had to attend school. However, like Macheikh Mbaye and Thio Mbaye, Lamine's mind remained with the sabars.

> Because I was seven years old, my mom told me that I had to go to school. My father brought me to school. But whenever I was at school, I would be dying to leave to go play sabar. I went to school, but I understood nothing.

> The teacher would tell my mom, 'your son, I don't know about him. He taps on the table; he plays the tables, like the sabars.' I would take my pen and play all the time, and the teacher would yell at me "Hey, you! STOP PLAYING!" He didn't like it when I played on the table, and I would be punished for this, all of the time. [laughing] (4/28/98)

Meanwhile, Lamine continued playing sabar with his group of friends, which included Lendor Mbaye, Karim Mbaye,[31] Assane Niang, and Issa Sow. For fun, they would organize *sabar*s for the young girls in the neighborhood. This was how they practiced. One day, their hard work earned them the opportunity to do what they had never done before: play in a real *sabar*. Their luck came when their uncle, Ali Gueye Seck, needed drummers for a program one evening. Lamine was eleven years old at that time.

> Ali Gueye Seck (my uncle), had his own group of percussionists. One day, he had a program, but all of his percussionists were off playing at other gigs. This was a big problem for Ali Gueye because he had nobody to accompany him. So he came to our house, and saw Thio's mother, Agida Seck. Agida said, "Well, take the kids—they're here!" We had already gone to sleep. But Agida convinced him that we played well and he should take us. We were still young and had never played on real sabars—only tomato cans and mortars. But Ali Gueye was desperate, so he agreed, and came to get us. So Lendor, Assane Niang, and Issa Sow and I went with him.
>
> We took a taxi. We were so-o-o excited—our first time really playing! And we were going to play on real sabars! But he scared us too. He said, "You better play well!" But we said, "Yes, we are real percussionists, we won't disappoint you." So during *saaji* [warmup], we played. There were us four kids, one other older guy, and Ali Gueye—we were just six. When the women came, they said, Ali Gueye, but these are kids! How can they accompany you? He said, "You'll see." And we showed them.
>
> But the sabars were heavy. (We carried them standing up.) We got tired quickly. But Ali Gueye wouldn't let us give up; he would yell at us and hit us. We were scared and tired. Issa Sow even began to cry because he was so tired. But we played well. Afterward, they gave us each 300 cfa. We were so excited with 300 cfa! After walking home, I arrived around one o'clock in the morning. My mom was worried that I was home so late, but I told her we played well, and I gave her 100 cfa. I kept my 200, and in the morning, I went to the corner store and bought lots of things—peanuts, chewing gum, and mint candies. (8/12/99)

This was the beginning of Ali Gueye's "kiddie" sabar group. Because they all enjoyed working together, and the audiences enjoyed seeing the kids play, the group was a success. Although his memories of the children's group include some rough moments (due to Ali Gueye's strict disciplinarian style), Lamine gives Ali Gueye credit for helping them to become good percussionists.

> We were very excited and happy to play with him. We liked his way of playing and the way he dealt with us. He was very serious and could be mean; we were afraid of him. But that's why we became such good percussionists. He wanted us to really play well, to use a good hand technique, and to play strongly. . . . We got very tired. But because we were afraid of him, we played well. . . .
>
> With Ali Gueye, we would even sleep over at his place . . . because by the time we finished playing, often it was nighttime, so we would just go to his place and crash. We were very young, but my mom didn't mind; we slept at his place, ate at his place . . . every day, we were at Ali Gueye's; we would even help him to shave skins and mount the sabars. We did a lot with him.
>
> Ali Gueye even bought matching outfits for us. Because we were doing so well. We would play at soirées—in Kaolack—we did a competition, we even competed against Omar Thiam's group.[32] And we won—we blew them away! It was in a big hall at the Chamber of Commerce. (8/12/99)

As Lamine began playing more often with older drummers, making some money, and even getting his own gigs, he decided to quit school. (He was twelve years old and in the fourth grade, or *quatrième*). He explained to his mother that he had thought through his decision carefully and that his mind was not on school; he wanted to play sabar. She finally agreed, but she suggested that Lamine take on a part-time job as well, since sabar was not as yet a full-time activity. So Lamine began working at his brother's friend's shop, where he did car repair and painting (*tôlier/peinture*).

Around the age of thirteen, Lamine moved to Dakar for six months. He stayed with his elder brother, Alassane Djigo, who had come to Dakar to further his career as a percussionist. Lamine started playing with singer Salaam Diallo. As Salaam's percussionist, Lamine began to gain some recognition as a talented young percussionist and was also able to earn a modest salary. However, he was not accustomed to life in Dakar and missed his friends, so he returned to Kaolack. A few years later, in 1988, he decided to go back to Dakar, realizing the lack of economic opportunities for percussionists in Kaolack and drawn by the possibilities of playing with music bands in Dakar. At first, Lamine lived with his brother Alassane at Niari Tali, and he never went to the HLM quarter. But after a while, Alassane introduced Lamine to Macheikh Mbaye's family at HLM,[33] and Lamine became acquainted with Macheikh Mbaye, Biran, and Thio. Although Lamine was still playing with the singer Salaam Diallo, he began playing with his uncle Thio Mbaye as well. Here he explains how he started playing with Thio, as well as how he came to live at HLM at Macheikh Mbaye's house.

> When I first arrived in Dakar, I played with Salaam and some other griots in the Niari Tali area. But after a while, I started hanging out with Thio more; Thio lived in Parcelles, which was a bit far, but I would go to HLM and find him there. He took me under his wing, and I began playing with him. We've played together ever since.
>
> I began living at HLM when I was sixteen years old. It was because I had friends there, like Niass. . . . He's younger than I am, but we became good friends. You see, I lived with my brother at Niari Tali, and it's not very far from HLM. So I would basically spend the day at HLM and then go back to sleep at Niari Tali. But then my brother moved to Patte d'Oie [when he got married]. So I began to stay at HLM, and I grew to really like it. When my brother's wife left [to go back to England], I was to return to his place, but at this point, I preferred to stay in HLM. Also, Macheikh Mbaye said that I should stay at his house, out of convenience, since I played sabar. . . . For example, sometimes they are asked to play, and there isn't time to go far and look for Lamine. So it's better if you sleep here, stay here, since you play sabar with the other kids. I agreed, and Alassane agreed, too. So I stayed. . . . You see, the head of the household, he is not my father; he's not even the brother of my mother; but he's a griot. Also, he helped to raise my uncle Thio Mbaye, and my brother Alassane Djigo. So the relationship went deep—he was like the father of my brother. That's why I went there; he was good to me. . . .
>
> There were times when I had problems, but I didn't allow myself to get discouraged, because I refused to return to Kaolack. It's not good to stay in Kaolack. Because there, even if you know how to play well, you won't be able to find much work. That's why Thio left, and Alassane left too. (4/28/98)

With some experience playing with Salaam Diallo, Lamine gained an interest in popular music bands. At the time, his brother Alassane played with the highly successful band Super Diamono and would bring Lamine along to watch, and sometimes even to play. In 1991, Lamine formed his first group, called Xiis. The group included Charles Ndoye (singer), Malick Diaw on guitar, and Charles' brother Massar on drumset. They once opened for Youssou N'Dour in a concert at the Sacre Coeur High School. After a while, Lamine left the group and started playing with the singer Moustique Mbaya[34] at LT, a small Dakar nightclub. It was the first "real" group Lamine played with in Dakar. Lamine played with Moustique for the next several years—first with Moustique's own group, Keur Gi—then with another group called Diaspora, for which Moustique sang. (Diaspora performed at the downtown club Fouquets, playing both *variétés*[35] and *mbalax*.)

In 1994, Lamine joined the Ballet Ousmane Cissé,[36] where two nephews of Macheikh Mbaye, Biran and Talla, also played. There, Lamine broadened his experience with both sabar and *djembé*, learning various different styles of African music. The Ballet rehearsed at the Centre Culturel Blaise Senghor, where Alioune Mbaye Nder and his Setsima Group also practiced. One day, Nder's percussionist did not show up, so Nder asked Lamine to rehearse with his band. Lamine practiced with them, and Nder liked his playing. When Nder's percussionist, Daouda Faye, permanently left the band (during a tour in France), Nder asked Lamine to join Setsima Group. After six months with Setsima, Lamine quit due to monetary disputes. However, during this entire period, he continued playing in Thio Mbaye's sabar group. Soon after Lamine left Setsima in 1995, Mapenda Seck incorporated Lamine into his mbalax band.

> Meanwhile, I was still playing with Thio's sabar group. We played *soirées sénégalaises*, *tànnibéer*s, *ngente*; after a while, Mapenda Seck noticed me and asked me to come play with him. At first, it was great; a lot of people came to hear us, and we played well [at RK, another small Dakar nightclub]. But you know how the music business can be. Sometimes it works, sometimes it doesn't. After a while we just went down the tubes. That's when I joined the Orchestre Nationale. I stayed there for about a year. The Orchestre Nationale is a governmental organization, so the government would pay us. . . . If there was a big affair, with the President, we would play. I played a lot there; [singer] Soda Mama was there as well, and even Moussa Ngom. . . . But meanwhile, I was still playing with Mapenda. After a while, Mapenda's group started to succeed again, and we began to play more. I played with Mapenda for about two years.
>
> Then one day [in 1997], one of Alioune Mbaye Nder's staff came to look for me and said he wanted me to come play that night with Alioune Mbaye Nder. So I came and played with Talla Seck,[37] and it was a big success. They told me that they wanted me to come back to Setsima. At first, I refused because I was still part of Mapenda's band. But afterward, I realized that Setsima was much more successful than Mapenda; it's the music business. . . . So I left Mapenda and joined Setsima. That's how I rejoined Setsima Group. (4/28/98)

Since then, Lamine has enjoyed a successful career with Alioune Mbaye Nder et le Setsima Group. The October 1997 release of their hit cassette *Lenëen* brought the group to the top of the charts and made the group the hottest mbalax band in the country for months to come. With Nder being dubbed the "new king of mbalax," the group aspired to compete on the level of mbalax giant Youssou N'Dour, with a CD released in France and several tours to Europe and North America.

Although Lamine was content with Setsima Group, he had dreams and aspirations for leading his own sabar troupe, a troupe that would travel internationally and promote the sabar. In his words,

> I play with Setsima Group because I like playing mbalax. But I love playing sabar more than I love mbalax. If I had my own sabar group, I would go far with it. Because if the sabar stays here in Senegal . . . there are many parts of the world where they don't know about sabar yet. So I would like to develop the sabar and make it known. . . . There are many rhythms in the sabar. The sabar can play jazz; it can play rock; afro—everything. I like Alioune Mbaye Nder, but Setsima is his group; if I had my own group of percussionists, that would be something else. (4/28/98)

There are some obvious differences in the experiences of these three percussionists, who grew up in different time periods. Macheikh Mbaye's stories are reminiscent of the colonial past, when world expositions and competitive events were rewarded with high state honors and decorations. His professional experience as a percussionist included his involvement in various national ensembles—ballets and drama troupes. With Thio Mbaye, we see a shift in employment from ballets to the mbalax scene, as Thio's career flourished with the rise of mbalax and both its immense popularity in Senegal and its increasing international presence. The cassette recording industry paralleled this rise of mbalax, and in turn made possible such projects as Thio's solo cassette, *Rimbax*. We then have Lamine Touré, who in his mid-twenties has already enjoyed a successful career with an *mbalax* band, has toured Europe and North America, and has dreams of leading his own sabar troupe that will tour internationally and experiment with different genres of music.

Although they represent three different generations, the three percussionists share many common life experiences. All three began drumming at an early age, essentially growing up in a family sabar environment. They all had some degree of schooling but eventually quit school to pursue sabar. Although Macheikh Mbaye was born in Dakar, Thio Mbaye and Lamine Touré both migrated from Kaolack to Dakar in hopes of greater work opportunities as percussionists. But perhaps the most striking thing that these three share is their sense of family pride—they are proud of being *géwël*, and proud of being percussionists, but more specifically, they are proud of their family and their ancestors. It is these ancestral roots that we will turn to in the next section.

Selective Genealogies: Remembering Past Generations

In the three biographical sketches presented above, the *géwël* all situate themselves within a long line of percussionists. Tracing genealogies, and in particular invoking the names of particular ancestors, is an important part of *géwël* identity. As studies on genealogical method have shown, genealogies that are orally reported are not only primary documents from the past, they also "reflect the uses that the present society has for its own history" (Irvine 1978). Wolof genealogies are no exception.

According to Judith Irvine, Wolof genealogies "must be seen in the context of a society much concerned with distinctions of rank and relations of patronage, and in which prevailing ideology links both of these to birth and family" (Irvine 1978, 653). Although Irvine's study deals primarily with griot recitations of noble lineages, the same observations can be made of *géwël* lineages. Irvine gives an example of the genealogical praise-song for a woman of noble origin named Nogoy Samb. In the course of the text, the *géwël* connects Nogoy Samb's ancestry to the founder of the village, to another former village chief, and to the well-known ancestors of a local family of import (Irvine 1978, 659). Clearly, linking the woman to ancestors of high status is the *géwël's* way of praising the woman and thus increasing her own status.

Likewise, by connecting oneself to ancestors who were well-known percussionists or performers, present-day *géwël* are able to validate and reinforce their own positions as transmitters of an ancient and important tradition. In this section, I will present some *géwël* of past generations in the Mbaye family who were repeatedly mentioned to me in interviews. Again, I will try to include their own words as much as possible so as not to compromise the vitality of the stories.

There is one ancestor in particular who is always mentioned with great pride and is regarded as the "great forefather" of the sabar tradition. Samba Maissa Seck, Thio Mbaye's grandfather and Lamine Touré's great-grandfather, was perhaps the greatest ancestor of the Mbaye family.[38] Samba Maissa Seck's parents, Soxna Niane and Saxaya Seck, are the oldest generation of the family that I was able to trace, but Samba Maissa Seck was the earliest ancestor who was commonly mentioned in my interviews.

According to Mari Sow (Lamine Touré's mother), Samba Maissa Seck was in fact not originally from Kaolack, but was born in Thies. As a young drummer he performed throughout Senegal, and finally in his mid-twenties settled in Kaolack. The story goes that one of his *geer* (Diodio Diaw) was celebrating the wedding ceremony of his daughter, so Samba Maissa Seck went to Kaolack to play at the wedding. After the ceremony, Samba Maissa Seck played so well that the *geer* asked him to stay in Kaolack and bought a house for him. It was in this way that Samba Maissa Seck settled in Kaolack.

When talking about her sons, Alassane Djigo and Lamine Touré, Mari Sow said:

> All in all, this is our tradition. They [Alassane and Lamine] inherited it because their great-grandfather used to play the drums, Samba Maissa Seck. And he was known throughout the world. All those drummers in Senegal know him, and since he was the father of my mother, and I am the mother

of Alassane and Lamine, it is natural that they play sabar. They must play sabar. It was a legacy. That's why they are playing; it's their tradition. (5/8/98)

Stories of Samba Maissa Seck include accounts of his mystical powers. Samba Maissa Seck could recite mystical formulas into his drum sticks, so that when his competitors would start playing, their drum heads would pop, or they would develop big wounds on their hands. These mystic abilities were also used in a positive manner: Samba Maissa Seck was known for his ability to marry off unmarriageable women. The story goes that he would hold a *sabar* for such a woman, then ask her to sit on the sabar; after he recited various mystical chants, a man would turn up with a dowry within three days, without fail (Sow 7/2/98).

According to his descendants, Samba Maissa Seck's drumming abilities were so great that he was given a woman as a reward. In Mari Sow's words,

> My grandfather played everywhere, even in Mali. The president of Mali at that time asked him to go play in Mali. He played so well that they gave him a wife in Mali as a present. When my grandfather, Samba Maissa Seck, came back from Mali, he was accompanied by the woman he was given. My grandfather went to Mali, played so well, that he was given a woman as a present. That woman was Mbenda. Actually, when the woman came, we did not know what her name was, so my grandpa called her Mbenda. . . . That's how it was. This is just to tell you that my grandfather was an artist. (5/8/98)

The generation after Samba Maissa Seck included such names as Ali Gueye Seck, Sr. (not to be confused with his nephew with the same name, who led the "kiddie" sabar group in Kaolack in which Lamine played when he was little), Yimougoor Seck, Njouck Seck, Agida Seck, and Massaer Mbaye. Because these people were the parents and foreparents of the *géwël* I interviewed, I heard many stories about this generation. Ali Gueye Seck and Yimougoor Seck took over their father Samba Maissa Seck's tradition when he passed away; they, along with Massaer Mbaye (who married their sister, Agida Seck) were frequently mentioned as the greatest drummers of that generation. The women, Njouck Seck and Agida Seck, were also recognized for their accomplishments.

Njouck Seck is remembered as a great dancer and singer in the early years of Independence in the 1960s (see Figure 4.7). In the words of Mari Sow, reminiscing about her mother,

> Njouck Seck would praise Senghor [the first president of Senegal]. At that time, Ibrahima Seydou Ndao was a supporter of Senghor. Anytime Senghor came over, my mother would sing for him. [With her sister-in-law] they would sing for Senghor, and that night there would be a *tànnibéer*. They would dance

> for him to make him happy, then afterward, the *tànnibéer* would be over. Everybody knew my mother. She would sing for Ibrahima Seydou Ndao so well that one day he gave her a car. At that time, you would not have cars like nowadays; cars were rare. And Senghor gave her a check—a LOT of money, you know, at that time, in 1961. (7/2/98)

Njouck Seck also is remembered for her beauty and wealth. Before she died, her health declined and she lost her sight. According to the doctor's diagnosis, it was the glare of all the gold jewelry that she wore that destroyed her eyes. Soon after, she passed away. Whether or not this was the true reason for her blindness, the story paints Njouck Seck as a woman whose great talents were rewarded by wealth and prosperity.

Njouck Seck's sister, Agida Seck, is remembered for her skills as a dancer and as one of the first female sabar players. A story about Agida and her husband, Massaer Mbaye, is proudly told by their son, Karim Mbaye:

> My mother was the first woman to play the sabar in Senegal. She was called Agida Seck; she was my mother, and she was the first one ever, the first

FIGURE 4.7. Njouck Seck (Lamine Touré's grandmother); courtesy of Lamine Touré

> woman ever to play the sabar in Senegal. Yes, my father told me a story that one day, he and Ali Gueye Seck came to Dakar for a meeting we call *congres*. . . . He had a real *grand boubou* [robe] on; we call it *jam put*. Aladji Mansour Mbaye introduced my father to the public, saying he came from Kaolack to participate, and he came with his delegation and crew, so people expected something very extraordinary from my father because they had heard about him. So they all have their sabars on, but when they came inside the circle, my father was given the microphone, and then all of a sudden, the bag he had with him was full of pigeons! He had about ten pigeons in the bag, and a rifle (*maq doom*). So one by one, he took the pigeons out, and as each pigeon flew away, he shot it. After this, he started to play a *bàkk*, a *bàkk* that all people from griot families would understand. And after that, my father told me that my mother came inside the circle, and my father gave her the sabar, and my mother was leading the whole *batterie*, and that was the first time people ever saw a woman playing the sabar. That's my mother, Agida Seck. (8/16/98)

Family as Transmitter of Tradition and Producer of Knowledge

As is evident from the life histories presented above, the family is the center of the young *géwël's* learning environment. Born into a household where sabars are everywhere and many of the family members are sabar players, a *géwël* child's baptism is only the beginning of a life-long exposure to sabar. As was mentioned by both Thio Mbaye and Lamine Touré, many youngsters begin drumming as *fo* ('play'), creating little sabars out of tomato cans and leftover pieces of skin. The less ambitious may use plastic water jugs as drums; the more ambitious may advance from tomato cans to leftover mortars. In any case, young children from *géwël* households can be found in many doorways and on streetcorners, diligently playing their makeshift drums.

As the young *géwël* becomes more interested in sabar, he will start accompanying family members to their various performances (such as baptisms, weddings, *turs*, and *sabar*s or *tànnibéers*). As a child, he will be expected to help carry the drums to the performance site, to keep the drumsticks and distribute them as drummers break their sticks and need new ones, and to carry out other small tasks (such as fetching water or cigarettes for the drummers).

Through careful observation and repeated exposure to the *rythmes* and *bàkk*s, the young *géwël* will become familiar with the family repertory—both standard *rythmes*, and *bàkk*s particular to the family. He can be seen sitting behind the other drummers, tapping out the rhythms on his lap. If lucky, he may be allowed to play during *saaji*, the warmup period before the full audience arrives for a *sabar* or *tànnibéer*. The young *géwël* will eventually be allowed to play in the ensemble itself, albeit on less important occasions (such as small neighborhood *sabar*s organized by teenage girls, or a small *tur*).

There is little patience for beginners and even small mistakes, so a beginner should expect harsh words of criticism. Over the course of my field research, I observed this phenomenon with Lamine Touré's younger brother, Vieux Touré. In 1997, Lamine's mother had sent Vieux from Kaolack to Dakar to be looked after by Lamine, in hopes that Vieux could begin to learn the ropes of sabar playing and, in the future, earn money as a musician. Vieux was usually present at sabar events in which Lamine played, though depending on the event, he would sometimes just carry the sticks or play during *saaji.* On the few occasions when he did actually play, he was constantly being yelled at and insulted by his brother, and his playing was usually cut off by Lamine or another more senior player snatching the drumstick out of his hands. However, by 2005, he had become one of the best players in the group.

Despite the verbal and, at times, physical abuse, young *géwël* persist, for it is only repeated exposure and repeated effort that will eventually give them the experience to play well and hold their own. Within a group, there is always a clear hierarchy in terms of experienced versus inexperienced players. For example, in Thio Mbaye's group, Group Rimbax, Macheikh Mbaye (Jr.) was one of the newest and least experienced members in the group in 1997, and he was constantly reminded of this fact. However, Macheikh had to swallow his pride and accept the occasional put-down or insult in order to learn to become a better player. Years later, a younger and less-experienced brother would join the group, and Macheikh might be in a place to give that person advice. There is a real "pecking order" among the family sabar players; but it is precisely this hierarchy and respect for the more experienced that allow the young sabar player to learn and to advance.[39]

It should be noted that there is no formal apprenticeship in the sabar tradition: nor do *géwël* give each other formal "lessons."[40] As Macheikh Mbaye states, "Nobody ever taught me how to play. . . . Nobody just took my hand and showed me the way to play." But rather he was surrounded by drums and grew up with the drums, so it was natural for him to learn how to play. However, more experienced drummers often take the less-experienced drummers under their wing. For example, although Lamine Touré is only a few years their elder, Macheikh Mbaye Jr., Massala, and Moustapha Niass all cited Lamine as their mentor and have on repeated occasions mentioned how much Lamine has taught them and how much they learn from watching him play.

The family atmosphere is a center for sabar care and maintenance in addition to learning. At Macheikh Mbaye's HLM household, the sabars have a room of their own. There is a never-ending cycle of wear-and-tear—drumheads break constantly, and drum shells occasionally need to be oiled, revarnished, or patched up. The household is a center for sabar preparation as well. Mounting drumheads is no simple matter, and only a few family members are highly experienced in doing so; the others help out with tasks delegated to them. In the Mbaye family, Thio Mbaye, Karim Mbaye and Lamine Touré are the ones who typically lead and supervise a head-mounting venture. In preparation for an upcoming *tànnibéer*, Lamine Touré will purchase several goatskins for drumheads. After soaking the skins, he will ask his younger brother Vieux to undertake the boring but meticulous task of shaving the skin (although time-consuming, skin-shaving requires great care since just one wrong move with the razor blade will cut and thus ruin the skin; this task is made less pleasant by the multitude of flies that are always attracted to the wet, smelly skin).

The less experienced relatives help by oiling the wood with palm oil, and with various steps in mounting skins. Although Lamine will be in charge of the important steps, the others will help with simpler tasks (such as finishing lacing the *mees* through the head).

Family as Performance Troupe: Group Rimbax

The importance of family to the Mbaye percussionists is perhaps most clearly manifested in the existence of the family sabar group Group Rimbax. Although family members traditionally play together, the formation of "official" family sabar troupes (with an official group name, a manager, etc.) is a fairly recent phenomenon. The Mbaye family sabar group was founded in the early 1990s by Thio Mbaye, the leader of the group, who felt he wanted to have his own sabar group in the same way a singer leads a mbalax band, with semiprofessional management and possibilities for international touring. The group name comes from a sabar sound that is in part a signature rhythm of Thio's. He explains:

> Rimbax is a sound that is among the most difficult to produce on the sabar, and it's a sound I love a lot; so I wanted to give my group this name. It's "pax, pax, pax." So Rimbax Papax, it's a sound one plays; my album has the same name. It has given me good luck because the album has been a success, and I have toured all over the world promoting my album. (5/23/98)

Group Rimbax consists of a roster of percussionists from the extended Mbaye family—mostly from the younger generation, with a few exceptions. The group roster varies slightly depending on who is available, but the core members of the group remain the same. Although many of the members also play in popular music groups, their allegiance is to the family sabar group. For example, Lendor Mbaye[41] played with Souleymane Faye, Karim Mbaye plays with the group Njollor, and Khalifa Mbaye plays with the Ensemble Lyrique Traditionnel. But family ties bring the percussionists together to play with Thio and make the group special to all of them. In Thio's words,

> With my group, Group Rimbax, . . . I have the chance to have a group that I want because I play with—for the most part—my brothers, and my sons/nephews, too. Someone like Lamine Touré, he's my son/nephew. Because I am the brother of his mother. I also have two brothers, Lendor and Karim, in the group; I have Khalifa and Biran, their father is the one who raised me, Macheikh Mbaye; so there are only brothers and big brothers. . . . It's family. (5/23/98)

Various members of the family, such as Macheikh Mbaye Jr., express allegiance to the family group:

> We all belong to Rimbax because Thio did a lot for us. If we know about sabar now, it is thanks to Thio. The guys in Pikine (a suburban quarter) . . . , they're just friends. But I belong to Rimbax. Rimbax is my group, the real one. You know my family lives in Pikine, so when they have a *programme* and I happen to be there, they will ask me first if I have something to do with Thio. If I don't, I could play with them on that particular *programme*. But they know that Rimbax is my group. (7/25/98)

Managed by Thio's longtime friend, Doudou (who arranges transportation to and from events and manages all financial dealings), the family sabar group performs at naming ceremonies, weddings, *turs*, wrestling matches, neighborhood dance events, political rallies, and *soirées sénégalaises*. Of these, naming ceremonies, *turs*, and neighborhood *sabar*s/*tànnibéers* are the most common. The size of the group depends on the type of event for which the group is needed; for example, a small *tur* may call for just three or four percussionists, whereas a full-fledged *tànnibéer* could require as many as sixteen. And although Thio Mbaye is the official leader of the group, if Thio is abroad or unavailable, he will pass on the leadership role to either his brother, Karim Mbaye, or to Lamine Touré. Karim explains:

> I have another sabar group, and I am the leader of that group. It's like another version of Rimbax; we call it *Deuxième Rimbax* ('Rimbax no. 2'). Deuxième Rimbax is something like Rimbax—you know, the same. If somebody wants to organize a *tànnibéer*, and if he calls Thio and the price does not match the level of Thio's fame, Thio will pass the gig to me. So I'll go with my family, and we will play without Thio. I might be the leader, but after the *tànnibéer*, we all share the money, and we have good relationships among us. (8/16/98)

As an ensemble, the percussionists are accustomed to playing together, and they thus have the same "style" and, of course, the same repertory.[42] Each percussionist also shows his strength on a certain part (instrument) in the ensemble, as Thio once explained:

> It usually goes like this. Lamine, he always plays *mbëng-mbëng*; Niass and Karim too—it's like a team. On the *cól*, it's usually Mbaye Samb; I had another brother named Momar Ndiaye but he's in Kaolack right now . . . , but he, too, and Mbaye Samb, and Khalifa. Also Mini Mbaye. Mini Mbaye—when he's here, he plays *cól*, or often the *nder*. But we don't change around that much. We respect the same instruments. Each percussionist has his instrument. Yes, . . . I am proud that each one has his strength on a particular instrument. They are all very strong players. (5/23/98)

The boom in Rimbax's popularity was due in large part to the release of Thio Mbaye's solo cassette of the same name in 1993. The success of the cassette *Rimbax* helped to blur the boundaries between traditional and popular use of sabar by bringing the traditional sabar group into the nightclub scene. Up until 1993, one could only hear sabar in nightclubs when it was in the context of an mbalax band. The domain of traditional sabar groups remained outdoors and on the street; for example, outside the house of a baby who just had a naming ceremony, or at a *tànnibéer*.

Because of the success of the cassette "Rimbax," the proprietors of the popular Sahel nightclub in Dakar collaborated with Thio Mbaye and came up with the idea of holding a sort of *tànnibéer* inside the nightclub, with an entry fee. In this way, Thio and his Group Rimbax invented the "*soirée sénégalaise*," which, at the turn of the twenty-first century, has become a tradition in its own right and is a weekly event at most major nightclubs in Dakar.[43]

Family as Creator and Owner of Sabar Repertory

In addition to serving as a learning environment and a performance group, the family also has an enormous impact on the sabar tradition in that each family has its own unique repertory—that is, the *bàkk*s that are composed and in a sense owned by each family. These *bàkk*s are an extremely important part of the *géwël* percussionist's repertory because they distinguish one drummer from another, or more importantly, one family from another. Each family has its own repertory of *bàkk*s that become signifiers or markers (emblems) of that particular family's identity. This topic will be explored further in Chapter 5.

Conclusion

The family is a fruitful unit of study when looking at Wolof *géwël* because of its central role in the production and dissemination of *géwël* knowledge. A case study of the Mbaye family, one of three major percussionist families in Dakar, shows the importance of familial ties in learning, performing, and professionalization of sabar. Through the life histories of Macheikh Mbaye, Thio Mbaye, and Lamine Touré, we can see how the success of sabar in popular music has enhanced *géwël* identity in the contemporary period. In the next chapter, we will turn our attention to the instrument which has played such an important role in maintaining the Wolof *géwël's* status in modern-day Senegal: the sabar drum itself.

5

If a Snake Bites You, You Will Think of Death

SABAR REPERTORIES

Ku jaan matt	If a snake bites you
sama xel dem ci dee	you will think of death
ba ngay dundu	whether you live
ag ba ngay dee yepp	or whether you die
sama xel dem ci dee	you will think of death

THE WOLOF SABAR REPERTORY is infinitely vast, changing over time, and varying from one griot family to another. Two recent recordings[1] provide fine examples of sabar, though to my knowledge, thus far there exists no detailed documentation or musical analysis of this repertory other than my own. In this chapter, I hope to fill the gap by transcribing and analyzing some key components of the sabar repertory as I learned them from the Mbaye family from 1997 to 2005.

This chapter will begin by examining how Wolof *géwël* talk about their music, introducing some basic musical terminology used by sabar players, including two important concepts: *rythme* and *bàkk*. Transcriptions and analyses of standard dance *rythmes* (short rhythms) and selected *bàkk*s (musical phrases) played by the Mbaye family will illuminate the broader discussion of history, development, and change in the Wolof sabar repertory. In particular, a look at the transformation of the spoken word into *bàkk*s will explain how *géwël* percussionists in contemporary Senegal have empowered themselves and managed to maintain their status in a modern context.

Discussing Music

Wolof *géwël* do not have a large, specialized vocabulary specifically for talking about sabar. Musical ideas are most often expressed through action or through verbal exchanges using words otherwise common to everyday life. For example, mistakes are often addressed by a disapproving look or shake of the head from another drummer. (And if the mistakes continue, this could lead to a painful blow with a drumstick!) Some common verbal reactions to mistakes or poor playing might include "*Taxawal*!" ("Stop it!"),"*Baaxul*!" ("It's bad!"), or a more forgiving "*Ya ngi dem*!" (which is literally 'you're leaving', meaning "You're getting off track"). Good playing is affirmed by smiles, nodding of heads, and exclamatory remarks such as "*Ey way*!" (an interjection showing happiness), "*Foofu la de*!" ("That's it!"), or "*Waaw waaw*!" ("Yes, yes!"). When a fellow percussionist is playing exceptionally well, he is congratulated by a quick twisting motion of the others' fingers on his head or through a monetary bill shoved into his mouth.[2] In postperformance discussion, sabar drummers may say, "*Tu as bien joué*!" ("You played well!"), or "*Neexoon na torop*!" (literally, "It was very delicious!"); other comments may include a discussion of tempo (as being too fast or too slow) or the quality of the sound (such as the drums not being well tuned beforehand). In talking about specific *rythmes* or *bàkk*s that they played, *géwël* refer to *rythmes* by their specific given names and refer to *bàkk*s using mnemonics. Otherwise, strictly musical terms are rarely employed, which should not be surprising, considering that Wolof *géwël* learn through observation and action rather than explanation.

Within the somewhat small musical vocabulary used by Wolof *géwël,* two main concepts have emerged as fundamentally important: *rythme* and *bàkk*. For the most part, everything that a percussionist plays fits into one of these two categories. The Wolof have incorporated the French term *rythme*[3] to denote a standard set of rhythms that are played at events such as naming ceremonies and *tànnibéer*s. In general, each *rythme* accompanies a particular dance. These *rythmes* are usually short and simple and have specific names, such as *ceebu jën* (named after the national Senegalese dish of fish and rice). The names of these *rythmes* and the dances that accompany them are familiar to the general Senegalese public: most Senegalese women know how to dance to these *rythmes* and often request them by name.[4] *Rythmes* have been part of the sabar repertory for a long time,[5] and the *rythmes* themselves have not changed, although the popularity of some have faded or changed with time. The *rythmes* are standardized, so they remain the same whether played by one family or another.

In contrast to the *rythme* is *bàkk,* a Wolof term that *géwël* use nowadays to refer to what they translate as "musical phrase." The *bàkk*s are the sites of *géwël* creativity. Some *bàkk*s represent verbal text; some are dedicated to particular people or families; others are simply creative compositions or examples of virtuosity. *Bàkk*s can be handed down from generation to generation, some unchanged, others modified over time; and every day, new *bàkk*s are created, whether by an individual or a sabar group as a whole. Although *bàkk*s can be played by an entire sabar troupe in unison, they are typically overlaid on the *rythmes* of *Kaolack* or *lëmbël,* which will be described later.

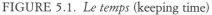

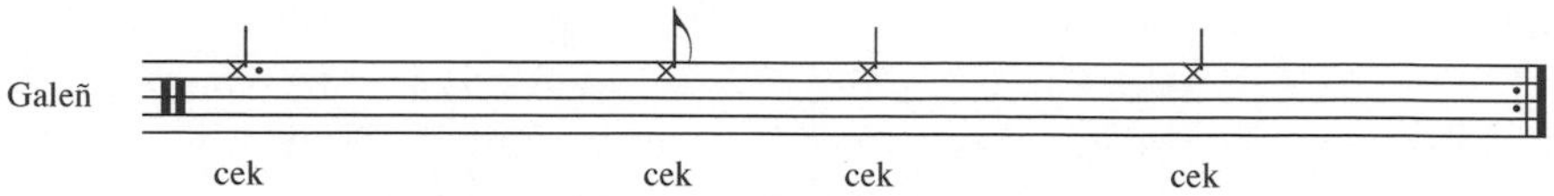

FIGURE 5.1. *Le temps* (keeping time)

The *bàkk*s are an extremely important part of the *géwël* percussionists' repertory because they distinguish one percussionist from another, or one family from another. Because each family has its own repertory, it develops its own *bàkk*s that become signifiers or markers of that particular family's identity. *Géwël* percussionists are always listening to what other sabar groups are doing—what *bàkk*s they play, etc. In this way, there is friendly competition that involves building on one another's *bàkk*s, trying to be innovative, and trying in some way to "outdo" one another in the quality of a *bàkk*—its catchiness, as well as its virtuosity. Thio Mbaye says outright that he takes pride in creating *bàkk*s that are difficult to count, and that often his *bàkk*s are interesting and difficult because they feel *contretemps*, or against the beat.

The concept of a steady beat, or time (*le temps*) is a basic concept in sabar drumming. *Le temps* is kept by tapping the *galeñ* (drumstick) on the side of the drum, creating a clicking sound, in the pattern shown in Figure 5.1 (CD Track 1).

Sabar rhythms always have a clear beat; even if that beat may not be externally obvious, it is kept by the accompaniment parts (that is, the *mbalax* and *talmbat* parts).

In the following section, we will explore the repertory of dance *rythmes* in greater depth. Although sabar playing can be found in a variety of contexts, the most common context involves dancing, so that is where we will begin.

Rythmes: History, Development, and Change

The term *rythme* is borrowed from the French and is used to refer to a set of standard rhythmic patterns, each of which have specific Wolof names. *Rythmes* are generally shorter, repeated small phrases, whereas *bàkk*s tend to be longer and more elaborate.[6] The *rythmes* that will be explored in this chapter include the following: *ardin, farwu jar, ceebu jën, baar mbaye, Kaolack/ndëc/mbalax, lëmbël/ventilateur, mbabas, dagañ, niari gorong* and *yaaba composé*. During the period of my research (1997–2005), only *ardin, farwu jar, ceebu jën, baar mbaye,*

Kaolack and *lëmbël* were standard *rythmes* in the sabar repertory in Dakar.[7] These six standard *rythmes* will be the focus of my transcriptions and analyses.

Rythmes are intricately linked to dance. The close relationship between *rythmes* and dance likely accounts for the standardization of these *rythmes*: all Senegalese women learn to dance to this particular set of *rythmes*.

Thio Mbaye explains that there are old and new *rythmes*:

> There are *rythmes* that exist for one month, two months, six months, one year . . . or *rythmes* that stay. . . . Something like *ceebu jën* is an original. It's a *rythme* that's been around for centuries, you see? . . .There are *rythmes* that never change. (5/23/98)

Changes in *rythmes* and *bàkk*s are cause for some degree of reminiscence among *géwël* of all generations. During my interview with Daaro Mbaye (older generation) and Lamine Touré (younger generation), Daaro Mbaye spoke of *rythmes* that he used to play: *ceebu jën, mbabas, dagañ, baar mbaye,* and *yaaba ndar*. He also spoke of a *rythme* called *yangap*, which is no longer played. Lamine Touré lamented the loss of this *rythme*:

> There was a *rythme* called *yangap*. But even I don't know how to play it. He [Daaro Mbaye] knows how to play it. *Yangap* is a very old *rythme*. My grandmother, Njouck Seck, danced *yangap*. So, the times change. Since the days [Daaro Mbaye] played. Now there is *musique*.[8] It's not the same. The percussion of the past, it was more pure. It was better than it is now. (7/3/98)

At a *sabar, tànnibéer, ngente* or *mariage*, the *rythmes* normally occur in the following order:[9]

1. *Ardin*
2. *Farwu jar*
3. *Ceebu jën*

4/5. *Baar mbaye* (sometimes *Kaolack* may be interchanged with *Baar mbaye*)

5/4. *Kaolack* (also called *mbalax* or *ndëc*)

6. *Lëmbël*[10]

Although *rythmes* may be played more than once (for example, after *baar mbaye*, the drummers may play *ceebu jën* again), the above list reflects the general order of first appearance of these *rythmes*.

Transcribing Sabar Rhythms

Ethnomusicologists have long debated the pros and cons of using Western forms of notation for African music.[11] I have purposely chosen to transcribe the *rythmes* and *bàkk*s using standard Western musical notation in conjunction with vocal mnemonics. After experimenting with different forms of notation including variations on the Time Unit Box System (TUBS) used by James Koetting (1970), I decided to use Western musical notation because (1) it is accessible to readers, and (2) when used in conjunction with mnemonics and a key to drum strokes, it accurately conveys the rhythmic properties of *rythmes* and *bàkk*s. All musical transcriptions are original transcriptions of *rythmes* and *bàkk*s as performed by the Mbaye family.[12]

Although there are just three basic hand strokes in sabar technique (*gin*, *piṇ*, and *pax*), the combination of different stick and hand strokes produces a multitude of different sounds. My musical transcriptions of the *rythmes* will be accompanied by mnemonics that denote what playing technique is used to produce the sound. Below is the key to the drum strokes played on the sabar (with notes on *cól* technique, particularly, since it differs from the others). The sabar is generally struck directly with the left hand and with a stick held in the right hand (though left-handed drummers sometimes use the right hand and hold the stick in the left hand).

Géwël percussionists commonly use vocal mnemonics to represent drum strokes and combinations of drum strokes. Although these mnemonics are generally similar, there is no standardized system of mnemonics, and the same drum stroke may be called by several different names, depending on how it is combined with other strokes. In the key below, I explain the movements and sounds that correlate with the basic mnemonics. This key will be followed by the notational symbols used for musical transcription[13] (CD Track 2; see Figure 5.2).

KEY TO VOCAL MNEMONICS

gin left hand strikes the center of the drum, creating a resonant bass sound (see Figure 5.3).
[on the *cól*: left hand strikes edge of drum; like *pin* on *mbëng-mbëng*.]

pin left hand open stroke (struck near edge of drum head). Hand bounces off (see Figure 5.4).

pax left hand strikes the edge of the drumhead, primarily with the fingertip pads, and the hand is left there (instead of bouncing

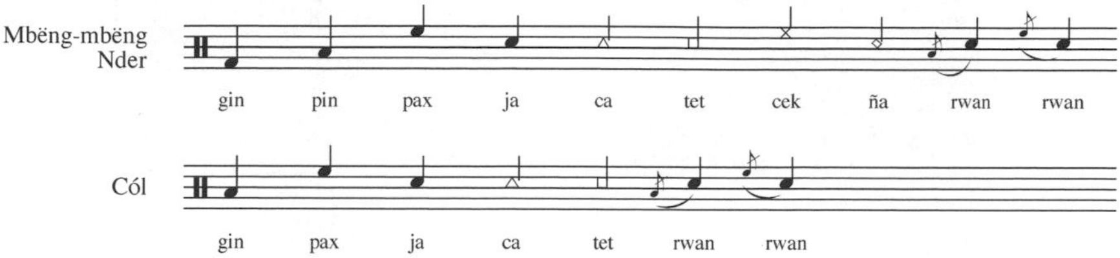

FIGURE 5.2. Key to vocal mnemonics

off), creating a sharp, slap-like sound (in contrast to *pin*, which is allowed to resonate) (see Figure 5.5).
[on the *cól*: hand, sometimes with thumb tucked under, hits the center of the skin.] Also known as *pa, bax,* and *ba.*

ja stick stroke, played with the right hand; the stick hits the skin and bounces off freely. Also known as *jan, tan, tën, ta, tas, sa, ya, ra,* and *dam.*

ca stick stroke; similar to *ja*, but hit flat against the skin, so that the length of the stick has contact with the skin. Also known as *céx.*

tet stick stroke; left hand dampens the edge of the drum before and during the stick stroke, creating a higher-pitched, sharper sound. Also known as *te* or *tek.*

cek stick stroke; stick taps edge of drum head, creating a non-resonant clicking sound.

ña stick stroke; hits at tip of stick and stays on the skin.

rwan *pin* or *pax* immediately followed by *ja*. This combination occurs frequently enough to be notated as a unit. Also known as *rwa* or *ram*. For example, *rwan* followed by *pax* can be notated as "*rambax.*"

In transcribing both *bàkk*s and *rythmes*, I have provided composite vocal mnemonics in conjunction with Western musical notation. Because the mnemonics are used to learn *rythmes* and *bàkk*s and to explain them, it is more appropriate to notate them in that way, rather than breaking them down into individual drum strokes. Basic mnemonics for individual drum strokes can be found in the key above, though there are inevitable variations as different drummers may use different consonants, and combinations of strokes create more complicated composite mnemonics. Although I will be examining some *bàkk*s that derive from speech, I should note that there is no direct correlation between specific words or syllables and specific mnemonics. Rather, the

5.3

5.4

5.5

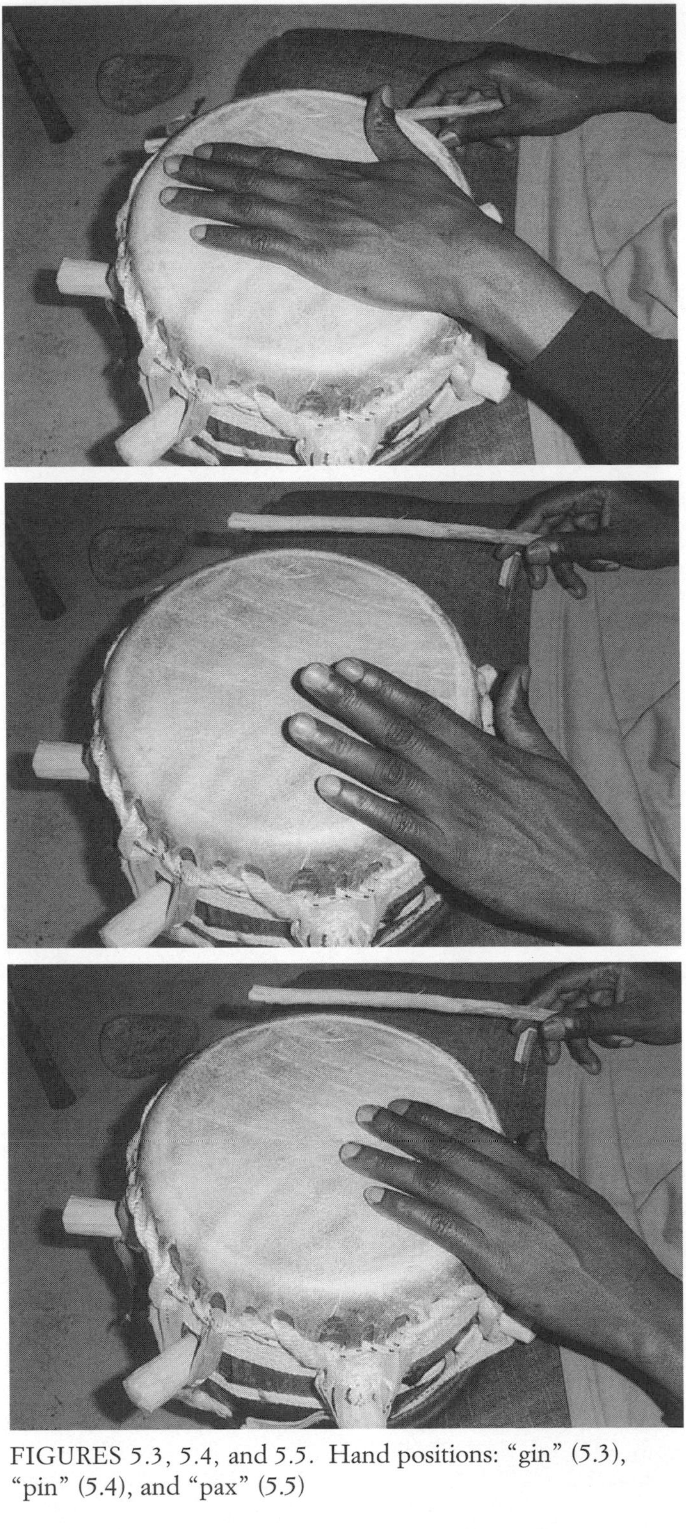

FIGURES 5.3, 5.4, and 5.5. Hand positions: "gin" (5.3), "pin" (5.4), and "pax" (5.5)

mnemonics should be seen as a way of vocally representing drum patterns that are inspired by speech.

A Typical Sabar Event

Every sabar event begins with two musical phrases: *ya ñu moom* and *tagumbar*. The *ya ñu moom bàkk* comes from the saying:[14]

Ya ñu moom, Bamba,	We belong to you, Bamba,
ya ñu moom	we belong to you
Bu ñu dunde, bu ñuy dee yëpp	Whether in life or in death
Ya ñu moom, Bamba,	We belong to you, Bamba,
ya ñu moom	we belong to you.

Cheikh Amadou Bamba (1853–1927), founder of the prominent Mouride sect of Islam, is perhaps the most respected religious figure in Senegal, not only for his religious status, but also for his legendary defiance against the colonialists. Thus it is fitting that this Mouride invocation praising Bamba has become a standard opening for every sabar event (CD Track 3; see Figure 5.6).

Before *ya ñu moom* was introduced to the repertory, Wolof *géwël* would begin sabars with *tagumbar*. (Currently, *tagumbar* immediately follows *ya ñu moom*.) *Tagumbar* is a special *bàkk* that is believed to protect the sabars—like a *gris-gris* for the sabars, so to speak. The *tagumbar bàkk* has its origins in a proverb, the words of which are now lost. Nevertheless, *tagumbar* is always played by the lead drummer at the beginning of any sabar event. *Tagumbar* is a *bàkk* that is very much respected, and everybody, regardless of family affiliation, plays it in exactly the same way. It is a mark of the true griot and is necessary for the protection of the sabars and generally successful nature of

FIGURE 5.6. *Ya ñu moom*
Note: There exist several versions of this *bàkk,* as performed by the Mbaye family. The above transcription is the simplest version, and the first I was taught.

the sabar event. Unlike *ya ñu moom, tagumbar* is played solo by the group leader. It can be played on the *nder, gorong yeguel*, or *cól*—whatever instrument is leading the group (CD Track 4).

After *tagumbar,* the group will typically launch into a number of different *bàkk*s to show off their virtuosity and catch the spectators' interest. Although there may be more *bàkk*s interspersed during the *sabar* (and certainly *bàkk*s are played in conjunction with some *rythmes*, namely *Kaolack* and *lëmbël*), the majority of the *bàkk*s will be showcased at the beginning of the *sabar* event before the women begin to dance. Then the players launch into *jël* (a preparatory rhythm) immediately followed by *ardin*, and dancing begins shortly thereafter.

The following section introduces the transcriptions and basic descriptions of the parts of standard *rythmes* of the sabar repertory. Most of the *rythmes* are short patterns, played repeatedly in a very fast tempo. In the context of a dance event, these *rythmes* would make up the bulk of the repertory, with some *bàkk*s overlayed on *Kaolack* and *lëmbël*; meanwhile, the lead drummer (usually playing the *nder*) and a *cól* player (playing the *tulli* part) would do extensive soloing/improvisation. The accompaniment parts (that is, *mbalax*, played on the *mbëng-mbëng*; *mbalax nder,* played on a *nder*; and *talmbat,* played on a *talmbat* or small *cól*) generally play without much variation, except for an occasional flourish (called *sëxët*), but they rarely improvise. (In these examples, I have transcribed basic *tulli* parts; however, one should note that these are just basic parts from which the *tulli* player will stray extensively.) The lead drummer is the primary improviser, gaining inspiration from the dancers, and inspiring them in return. How the various parts fit together will be discussed more completely in the ethnographic description of a *tànnibéer* in Chapter 6; what follows is a description of the basic parts of the dance *rythmes.*

Ardin

The rhythm *ardin* is the one *rythme* that is *not* danced. This *rythme* that introduces all other *rythmes* is played after *ya ñu moom, tagumbar*, and the exposition of *bàkk*s. Often preceded by *jël*, a preparatory rhythm led by the *dirigeur*, *ardin* always segues into *farwu jar,* when the dancing begins. Usually played only for several minutes,[15] *ardin* signals to the audience that the dancing will begin shortly. *Ardin* is characterized by the closely interlocking *mbalax nder* and *mbalax* parts (CD Tracks 5 and 8; see Figure 5.7).

Farwu Jar

After playing *ardin* for several minutes, the *dirigeur* (lead drummer) will play a short phrase (*transfer*) that launches the ensemble into the opening dance

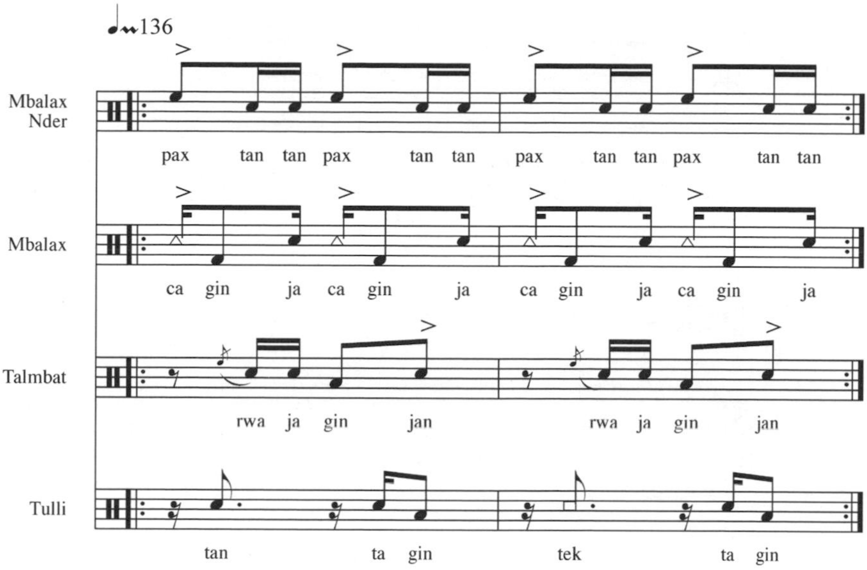

FIGURE 5.7. *Ardin*

rythme, *farwu jar*. In Wolof, *farwu jar* means 'worthy boyfriend'. The complete phrase goes like this:

farwu jar, ndigg tall lay doxe, raas niangal	[what the lady says]
caaga woo dootina	[what the man says]

Literally, this means "a worthy boyfriend can walk proudly (keep your chin up), just walk without a care, the woman is ready (for action)." This *rythme* was originally played for couples (to encourage courtship), and both men and women would dance it, but nowadays, as with all sabar *rythmes*, it is danced by women (CD Tracks 6 and 9; see Figure 5.8).

In contrast to *ardin, farwu jar* has a triple subdivision as opposed to a duple subdivision. The incessant, evenly spaced triplet notes make the rhythmic cycles "roll" from one to the next. Nonetheless, the first beat of every group of three notes is stressed with the "*ca*" sound, providing a steady beat for the dancers' feet to follow. Westerners may have difficulty hearing the time properly in *farwu jar* because the Western ear is often drawn to hearing the bass note (*gin*) as the downbeat, whereas it is the *ca* (in *ja ca gin*) that is the primary beat. In *farwu jar*, the *mbalax nder* is next in importance to the lead *nder*, as it helps to control the tempo.

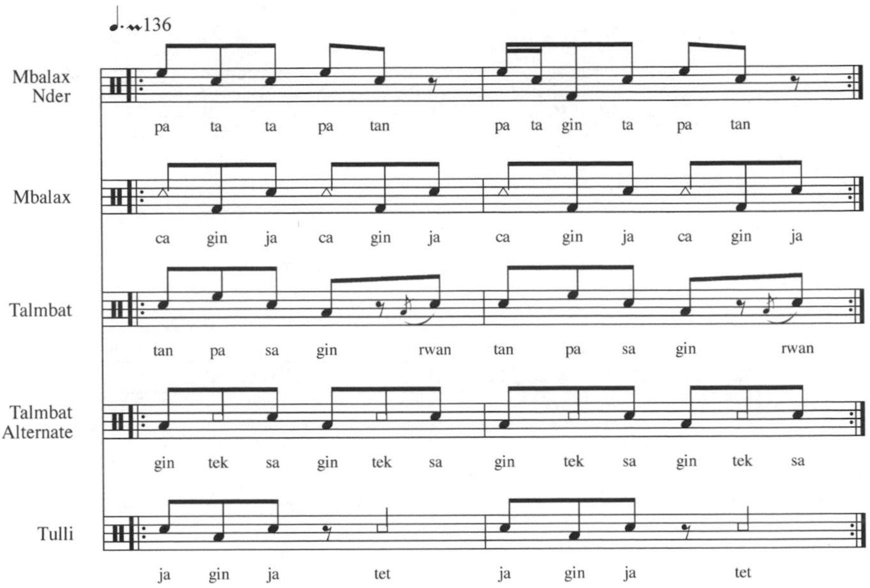

FIGURE 5.8. *Farwu jar*

Ceebu Jën

The rhythm *ceebu jën* is named after Senegal's national dish of fish and rice, considered by all to be the tastiest of all Senegalese dishes. It is the most difficult *rythme* for the percussionists to play and for the dancers to dance, due to the rapid tempo. Although the *mbalax* rhythm itself may seem deceptively simple, a mere attempt to tap it out on a table at the appropriate speed for more than a minute will give the reader some appreciation of the *rythme's* difficulty. It takes stamina to play *ceebu jën*, and novices dread playing this *rythme*. The Mbaye family prides itself in playing *ceebu jën* at a faster tempo and for a longer duration than any other sabar group.

Because of the rapid tempo, when the entire ensemble is playing, it is the lower-pitched *gin* sound in the *mbalax* part that comes out the strongest, providing a constant beat. If the percussionists ever tire, they may momentarily rest their stick hands, but they must always continue the *gin* sound (*ndën,* or bass note) in full force (CD Tracks 7 and 10; see Figure 5.9).

Baar Mbaye (nos. 1 and 2)

The rhythm *baar mbaye* originated from the *bëkëtë* ritual. *Bëkëtë* is a ritual celebrated by the Lebou people of Ndiagne Ndoye and Ndiagne Mbaye ancestry. It is performed as a ritual of protection on the eighth day of the child's life (the day of the naming ceremony, or *ngente*), to protect the child from evil spirits, evil tongue, evil eye, accidents, etc. As the *géwël* chant "*Bëkëtë, bëkëtë baar mbaye*" and play the *baar mbaye rythme*, the family goes through an elaborate ritual (to be explored in detail in the following chapter). When the drums play "*Bëkëtë, bëkëtë*," people answer, "*Rapp wu aay, yallaa na la tegge doom*" ("Be protected from the evil spirits, evil tongue, evil eye").

Although its origins lie in the *bëkëtë* ritual, today *baar mbaye* is an integral part of the dance repertory and one of the most popular *rythmes*. There are two different versions of *baar mbaye*, both of which I have transcribed below. The *tulli* solos extensively and also plays out a rhythmic representation of the text, "*Bëkëtë, bëkëtë, baar mbaye*!" (CD Tracks 11 through 14; see Figures 5.10 and 5.11) *Baar mbaye* No. 1 is characterized by a gradual speedup in tempo that relaxes again (Tracks 11 and 12). In both versions of *baar mbaye*, there is no *mbalax nder* part; there is only a lead *nder* part, which the accompaniment parts follow.

Kaolack/Mbalax/Ndëc

The *rythme* named *Kaolack*, *mbalax*, or *ndëc* is the most important of all *rythmes* because it is the primary *rythme* used in *musique*, or mbalax music.[16] This *rythme* is called *Kaolack, ndëc,* and *mbalax* interchangeably. *Ndëc* is the name

FIGURE 5.9. *Ceebu jën*

FIGURE 5.10. *Baar mbaye* No. 1

of the *rythme*, but it is more often referred to as *Kaolack*, its city of origin. To make matters even more complicated, this *rythme* is also commonly referred to as *mbalax,* which itself has multiple meanings. The word *mbalax* literally means 'accompaniment'. However, due to this *rythme's* use in the popular music genre, *mbalax* has come to mean the popular music genre itself as well (to the Senegalese and the rest of the world). However, Wolof percussionists themselves refer to the popular music genre as *musique* and reserve *mbalax* for 'accompaniment'. For our purposes, I will refer to this *rythme* as *Kaolack* to avoid unnecessary confusion.

Kaolack is the primary rhythmic accompaniment onto which most *bàkk*s are overlayed. *Kaolack's* flexibility and ability to accommodate *bàkk*s is undoubtedly related to its prominence in *mbalax*, the popular music genre. It is

FIGURE 5.11. *Baar mbaye* No. 2

unclear whether the *rythme's* success in traditional sabar repertories led to its use in popular music, or its use in popular music has perpetuated its general popularity. Both are probably true, as it is a fluid multidirectional relationship. In Lamine Touré's words,

> *Kaolack* is the richest *rythme* of all in sabar. If you play *musique*, you must play *Kaolack.* If you don't play *Kaolack,* it won't work. Because it's *Kaolack* that makes people dance. If you play something else, people won't dance. To make people move, if you play *Kaolack,* it will make everybody dance. Everyone loves to dance *Kaolack*. Because it's . . . it's the *rythme* that is the best, of all sabar *rythmes*, it is the best of them all. Not just for me, for everybody. For all the griots here in Dakar, and in Kaolack—it doesn't matter where . . . they know *Kaolack* is the best. It's the richest *rythme*; it's the Kaolackois [people of Kaolack] who created it—my forefathers created this *rythme*. So now, this *rythme* is the richest rhythm in sabar. (8/5/99)

Regardless, *Kaolack* will likely remain the most important sabar *rythme* due to its place in Senegalese popular music. For the Mbaye family, this *rythme* also holds special importance because it comes from their hometown, and they have special claim to it, since it was their forefathers who created this *rythme*.

In *Kaolack,* the *mbalax* part is the defining feature. The *tulli* part in particular can vary because the *cól* typically solos during *Kaolack.* This transcription includes typical variants on the *mbalax, talmbat and tulli* parts (CD Tracks 15 and 16; see Figure 5.12).

Lëmbël

The *rythme lëmbël*, also known as *ventilateur*, originated from the Lawbe people (the woodworker's caste). *Lëmbël* is typically played at the end of a *sabar* event. For the *lëmbël* dance, women lift up their outer dresses and wraps and openly display their *beeco.*[17] With their backsides facing the spectators, they put their hands on their knees and suggestively swirl their buttocks in a circular motion (hence the name *ventilateur*, French for 'electric fan'). Pairs of women compete to see who can best move their buttocks, as the spectators cheer the dancers on. Numerous *bàkk*s are played in conjunction with *lëmbël.*

The feeling of *lëmbël* is a fast grouping of six beats, with three repeated notes over the bar line. These give the feeling of a constant "turning," which appropriately accompanies the dance (CD Tracks 17 and 18; see Figure 5.13).

The *ventilateur* has been enormously popular since the early 1980s (Heath 1994, 97–98). One version of the *taasu* [oral poetry] performed during the *ventilateur* is provided below:

Wantilatér, kilimatisér	Electric fan, air conditioner
Ngelaw lë ci biir	There is wind inside
Man sax nelaw naa	I went to sleep
Suma yaay sax nelaw në	My mother went to sleep
Bo më de raay	If you caress me
Raay më ci leex	Caress me on the cheeks
Li ci des dañu më ko tere.	Everything else is forbidden to me.[18]

Rythmes Less Often Played

In the course of my fieldwork, I found several *rythmes* that were performed occasionally, but were clearly falling from common use. However, since they were once staple *rythmes*, I will discuss them briefly in this section. These *rythmes* are *mbabas, niari gorong*, and *yaaba composé.*

Mbabas originated from another dance called *dagañ.*[19] *Dagañ* would be played with one person on *tulli,* one on *mbalax,* and one other on *tama* (small hourglass-shaped talking drum). *Géwël* percussionists transformed *dagañ* into *mbabas* by replacing the *tama* with the *gorong mbabas*, which had a high sound akin to the talking drum. Thereafter the *rythme* was called *mbabas*. *Mbabas* was created in the mid-twentieth century by people of the generation of Macheikh Mbaye, Doudou Ndiaye Rose and Vieux Sing Faye.[20] Although it is still played on occasion, *mbabas* is another *rythme* that seems to be headed toward the rhythmic repository. Upon being questioned as to why *mbabas* is hardly played,

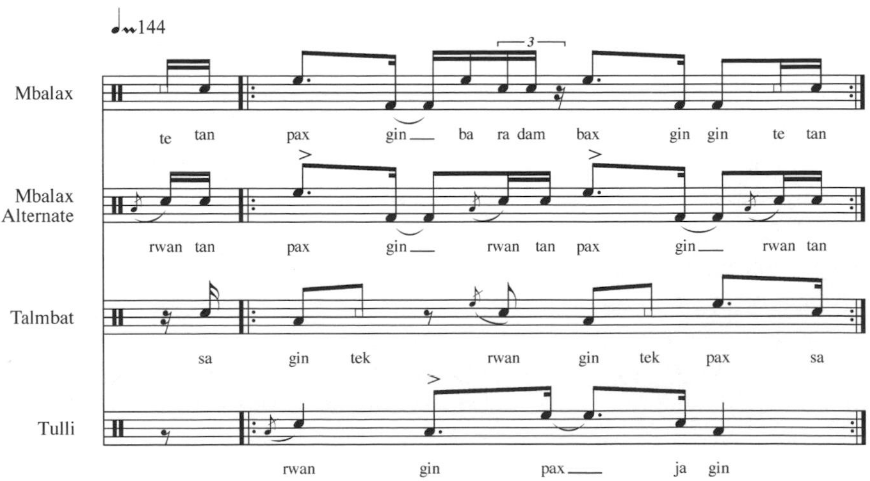

FIGURE 5.12. *Kaolack/mbalax/ndëc*

FIGURE 5.13. *Lëmbël*

several percussionists have described it as being "less interesting" than the other *rythmes* (CD Track 19).

Another *rythme* that is played less often than before is *niari gorong.*[21] *Niari gorong* shares the same *mbalax* pattern as *farwu jar*. However, *niari gorong* is led by the *cól* (as opposed to *farwu jar*, which is led by the *nder*). The name *niari gorong* literally means 'two gorong drums', the *gorong* being another name for the *cól. Niari gorong* was originally played by just two *gorong*s, though it eventually came to be played by the entire sabar ensemble. *Niari gorong* is also said to be the dance in which the *beeco* originated. In Dakar, *niari gorong* is still played at *tur*s (women's association meetings)*, ngentes* (baptisms), and *sabar ngoon.*[22] During *sabar ngoon*, it would be played between *Kaolack* and *lëmbël. Niari gorong* is no longer a part of the standard *tànnibéer* repertory in Dakar, though it is still played at *tànnibéer*s elsewhere in the region, because it has been slowly replaced by the nearly identical *farwu jar.* With the *nder* (as opposed to *gorong*) being used as lead drum most frequently, the shift to *farwu jar* is natural (CD Track 20).

One more *rythme* that is played with less frequency is the *rythme yaaba composé. Yaaba composé* is basically a slow version of *baar mbaye* No. 1. Also known as *yaaba ndar, yaaba composé* originated in Saint Louis (the city the Wolof call Ndar) and was originally danced by fishermen's wives. Although all women now dance this *rythme*, *yaaba composé* is most appropriate for older women due to its slow tempo, which makes dancing easier (CD Track 21).

Today, *yaaba* can sometimes be heard at *ngentes*, when more mature women come out to dance. Earlier in the century, *yaaba* became one of the most popular dance *rythmes* (for example, in the time of Lamine Touré's grandmother, Njouck Seck), along with *yangap*, another *rythme* that is no longer played. The faster but similar *baar mbaye* appears to have replaced *yaaba* at *tànnibéer*s, and it is perhaps just a matter of time before *yaaba* becomes yet another *rythme* of the past.

Bàkk: History, Development, and Change

In Arame Fal's *Dictionnaire wolof-français* (1990), "*bàkk*" as a noun is defined as "a song or rhythm for marching, a praise, a hymn." As a verb, it means "to sing praise to the rhythm of tam-tams/drums" (Fal 1990, 40, trans. mine). This original emphasis on song and praise is very important in considering the changing meaning of *bàkk* over time, which relates to the primary argument of my book: the shift from spoken word to what I will call the "drummed word" (that is, instrumental music), and how this has empowered *géwël* percussionists in modern-day Senegal and allowed them to maintain the status and importance of griots in a new and modern context.

In casual conversation, the concept of "praise" or "praise-singing" is not referred to as *bàkk* but rather *woyaan*, which means to praise or flatter, from the root *woy*, meaning 'to sing'. In the literature, the word *bàkk* has been referred to as "special tunes which are requests for money" (Leymarie 1978, 206), and as a verbal art form performed by men at wrestling matches (McNee 1996, 38).

However, among *géwël* percussionists today, *bàkk* is a strictly musical term, referring to a musical phrase played on the sabar drums. In contrast to *rythmes,* which have specific names such as *ceebu jën*, *bàkk*s lack specific names, and are instead referred to by saying "*bàkk bi*" ('this *bàkk*'), followed by either a verbal mnemonic of the *bàkk*, or an actual performance of it.

Thio Mbaye explains the difference between a *bàkk* and a *rythme*:

> A *bàkk* is a phrase, like you would say in talking about music. For example, when you play "*gin gin tan tan bak ten, ta ra ra gin pa tak tak boom, pax*" on the sabar, one would say, "Hey! You hear the *bàkk* he's playing?"

> It's called a *bàkk.* But you could call it a phrase . . . *Ceebu jën, mbabas,* all of those are *rythmes*. Even Tyson is a *rythme*. It's *jak jak jak jak gin, gin gin, jak jak jak gin* . . . it's a *rythme,* because it runs/pours [*couler*]. But a *bàkk,* when you play it, there are refrains, one stops, one restarts, one slows down, you see? One changes the tempo; one increases the tempo; these are *bàkk*s, phrases. (5/23/98)

Bàkk: Historical Representations of Spoken Word

The modern concept of the *bàkk* (as explained above by Thio Mbaye) as a purely musical phenomenon is not shared by percussionists of the elder generation. Macheikh Mbaye explains his view.

> You know, now people just follow their inspiration. All those people could not explain exactly what they mean when playing a special *bàkk*, so they just follow their inspiration and put it into a rhythm. It's just like notes put together; that's what's happening now. But in the past, our forefathers would not play that way. In the past, the *bàkk*s that our forefathers would play, they spoke. For example, say there were two rivals living in the same neighborhood dating the same woman. If there was a *sabar* ceremony, then after a while, if one of the rivals had some problems with the girl and the girl wanted to just praise the other one, she would just go talk to the drummer and be like, "*Ku lamb yate, diagu fan nga nabe*" ("If you don't love me, I have somebody else"). So, it was very meaningful, and then the griot would just play it and turn it into a rhythm. . . . So all in all, it was like proverbs or words turned into *bàkk*s. But nowadays, we don't have it anymore; what we have is like notes put together, in harmony, just to, like they just invent *bàkk*s as rhythms, but they don't have any meaning. (8/12/99)

As explained by Macheikh Mbaye, originally *bàkk*s were rhythmic representations of spoken word. Although Wolof is not a tonal language, it can nonetheless be represented through first transforming the spoken word into rhythmicized speech, and then translating this into a drummed pattern.

There has been considerable interest in the topic of drum languages, "talking drums," and speech surrogates in Africa and elsewhere.[23] In sub-Saharan Africa, the most notable work includes that of Carrington (1976), Nketia (1963), Ong (1977), Locke (1990) and Agawu (2003). In Nketia's study of Akan drumming, Nketia identifies three modes of drumming, which he calls the speech mode, the signal mode, and the dance mode (Nketia 1963a, 17–31). Drummers utilizing the speech mode reproduce as closely as possible the original speech; those using signal mode convey messages through more symbolic terms. Wolof *géwël* make use of *bàkk*s in both speech and signal modes;

although *bàkk*s nowadays may not have meaning in terms of spoken words, I will argue that they gain another level of meaning by becoming signifiers and markers of an individual or family's identity.

Lamine Touré also recognizes the verbal origins of the *bàkk*, though his view of the "modern" *bàkk* is broader than Macheikh Mbaye's, reflecting their generational differences:

> Nowadays, we create *bàkk* with the sabar—I think of the sabar, and I create a *bàkk*. But before, when the older generation created *bàkk*s, it was from speech. . . . It's not the sabar that created the *bàkk*—it is speech. If you tell your *géer*, "*Cow li cow li, yow la! Ja gin ja gin jan*!" ["We're talking about you!"]—We play that now, but it's been around for a long time. . . . All *bàkk*s came from speech. Because our forefathers, such as Massaer Mbaye or Ali Gueye Seck, when they created *bàkk*s, why did they create them? Because they spoke of good things. If he saw his *géer* and praised him, if he said, "*Da nga baax*" [and played] *rwa gin jan, da nga baax, rwa gin jan* . . . , it would happen like that. That is the origin of *bàkk*s. But now, there are *bàkk*s that we play, which are not derived from speech—because things change and develop with time, with the sabar. There are many *bàkk*s that we play now that came from speech, but now that element is lost. Now it comes from the sabar. (8/17/99)

As Lamine Touré mentions, there exist many *bàkk*s today that have their origins in spoken word, but those origins are now lost. Because there is no one-to-one correlation between drum stroke and word (or even syllable), it would be very difficult, if not impossible, to reconstruct a forgotten text from an existing *bàkk*. However, by looking at more recently invented *bàkk*s, we can better understand the creative process that transforms the word to the drum.

A simple but vivid example of this creative process is the "How are you?" *bàkk*. This *bàkk* was created from the *taasu* (spoken word poetry) of an especially gregarious *géwël* at a *tur*.[24] Because I was filming the event, this woman decided to focus her attentions on me and my video camera, much to the delight of the others present. Knowing that I was American, she appropriately created some *taasu* in English. This began with "How are you?" which she then repeated until she settled into a comfortable rhythmic pattern. This, coupled with "Good, fine," was quickly transformed into a *bàkk* by Karim Mbaye, which in turn was played by the entire ensemble.

In Figure 5.14, I have transcribed the rhythmic properties of the spoken word followed by the *bàkk* in the same manner the *bàkk* was created. Although this is a fairly simple *bàkk* rhythmically speaking, the example clearly illustrates the process of how spoken word can so easily be transformed into rhythm. Although the *bàkk* does not mimic the vocal rhythm exactly, it draws on the basic rhythmic structure and improvises on it (CD Track 22).

Members of the older generation (such as Massaer Daaro Mbaye and Macheikh Mbaye) showed me examples of old *bàkk* that they used to play. All correspond to traditional proverbs, including *bàkk*s recounted by Daaro Mbaye:[25]

> *Ku jaan matt, sama xel dem ci dee, ba ngay dundu, ag ba ngay dee yepp, sama xel dem ci dee.*
> If somebody is bitten by a snake, you will think of death. Whether you live or die, death is all you will think of.
>
> *Golo wacc leen seen morom yeek.*
> You monkeys get out for your equals to climb.
>
> *Ñay manu ci daqar dara gësëm gësëm baayi.*
> An elephant can't do anything to a tamarind tree; you will shake it, but after [that] you will leave it there because the tree is stronger.
>
> *Xaatup gaynde ndiaye, gaynde ndiaye, da ñu ko toñ.*
> If Gaynde Ndiaye [a lion] hits somebody, it is because they disturbed him.
>
> *Mbaara bukki, ni ku gisul mbaar, ni degguk sabam.*
> He who doesn't see the hyena can hear the cry.

According to Macheikh Mbaye, drumming was used as a form of communication before colonization. Take, for example, the first *bàkk* listed above: *Ku jaan matt, sama xel dem ci dee. Ba ngay dundu, ag ba ngay dee yepp, sama xel dem ci dee*, "If somebody is bitten by a snake, you will think of death. Whether you live or die, death is all you will think of." If a snake bit somebody at night in a village, people would call the *géwël*, and he would play this particular *bàkk*

FIGURE 5.14. "How are you" *bàkk*

at the village meeting place. Upon hearing the *bàkk*, anybody in the surrounding villages who could cure a snakebite would ride a horse toward the sound of the rhythm up to the place where the person lay injured. If there were no doctors in the neighboring villages, the griots in those villages would take their drums and play the same *bàkk*. So, from griot to griot, and village to village, the *bàkk* would spread all over the area, until a bush doctor would hear the sound and ride his horse to come rescue the patient. It was in this way that drumming was used as a mode of communication[26] (CD Track 23).

Musical Name Tags: Family *Bàkk*s

As I mentioned before, the repertory of *bàkk*s varies from family to family. For example, one of the primary characteristics distinguishing the Mbayène, Sing-Sing, and Ndiaye Rose families is their *bàkk*s. Each family has its own *bàkk* that serves as a sort of anthem—that is, when it is played, a member of that family will know that he/she is being called and will respond.[27] According to Macheikh Mbaye (ibid.), these *bàkk*s are as follows:

> NDOYE family: *Xambar bu jog, del ci gej, ëlëk mu taw, ci ngoon.*
> If you go fishing and see a dark cloud, return home because it will rain in the afternoon. (3/5/98)
>
> DIAGNE family: *Kameg ci Beer, gattam.*
> The oldest in Goree, f—k him.
> (Gorée island was called Beer before the French renamed it. This refers to historic dissention between the French—that is, the oldest in Gorée—and the Diagne's forefather, Musayes. Thus the *géwël* would praise the Diagne family in this way.) (3/5/98)
>
> GUEYE family: *Gueye gueye bësi, bi sa naqa jeex, ngaa cey kwook, gueye gueye bësi.*
> If you don't have any more millet, you put your [millet holder] into the cupboard. (8/12/99)
>
> MBAYE family: *Jaan dëngël, pax ma dëngël, niassateng mu ngi ci guy ga.*
> (The snake winds into its hole, but the *Niassateng* [another kind of snake] is in the baobab tree. [This is Macheikh Mbaye's family *bàkk*.])

Each of these family *bàkk*s consists of a proverb with a particular message. By turning these proverbs into drumming patterns, *géwël* can both mark their family's identity and give words of advice and wisdom through this process (CD Track 24).

Wordless Markers of Identity: The *Bàkk* as Creative Musical Composition

In recent times, *bàkk*s have come into existence not only as representations of spoken word, but as purely musical compositions. However, their meaning as markers of identity still holds strong. Rather than emphasizing text, instead the focus is on aesthetic creativity.

Thio Mbaye attempts to explain his creative process:

> It's kind of difficult to explain, because it depends on how you get inspired. For example, let's say I'm playing, and I look around the spectators and see someone who's marking time in another way that does not correspond with what I'm playing—I can be inspired by that. Sometimes I play, I enter in time and then go to the side and then return, you see? My rhythms are difficult to count. I can be inspired by the sound of an electric fan, by American or Japanese music I might see on the television—it's easy for me to find inspiration. (5/23/98)

In Group Rimbax, Thio is the primary creator of *bàkk*s, although all members of the group take part in the creative process. In Thio's words:

> I lead the rehearsals. But everything we play . . . everyone has the right to give his input/ideas. As for me, my thing is that I refuse to play anything that anyone else [that is, another group] has played. That's not allowed in my group. Since we created the group, everything we play comes from my inspiration. But that doesn't prevent the others from creating, too, and giving their ideas, too. For example, the other day, at the wrestling match, my brother Karim played two little things that we ended up keeping—we listened to it and liked it. (5/23/98)

Lamine Touré explains how he conceives of *bàkk*s:

> When you create a *bàkk*, you do it with pieces. For example, if I play *rwan pax, gin gin, rwan pax* is one part, *gin gin* is another part; then it's *patas, rambax, rambax, gin gin, patas rambax*—you see, I just created a *bàkk*! *Bàkk*s enter my brain easily . . . if somebody tells me to create a *bàkk*, it comes very quickly. It comes because I have the habit of creating them. Perhaps for creating a long *bàkk*, you need to take a lot of pieces and put them together; if you have a good brain, you won't forget it. . . . For example, if I want to create a *bàkk*, I will make sure all the pieces are in my head. I don't want to put together many pieces that aren't in my head; otherwise, I would forget it tomorrow. When I want to create a *bàkk*, all the pieces that I want to put in the *bàkk*, they must be very clear in my head, so that I

> don't forget them the next day. We also form *bàkk*s like—. . . . For example, if I go, *Rampax! Gin gin, gin gin, rampax!* And the other percussionists complete the idea. You know? Long *bàkk*s come like that. If you see a really long *bàkk*, chances are more than one person created it. (8/7/99)

A Group Emblem: "*Le bàkk de spectacle*"

Although all of the *bàkk*s played by the Mbaye family group, Group Rimbax, are markers of their group identity, there is one *bàkk* that remains the signifier par excellence. This *bàkk* is referred to as the *longue bàkk* ('long bakk') or, more commonly, the *bàkk de spectacle* ('showpiece *bàkk*').[28] The *bàkk de spectacle* is considerably longer than any other *bàkk* in the group's repertory and is the longest *bàkk* I have heard anyone in any group play.[29]

When *géwël* percussionists learn a *bàkk*, they usually break it down into both large sections and smaller phrases that are easier to grasp, indicated by line divisions in the mnemonic transcription. I suspect that *géwël* learn and retain *bàkk*s through what Daniel Schacter terms "elaborative encoding," associating new data with data already learned (1996, 44). Once a *géwël* percussionist has become familiar with certain common phrases or short musical patterns, he will have a sort of "rhythmic glossary" that will help him learn long and complicated *bàkk*s such as the *bàkk de spectacle* (CD Track 25; see Figure 5.15).

The diverse array of metric subdivisions (that is, changing meters over elapsing time) is just one indication of the enormous rhythmic complexity of this *bàkk*. Many of the phrases occur *contretemps* (against the beat) and syncopation abounds.

The transcription reveals some repetition of phrases. In performance, the leader may choose to repeat such phrases more than once, and the rest of the ensemble is expected to follow appropriately. This makes the length of the *bàkk* very flexible. One particular phrase is often repeated, as indicated in the transcription with a repeat sign.

For the most part, the *bàkk* is played in a very strict tempo. The one exception is near the end (measure 165); here, all eyes must be on the *dirigeur*, who will slow the *bàkk* to a near halt before resuming the fast tempo (measure 175).

According to Lamine Touré, this *bàkk* had its origins in speech (*parler*). However, none of the percussionists in the family could tell me what it stood for. The *bàkk* itself is originally attributed to Thio Mbaye's father, Massaer Mbaye. It was passed down to Thio, who made it more rhythmically complicated and also made it longer by adding another part (said to be composed by Macheikh Mbaye). The end result is the *bàkk de spectacle* as we know it now. Thus, although this *bàkk* had its origins in text, through time it has lost its

FIGURE 5.15. *Bàkk de spectacle* (continues on next two pages)

FIGURE 5.15. *Bàkk de spectacle* (continues on facing page)

FIGURE 5.15 Continued

textual meaning and has been adapted and modified to reflect technical and rhythmic virtuosity as well as musical creativity.

This *bàkk* serves as an important emblem of the Mbaye family sabar group. Without fail, the *bàkk* was played at every *sabar* event of theirs that I attended from 1997 to 2001, so in recent years, it has clearly been a fixture in their repertory. In addition to showing off the drummer's virtuosity, the *bàkk* serves to invigorate the percussionists themselves. When they play the *bàkk*, one can see the concentration in their faces, and the satisfaction they gain from playing it well.[30]

The *bàkk* is also a test of the percussionists' ability. For example, the newest members of the group are chided for not knowing how to play the *bàkk* perfectly, as it is a measure of one's rank within the group. Likewise, the *bàkk* specifically marks who is in the family group and who is not. Occasionally, distantly related players will come to perform with the group, but when that happens, those players will have to play *mbalax*, an accompanying part, while the others play the *bàkk*.[31] As a rule, the Mbaye family *bàkk* is never played by members of other families (such as Sing-Sing or Ndiaye Rose).[32] This is what separates the Mbaye family from other families, and why this *bàkk* remains such an important part of the Mbaye family sabar repertory.

When Thio Mbaye first played the *bàkk* for the members of the group, legend has it that Lamine Touré was the first to learn it. Some group members even claimed that upon first hearing, Lamine was able to play the entire *bàkk* immediately. Lamine Touré explains the story as he remembers it:

> The *bàkk de spectacle* is very, very long. But I was the first who was able to learn to play it. Thio gave it to us—he gave us the whole thing, the long *bàkk*. He didn't break it up. He gave the whole thing at once. We were all there, everyone in the group, and we all took it together. But when I came home, the *bàkk* came from time to time, when I was alone, it would come into my head . . . *rwan, rwan* . . . When I was alone and it was quiet, I began to think of the *bàkk*, and I knew it was in my head. The next day when we went back to Thio's, I took a sabar, and I told Thio, "Hey, listen." Thio said he wanted to see who would be the first to be able to play the *bàkk*. I came and I started to play it. He told me, "Really, I didn't believe you would be able to play it!" . . . So when Thio gave us the *bàkk*, it was so difficult, very long, and really not possible to learn in one day. Even if you are an amazing player, you couldn't learn it in one day. But I came, I took it, and in one day, I played it. The next day, when I came and played it with Thio, he couldn't believe it was me who was playing it, but I said, "Hey, it's me!" Also, I didn't forget it afterward. When I left Thio's, I thought about the *bàkk*. If you think about it a lot, you will learn it quickly and remember it. (8/17/99)

Lamine explains how he was able to memorize the *bàkk*:

> Sometimes I cut it, because I think, *rwan, gin rwan ja gin rwan, gin gin*, until it's all finished; then when I think some more, the next part comes; so when I think of *rwan gin rwan*, the other parts come. Before I finish one part, the next one comes. That is how I learned it. Also, if you learn a *bàkk*, you must have tranquility. If you have problems, you will forget the *bàkk*. You need to have a clear mind in order to learn a long *bàkk* quickly. When I was at Thio's, I had a clear mind. . . . Also, I like to learn things quickly, and I love the sabar. . . . . That's why I learn quickly. (8/17/99)

Lamine also comments on the importance of being able to learn a *bàkk* quickly, and he attributes the ability to supernatural factors:

> [Learning a *bàkk* quickly] is something I work on, because it's not good for someone to give you a *bàkk* and to not learn it for a long time—it's not good for a griot to be that way. It's in my blood; if you give me a *bàkk*. . . . You see, the sabar, it's not natural. It comes with *gris-gris*, it comes with *jinné*[33]—you know *jinné*? The sabar has a lot to do with *jinné*! Me, there are some things that I play—I don't know where I got them, but the sabar gave it to me. . . . Why do I learn quickly? Why does my brain do that? It's not me. Perhaps it's the sabar—It's the sabar that gave me this power. (8/17/99)

Having *Feeling*: Family Distinctions

Lamine Touré explains that in his extended family, the *bàkk*s that are created are all similar because they come from Kaolack. According to Lamine, it is important to have the same *feeling* ('feeling, way of playing, or style') as the other percussionists one plays with, and all of the percussionists who play with Thio Mbaye have the same *feeling*.[34]

Family rivalry shines full force as Lamine Touré talks about the difference between his family and another:

> The [other] family, the type of *bàkk* they play versus the type of *bàkk* we play is not the same—it's VERY different. [sings the signature rhythm of other family, then the signature rhythm of *rimbax*]. Their *bàkk* . . . it's nothing, but the *bàkk* we play, everyone loves it. Our *bàkk*s have *xorom* [salt/flavor], they have a lot of feeling; if other griots hear one of our *bàkk*, they will like it. You can listen to [the other family]'s *bàkk*, and you will like it, but not as much as our *bàkk*. (8/17/99)

The differences between the Mbaye and rival families is not only in their *bàkk*s but also in their way of playing the most important *rythme*: *ndëc/Kaolack.* Lamine Touré explains:

> Our *bàkk*s always work in the *rythme* of *ndëc*. Before, in Dakar, they didn't even know how to *mbalax*. It was the Kaolackois who taught the Dakarois how to *mbalax*. That's why when Thio was little, he was so popular in Dakar; when he played *mbalax*, the other griots couldn't believe it. Even myself, when I came here, and I played *mbalax*, everybody loved me. Because before, in Dakar, they would play "*te tan gaj, gin, te tan gaj, gin . . .*" it's not a good *mbalax*! In Kaolack, we did *parangaj, gin gin, te tan gaj, gin gin, parangaj, gin gin* [using a faster tempo] —it's not the same style. To play the *mbalax* of Kaolack is much more difficult; you must have *rapidité* (hand speed). We created things that surpassed all other griots. Our way of speaking and our way of playing, it's all different. If a player [from another family] comes to play *mbalax* with us, we won't like it. But if I go and play with them, they'll get a big surprise. They play well too; they are good percussionists. But we just don't have the same way of playing. We create *bàkk*s which are, frankly, much better than their *bàkk*s. Our *bàkk*s are more musical and will go well with everything. What they play is . . . too fast, their way of playing; they always play fast (*rapide*), regardless of the others. (8/17/99)

When it comes to discussing one's family's talents versus a rival family's, modesty is clearly not the objective. In a highly competitive atmosphere, a lot is at stake, so it is not surprising that otherwise modest people will be boastful in such a context.

Upon request, Lamine Touré provided me with some family *bàkk*s. Interestingly, when asked about these *bàkk*s, he spoke the *bàkk*s with mnemonics, whereas Macheikh Mbaye explained to me the Wolof proverbs for each *bàkk*. Lamine himself admitted that these *bàkk*s stood for words, but that he did not know what those words were.[35] This reflects the marked difference between the older and younger generations of *géwël* percussionists, as well as the gradual shift of emphasis from spoken word to musical creativity.

Conclusion

Together, *rythmes* and *bàkk*s form the staple repertory of *géwël* percussionists. Although historically, *bàkk*s were derived from spoken word, the original texts of old *bàkk*s are sometimes forgotten, and new *bàkk*s are often composed as purely musical creations without textual reference. However, when the original meaning of a *bàkk* is lost, the *bàkk* does not lose its history; rather, it gains a new autonomous meaning. In the process, the *bàkk* maintains its status as emblem of *géwël* identity and family. This shift from the vocal to the instrumental has allowed Wolof *géwël* to maintain their status in Senegalese society, but also has transformed their mode of expression.

Both *rythmes* and *bàkk*s are performed in a variety of contexts in Wolof culture. These performance contexts will be explored in the next chapter.

6

Dancing Fish and Rice

PERFORMANCE CONTEXTS

Sabar, sabar!
It doesn't belong to the Japanese
It doesn't belong to the Americans
It doesn't belong to the Spanish
It doesn't belong to the French
It doesn't belong to the North Africans
I say, it doesn't belong to the Chinese
I say, it doesn't belong to the Hindus
The lawbe is the one to carve the sabar
But the griot mounts the skin and beats it
Sabar, sabar!

—from Papa Ndiaye's
"Papa Ndiaye Guewel"[1]

THE SABAR IS AN INTEGRAL PART of Wolof culture and can be found in a variety of performance contexts. From neighborhood dance events to life cycle rituals, the sabar plays a vital role in negotiating different spheres: upper and lower caste, male and female, private and public, traditional and modern. In this chapter, I will discuss the primary performance contexts in which the sabar is played, including neighborhood dances, women's association meetings, weddings, baptisms, Muslim holidays, political meetings, wrestling matches, and *faux lion* spectacles. An examination of the role of sabar in these contexts will shed light on its impact on contemporary Senegalese culture as a whole.

Sabar: The Ubiquitous Dance Event

As mentioned before, the term "sabar" refers to both the sabar drum itself and the event at which it is played. In this section, we will explore this most common performance context of sabar drumming: the *sabar*.

The *sabar* is an organized dance event for women. Somewhat akin to block parties, *sabar*s are the most common form of entertainment and leisure in urban Senegal. During the *sabar* season, the sounds of sabar drums emanating from a *sabar* dance can be heard almost daily in the streets of Dakar. The spring and early summer seasons are the most popular time period for *sabars* because in the late summer (*nawet*, or rainy season), sabar drumming is officially prohibited, since it is believed that sabar drumming could drive away much-needed rainfall for the upcoming harvest season. However, despite the prohibition, the sound of neighborhood *sabars* can be heard year-round.[2]

Sabars can take place at various times of day, but the most common times are the afternoon or late evening. The afternoon *sabar* is appropriately called *sabar ngoon* (*ngoon* is the Wolof word for 'afternoon'); it takes place around 5 p.m. The night *sabar* or *tànnibéer* can begin anywhere from 10 p.m. to midnight.[3] The *tànnibéers* tend to be slightly more formal events organized by more mature women, whereas *sabar ngoon* are less formal and often organized by young women, teenagers, or even small children. In general, *tànnibéers* tend to last longer than *sabar ngoons*; the latter usually range from an hour to an hour and half, whereas *tànnibéers* generally last at least two to three hours. In the early 1960s and 1970s, before the advent of nightclubs, sabar dancing was even more popular than it is today. As a result, drummers would often play twice in a day; first in a *sabaru takkusan/ngoon* from 5 p.m. to 7 p.m., and then again in a *tànnibéer* from 8 p.m. to midnight.[4] According to some, *tànnibéers* date only to the latter half of the twentieth century because before that time it was difficult to provide adequate lighting for nighttime events.

Any woman who wants to can organize a *sabar*. There is always a sense of pride in the person organizing the *sabar*, for she will gain a reputation as a person of means and good hospitality (*teranga,* one of the most valued Senegalese virtues). More often, a *sabar* will be organized together by a group of friends who share the cost. On such occasions, the organizing women sometimes have special outfits made out of matching material, so that one can distinguish the hostesses.

Organization of a *sabar* can involve varying degrees of preparation. For any event, one must first procure the services of a sabar group and decide on the date and the payment.[5] Then it is necessary to rent chairs. (The formality of the *sabar* will be reflected in the type of chairs, which can range from cheap, rusting metal chairs to the higher-class plastic chairs, similar to what is used in the United States as porch furniture.) For a *tànnibéer*, one must also hire someone to set up a lighting system; sometimes, one might even choose to rent a sound system with a microphone (so that people can make announcements and speeches).[6]

Because *sabars* take place outdoors on street corners, it is also necessary to obtain a permit from the local police department to block off the street. Many *sabars* are closed down due to lack of permit, especially large *tànnibéers* that attract a large crowd and thus the attention of the authorities; however, smaller children's *sabar*s taking place on an underused street on an afternoon are likely to get away without a permit. As it is difficult to obtain a permit for a *sabar* during *nawet* (the rainy season), *sabar*s taking place during *nawet* are often held illegally.

Since dance is primarily a women's activity, *sabar*s are always organized by women and mostly attended by women. However, a *sabar* inevitably attracts a huge crowd; since it takes place on a neighborhood street corner, any interested passers-by might stop and watch. At a typical *sabar* event, mostly women attend, followed by a contingent of boys and girls, teenage and younger. Grown men are conspicuously absent, with the exception, of course, of the *géwël* drummers. There is a conspicuously gendered aspect to *sabar* events, with its male drummers and female dancers.

There is also a social class/caste aspect to *sabar* events, of which I was not aware for some time, since I had been associating with griot drummers during most of my fieldwork in Senegal. One *géer* friend told me he stayed away from *tànnibéer*s because they were "chaotic" and that "bandits hang out there—it isn't safe." Another *géer* friend told me that one of his sisters has a lot of *géwël* friends and she likes to dance a lot, so the others in the family sometimes tease her by calling her *géwël*. These anecdotes show that *tànnibéer*s and dancing are sometimes looked down upon as a lower-class activity.

Although I never surveyed the number of women at *tànnibéer*s who were griots, it is true that *géwël* are generally exposed to music and dance at an early age and perhaps are more prone to take part in such events. (*Géwël* also claim to be better dancers than *géer*, though I have seen some fine *géer* dancers as well.) Although *sabar* dance movements undoubtedly have a sexual/erotic aspect to them (in the movements and gestures themselves, as well as the lifting of dresses to expose sexy undergarments), it would be difficult to claim that dancing is necessarily a lower-caste event primarily for griots, since *géer* women do organize *sabar*s, and they can be rather "formal" events (opportunities for people to wear their finest clothing, to see and be seen).

Although a well-organized *sabar* may include printed invitations, a *sabar* is by nature a semipublic event because it takes place outdoors and is not cordoned off in any way. This makes it a popular form of free entertainment (with only the organizers absorbing the costs). Whereas entry fees to clubs can range from 2,000–5,000 cfa (US$4–10—a lot of money for the average Senegalese), and movie tickets also cost around 2,000 cfa, a neighborhood *sabar* is an ideal way to pass time dancing, socializing, and enjoying the music of sabar drums.

We will now move on to a description of a typical *tànnibéer* featuring drummers from the Mbaye family, based on yearlong observations of different *tànnibéer*s. Although this description is loosely based on a *tànnibéer* I observed (at Guel Tapée, August 11, 1999),[7] since each *tànnibéer* has its unique sequence of events, I will draw on elements from various *tànnibéer*s to give a more complete description of what one might observe on a typical summer evening in Dakar. A *sabar ngoon* would happen in much the same way, only it would take place during the late afternoon, might be a little shorter, and tends to be organized by younger women and children.

Tànnibéer: An Evening of Fun and Dance

It is shortly after 10 p.m. on a streetcorner in Dakar. Despite the late hour, the air is still very warm on this summer night. Some friends of the hostess are starting to set up plastic chairs in the form of a horseshoe, lining the sides of the street and blocking off one side. An occasional car drives up to the area, and the angry driver is told to turn around and find another route. A young man is climbing telephone poles and stringing lightbulbs from the poles and trees. With a flick of the switch, the dance space is suddenly showered with light.

Shortly thereafter, two taxis pull up, and the drummers unload their sabars from the trunks. One drummer asks a small child to tell the hostess that the drummers have arrived. The drummers pull up some chairs and start to play casually. One of the drummers, Macheikh, finds that his drum is out of tune. He goes to the side of the road and finds a rock with which he hits the drum's pegs to loosen them. After taking out the pegs and pounding them back in, he taps the drum lightly and nods with approval. "*Neex na leegi*!" he exclaims; "the sound is good now."

After some waiting around, the drummers start to play *saaji* ('warmup'). Not all of the drummers have arrived yet. Those who have begin to warm up their hands. Some younger brothers and other less-experienced percussionists in the family take this opportunity to play during *saaji*, for this is the only time that they are allowed to practice (since they are not yet deemed ready to play in the actual *sabar* itself).[8] In addition to playing standard *rythmes* such as *baar mbaye* and *Kaolack*, the drummers try their hands at various *bàkk*s. Those *bàkk*s that are more successful catch on, and soon the whole group is practicing them and nodding in agreement with each other. Perhaps this *bàkk* will be played during the *tànnibéer* proper.

Saaji also serves as a prelude, announcing that the sabar is soon to begin. Slowly but surely, spectators are drawn to the makeshift arena. Young women arrive, chatting animatedly with one another. Small children are immediately attracted to the sound of the drums, and some begin to dance around, only to be playfully shooed away by the grown women.

The women are all elegantly dressed. (Senegalese women are famous for their attention to style, beauty and detail, and a *tànnibéer* serves as clear evidence for this fact.) From the traditional *grand boubous*, the long flowing robes with headwrap and all, to the more recent styles of *ndokket* (a dress with puffy short sleeves and a slim waistline), from silks and the rich cotton *basin* to the intricately patterned and brightly colored *wax* cloths, the women's clothing is a feast for the eyes. Dressed in their best, the women chat with their friends, meanwhile eyeing other women to inspect the latest styles and choices of cloth. From clothing to jewelry to hairstyles, every woman seems to have taken great care in making herself look beautiful for the event.

It is nearly 11 p.m., and by now the drumming has attracted a decent crowd of spectators. Most of the seats are filled, and people are standing behind the seats. Small children are everywhere, and adolescents peer down from nearby rooftops and balconies.

Lamine Touré, who is *dirigeur* (leader) of this evening's *tànnibéer*, sets up his *nder* on a chair, facing his fellow drummers. The drummers are set up in a square horseshoe configuration, with three *cól* players seated in the back, and six sabars, three standing in a row on each side. Lamine looks around to determine whether enough of a crowd has gathered and decides that there is a sufficient crowd for them to start playing. After warming up a bit, Lamine Touré motions to the other drummers to stop playing. By raising his stick, he cues the entire group, which begins to play *ya ñu moom* in unison.[9] The familiar introductory phrases call attention to the drummers, and the *tànnibéer* has officially begun.

"*Ya ñu moom*" is immediately followed by the obligatory *tagumbar*, played on the solo, unaccompanied *nder*. *Tagumbar* is a special *bàkk* that protects the sabars, and it is always played at the beginning of a *sabar.* In addition to its protective element, *tagumbar* is also technically difficult to play, and all ears are on the *dirigeur* as he carries out this impressive *bàkk*. Occasionally the *tagumbar* is punctuated by verbal affirmations from the fellow drummers.

After *tagumbar*, the group launches into their signature *bàkk de spectacle*. The *bàkk de spectacle* is followed by a brief solo *nder* interlude, which leads into the *ndox bàkk*, another family *bàkk* and one recently popularized by its appearance in Cheikh Lô's top hit "Ndox." Afterward, the group plays the theme *bàkk* from the latest Balla Beye wrestling match (which featured Thio Mbaye et al.—see following section on music and wrestling).

After this initial exposition of *bàkk*s (lasting about fifteen minutes), the group launches into *jël,* a preparatory rhythm that segues into *ardin*. Although the drummers only play this *rythme* for a few minutes, it is an invigorating *rythme,* and the drummers become visibly excited by it, moving inward to play to each other as the drumming intensifies. Eventually the *rythme* segues into the *entrée*[10] to *ardin*. In less than a minute, the drummers have launched into *ardin*, the initial sabar *rythme*. *Ardin* is the first *rythme* played. The only *rythme* not danced to, *ardin* signals that the dancing is about to begin.

The crowd is constantly growing. Most spectators are watching the drummers, but others are still milling about, speaking to friends and moving chairs around for newcomers.

Lamine turns his drum so that he is now facing the crowd instead of the drummers. He then plays the *transfer*[11] from *ardin* to *farwu jar*, which signals for the dancing to begin. Immediately, the hostess/organizer runs out from the crowd into the middle of the circle, dancing in front of the drummers. (The hostess always has the honor of having the first dance.) After just ten seconds in the limelight, she retreats back into the crowd, as other women jump up from their seats to dance as well.

Sometimes one by one, sometimes with friends, women take turns dancing. There is no particular order; whoever feels the urge to dance can jump into the circle. Throughout the course of the evening, certain women who enjoy dancing reappear more often than others. Nonetheless, no woman generally stays in the circle for much longer than fifteen to twenty seconds. After this short period of dancing, each woman then quickly runs away, often looking embarrassed, jumping into the arms of her amused friends.

After about four minutes, Lamine plays the *transfer* that smoothly segues *farwu jar* into *ceebu jën. Ceebu jën* is the most difficult *rythme* to play due to its rapid tempo and it is thus a difficult *rythme* to dance to for the same reason. Still, this is no deterrent for the women, who continue to jump into the circle and dance, dust flying as their bare feet hit the ground with great force.

Although the dance is slightly different for each *rythme*, the basic movements are fairly similar for most of the dances (with the exception of *lëmbël/ventilateur*, which is discussed later). Sabar dancing is characterized by flailing limb movements, with each limb seemingly moving in a different direction. After a woman runs into the circle, she lifts her outer skirt wrap (*sër*) to expose the inner wrap (*bééco*). While she holds her clothing with one arm, the other arm flies around, upward and sideways, while her legs do the same. A turning and stomping motion between the legs alternates with an occasional leap. There is a constant twisting of the legs at all joints, especially at the knees and the upper legs (see Figure 6.1).

Facial expression is another important component of sabar dancing. Women roll their eyes upward (called *ragaju*) in what is meant to mimic sexual swooning (but has now become a central feature of the dancing). As each woman comes out and dances, there is some level of overt sexual tension between the dancer and the drummers, with the dancer being inspired by the drumming, and the drummers inspired by a good dancer (who can move her body with agility, exposing her undergarments at the same time).[12]

After several minutes of *ceebu jën*, the drummers stop playing, then immediately recommence. Stopping and starting is typical of sabar drumming when the leader wants to introduce a new tempo, the drummers are getting tired, or

FIGURE 6.1. Maguette Seck dancing

somebody wants to make a speech (or *woyang*, praising and asking for money). However, the discontinuous drumming does not detract from the overall flow of the multifaceted event.

Lamine plays a brief solo that starts the whole group into *ceebu jën* again. The drumming is intense, as is the dancing, and as one particularly good dancer finishes, the entire ensemble picks up its drums and moves toward her, encouraging her to dance some more. To the cheers of the crowd, the drummers surround the dancer, until she retreats again, and they move back to their original place. Soon one of the *cól* players comes to the front with the *cól* between his knees and begins to solo. Lamine continues to solo on the *nder*, though he lets up a bit as the dancers run up to the *cól* player, responding to the thunderous bass notes. (In sabar drumming, although there is one primary lead drum, this does not prevent other drums, especially the *cól*, from soloing as well, and in this way, the ensemble takes a sort of democratic approach to performing). As the *cól* inspires the dancers and the other drummers, one of the other drummers sticks a 500 cfa bill in the *cól* player's mouth for encouragement. After a few minutes, the *cól* player retreats back to sit with the rest of the *cól* section.

Now a good half hour into the *tànnibéer*, the drummers play the entrée to *baar mbaye,* chanting: "*Baar mbaye, bëkëtë bëkëtë, baar mbaye mbësu*!" After the introductory *bàkk*, they launch into the dance *rythme* proper. A popular *rythme, baar mbaye* has a more relaxed feeling and slower tempo than *ceebu jën*. (Refer to the rhythmic transcriptions in Chapter 5.) The women continue to dance as the drummers speed up to a near-chaotic tempo, then return to the slower, more relaxed *baar mbaye*.

After several minutes of *baar mbaye*, the group changes to the *Kaolack* rhythm. During *Kaolack*, one of the *cól* players comes out to solo again. The *mbalax* part of *Kaolack* is overlayed with some of the latest *bàkk*s. As Lamine introduces different *bàkk*s, the majority of the drummers play them. After each dancer has danced her sufficient time of ten to fifteen seconds or so, she is signaled to leave by a *danel*. (The *danel* is a short musical phrase played by the sabars to indicate that the dancer should leave; only played during *Kaolack* and *lëmbël*, the *danel*s change with time, as some go out of style and old ones are revived). Because *danel*s are repeated, the women begin to anticipate the *danel*s and dance accordingly, sometimes matching pelvic thrusts to the final drum strokes of the *danel*s, evoking shrieks and laughter from the spectators.

The drumming and dancing alternate back and forth between *baar mbaye* and *Kaolack*. Suddenly, the *cól* player signals the introductory *bàkk* to the famous wrestling rhythm *Tyson*. There is a call and response between the *cól* and the other drummers in this *bàkk,* which then launches into the recently popular *Tyson rhythm*. A woman jumps into the circle and mimics the stylized wrestler's movements of the *Tyson* dance, taking large steps and swinging her arms back and forth. A small group of male adolescents enters the circle as well, dancing in single file, until other young boys try to join in, and they are all eventually shooed away by the adults.

After *Tyson*, the drummers return to *baar mbaye*, which seems to be a favorite *rythme* of the evening. (The drummers often gauge which rhythms are more successful, and if there is one *rythme* that the dancers seem to respond to more than the others, they will return to that *rythme* more often.) After *baar mbaye*, they pause, and Lamine begins to *woyang*. He shouts praises of the other drummers and encourages the spectators to reward them with money. This period of *woyang* is a necessary component of every sabar and usually occurs when the sabar is well underway, somewhat closer to the end of the event.[13] Lamine is joined by one of the other drummers, as they shout praises to one another and start praising the organizer of the event. As she comes up and hands a bill to Lamine, she whispers in his ear the names of some of her friends, and they proceed to praise these other women, who are then of course obliged to come up and give money. Meanwhile, other random women come up to give money in their appreciation for the drummers, as the praising is occasionally punctuated by intermittent drumming. (One *bàkk* commonly played at this point is the one accompanying "*cow li, cow li, yow la*," which means "the hubbub is all about you!") After about ten minutes, the drummers have collected a sufficient amount of money, and they resume playing, launching into a fast-paced *ceebu jën* rhythm, to which the women vigorously dance.

The *tànnibéer* has been going full force for nearly two hours when the drummers turn to the final dance *rythme* of the evening, *lëmbël*. This *rythme* is accompanied by *bàkk*s and *danel*s, as well as some occasional *taasu* (spoken-word poetry with bawdy lyrics). The most overtly sexual of all the dances, the *lëmbël* dance is also called *ventilateur*, or "electric fan," which refers to the quickly rotating movement of the women's buttocks. During this dance the women hike up their outer wraps (or in many cases, dispose of them altogether, completely exposing sexy *béécos* and *bin-bin*, the strings of beads worn around one's waist). As they expose their *béécos*, with underpants peeking out from underneath, they grind their hips and swirl their buttocks in the faces of the drummers as they intensify their erotic eye movements, much to the amusement of the onlookers, who cheer them on with rhythmic clapping and shrieks of laughter. When an especially talented dancer does the *lëmbël*, she will be rewarded by people throwing their shoes and other articles of clothing at her feet. Occasionally one woman will be joined by another in the final steps of *danel*, with the two mimicking rhythmic pelvic thrusts to the shrieks of the spectators—then of course running back into the crowd.

The drummers become visibly excited by the highly sexual dancing, and occasionally a drummer will come right up behind a dancer as if he is about to grab her, much to the delight of the spectators. Despite the sexual nature of this dance, however, all actions are taken on a level of playfulness and entertainment. Young boys especially gather around to watch *lëmbël*, and they stare wide-eyed as the women expose themselves and swirl their buttocks in rhythmic fashion, ending with a punctuated pelvic thrust.

After a good fifteen minutes of *lëmbël*, the drummers suddenly return to *ya ñu moom,* and within seconds the crowd disperses, and the event is suddenly over. Children run around as the drummers gather up their drums, chairs are put away, and the event has come to an end in a sort of anticlimax. The drummers, tired, wait around to get paid, as they discuss the evening's performance—who played particularly well, and which *bàkk*s were successful. After some time, Lamine returns with the payment and distributes the money to the drummers as he sees fit. Soon taxis are hailed, and the drummers retire to get a good night's sleep after a long evening of physically demanding work.

In the context of the *tànnibéer*, the sabar facilitates an important social event for women. The *tànnibéer* allows women to socialize with one another as well as create a sphere for themselves where adult men are not present, with the exception of the male *géwël* drummers. This gender division is further accentuated in the next example, which specifically promotes female bonding. This example is the *tur*.

Women's Association Meetings: The *Tur*

The *tànnibéer* and the *sabar ngoon* are both semipublic events because they take place outdoors on streetcorners. Although they will mostly attract friends of the organizer and others from the neighborhood, technically anybody may attend the event. However, sabar drumming and dancing can also take place within the private sphere of a family compound. One context in which they can take place in either private or public (depending on the size of the event) is the women's *tur*.

The *tur* is a women's association meeting.[14] Also known as the *tontine*, the *tur* serves as a mutual savings system. In a country where saving money is nearly impossible for the average Senegalese because there is always someone else in need, the *tontine* allows women to pool their wealth and distribute it evenly. Once a month, the group of friends or extended family members meets and contributes to a common fund. Although the monthly contribution may be a relatively small amount per person, the total pool becomes a sizeable amount of money. Each month, a different woman wins the money (either by chance, such as drawing names from a hat, or in a determined order), and that woman will host the next *tur*. Fairness is guaranteed by careful bookkeeping and mutual trust. In this way, each woman has her turn to keep a large sum of money she would otherwise not have been able to save up on her own. In addition, the *tur* is an important social occasion—a time to catch up with friends, share the latest gossip, talk about one's husbands and children (or boyfriends), reinforce female bonding, and dance sabar.

At a typical *tur*, the hostess provides snacks and refreshments, often making fresh juices and *fattayas* or *pastels* (small fried pastries containing meat or fish, dipped in a spicy sauce—similar to Indian samosas). Sometimes she hires a DJ and rents a sound system to provide music for dancing within the compound; other times, a woman will hire a sabar group and provide live drumming instead.[15] Depending on her means, she may hire just a small ensemble (three to four drummers) to play within her compound; a more elaborate *tur* would be similar to a *sabar ngoon*, taking place outside on the street.[16]

Even if the *sabar* dancing takes place in an outdoor venue such as the street, the *tur* is essentially a private event, and for this reason, the women feel even less restricted than at a *tànnibéer*, and are thus more likely to dance without restraint. (This is true of women from all socioeconomic levels and castes—even *géer* women, while expected to act with more restraint in public situations, dance in a provocative manner when in the company of their close friends in a private event.)[17]

For example, some of the least-restrained (wildest!) dancing I witnessed during my year in Senegal was at the *tur* of my good friend and domestic employee, Samuella Faye (February 22, 1998, at Grand Yoff). The *sabar* at this *tur* was more like a real *sabar ngoon*, with five drummers (led by Karim Mbaye) animating and nearly 200 people (women and children) gathered around to watch and dance. The energy level was high, and there was a strong sense of female comraderie, with women chatting animatedly and laughing with their friends. Likewise, the dancing was extremely energetic and was less restrained in that the women readily lifted their skirts and exaggerated their body movements and eye movements. When it came to *lëmbël*, they held a *lëmbël* competition (see section on *soirée sénégalaise* later in this chapter). Two women at a time would dance the *lëmbël*, after which one would be determined the winner (based on who earned the loudest cheers from the spectators). During the *lëmbël* competition, the women completely removed their outer skirts to expose their *béécos* and *bin-bin*, and wiggled their behinds like I had never seen before, with lots of *ragaju* (eye movements), as the crowd cheered them on and threw clothes and shoes at them when they danced well. Some women even flashed their underwear on purpose, momentarily lifting up their *béécos*. This of course excited the drummers, but was primarily a way of entertaining the crowd and having fun with female friends.

In addition to *lëmbël*, the rhythms of *niari gorong* and *mbabas* are typically played at *turs*, as well as the latest dance crazes. The ensemble will often include a *tama* (small talking drum), which is sometimes featured as a solo instrument during *lëmbël* and *niari gorong*.

The *tur*, like the *tànnibéer*, is an occasion in which the sabar ensemble provides music for women to dance. However, the semiprivate nature of the *tur* allows women of all castes to feel even less restrained in their behavior, especially in dance. The *tur* is not only an occasion for financial empowerment, but for social empowerment as well, and the sabar drums contribute to this social aspect in a vital way.

Life Cycle Ceremonies: *Mariages* and *Ngentes*

Sabar drumming is an extremely important part of Senegalese life cycle ceremonies. In this section, we will discuss two life cycle ceremonies in which sabar drumming and dancing occurs: the *mariage* and the *ngente/baptème* (naming ceremony). Two other important life cycle ceremonies, the *kasak* (circumcision ceremony) and the *laaban* (virginity declaration) have fallen out of practice and are rarely performed in modern-day Dakar.[18] Because I was not able to witness either of these ceremonies firsthand, I do not feel qualified to discuss either *kasak* or *laaban*.[19]

Because sabar drumming at a *mariage* serves a very similar function to that at an *ngente,* I will focus specifically on the *ngente*. Both are of course private events, and both take place during the day (thus called *sabar yendo*, or daytime *sabar*). At both weddings and naming ceremonies, the *sabar*s take place in the afternoon, after the rituals and ceremonies are completed and the celebration is to begin.[20]

At an *ngente* or *mariage,* a large tarp or open-sided tent with chairs under it is usually set up in the street outside of the house. The tent symbolizes a sort of extension of the household, keeping the event an essentially private affair, despite it being in the "public" street. This distinguishes it from a *tànnibéer,* which never takes place under a tent and is always an open, public event.

An *ngente* is usually an all-day affair. In the morning, the men (male relatives and other distinguished friends of the head of the household) come to pay their respects and praise the baby. It is in the morning that the baby is named as well.[21] *Laax*,[22] which is also served at *Korité* (a Muslim holiday to be discussed later), is traditionally served on the morning of an *ngente.* Lunch will be *ceebu yapp*, a rice and meat dish, cooked with the sacrificial sheep. The men slaughter a sheep in the morning, after which the women griots busily prepare cooking it.

Although all sorts of friends and family visit the household throughout the day, the men primarily come in the morning, whereas the afternoon is the time for women (and, not so coincidentally, is also when the *sabar* takes place). All guests bring a small monetary gift (*ndawtal*) to the mother to congratulate her and to help with the costs of the *ngente* (which can be an expensive affair, between renting chairs, the sabar group, and providing food and drink for everyone).

In contrast to its role at a *tànnibéer*, which is a dance event that is also an occasion for drummers to show off their virtuosity and showcase *bàkk*s, the sabar's role at an *ngente* (and *mariage*) is more purely functional: to accompany dance. Thus the drummers primarily play dance *rythmes* (after *ardin, farwu jar, ceebu jën, baar mbaye*, and *ndëc*.) They play *bàkk*s embedded in *Kaolack/ndëc*, but they do not play many other *bàkk*s (to do "demonstrations," as they would do in a *tànnibéer*). Normally they play a first set for an hour or so, break for a big late lunch, then resume playing in the later afternoon. Naturally, the drummers also engage in *woyang*, praising the mother of the baby or whatever other prominent people are around, thus eliciting money from them.

Thio Mbaye explains how a *tànnibéer* differs from an *ngente*, in terms of what is played on the sabar:

> For example, if I play in a big *tànnibéer*, how I play won't be the same as how I play at a baptism. When one plays at a baptism, it's not necessary to do lots of demonstrations, and one plays for the dance, for the people to dance. That's the difference. For example, if I'm playing in a nightclub [at a *soirée sénégalaise*], I will play more attractions, create more *bàkk*s, and

> play complicated phrases . . . in general, in *tànnibéer*s also, the first ten minutes or so, we play demonstrations; then we play the dance *rythmes*. Also, when I play at an *ngente*, I might play with just five or six sabars; but a full-fledged *tànnibéer*, we play with twelve sabars, eleven or twelve. So it's not the same thing. (5/23/98)

A Special *Ngente* Ritual: *Bëkëtë*

In addition to the naming, dancing, and other festivities common to all Senegalese baptisms, people of Lebou origin, descended from Diagne Ndoye and Diagne Mbaye, celebrate a special *ngente* ritual called *bëkëtë*.[23] Since Mbayes are of *géwël* origin, the Mbaye family considers the *bëkëtë* ritual an important *géwël* tradition and performs it every time a new baby is born into the family.

Bëkëtë is a ritual of protection.[24] As Macheikh Mbaye explains,

> *Bëkëtë* is a means of protecting the child. When the child is eight days old, we will celebrate *bëkëtë* in order to protect him. We will protect him from the evil spirits, from any kind of accident, from evil tongue (*caat*)—because some tongues will destroy anything when they talk about it. We will protect him/her also from evil eye; that's what *bëkëtë* is all about—to protect the survival of the child, that's all. (3/5/98)

In order to celebrate *bëkëtë*, the following basic ritual items are necessary: a vase (*ndaa*), a basket (*laayu*), three woven wraps (*sër*), a machete, a bundle of cotton string (*fale*), a mortar and pestle, and millet. In addition, sabar drums are an integral part of the ritual. The *bëkëtë* ritual takes place on the afternoon of the *ngente*, before the *sabar* dancing proper. First comes a procession leading into the ritual space (usually just the street, as in a *sabar*). The procession consists of female members of the family (sisters of the father of the child), and a mistress of ceremonies, usually an elderly female griot. The baby is carried by one of the women in a basket on her head. First they put a wrap on the basket, then put the child on the wrap, then wrap him/her up with the other two wraps. The baby is followed by a designated person (usually an elder sister of the father) and the mother of the baby. These two must crawl on all fours with a piece of cotton string strung between their mouths. This is to prevent the mother from either smiling or laughing—if she were to smile or laugh, the ritual would be destroyed. Even if people try to make her smile or laugh, she must stand firm until the end of the ritual. As a result, the mother looks very solemn, often just staring at the ground as she crawls on her hands and knees. The sister holding the baby also maintains a solemn face and neither smiles nor talks.

As the procession begins, so does the drumming. The ensemble (in the case of Oulymata's *ngente,* only three drummers—two *mbëng-mbëng* and a *cól*) plays *baar mbaye*, and the women repeatedly chant, "*Bëkëtë bëkëtë, baar mbaye*!" They may switch back and forth between *baar mbaye* no. 1 and no. 2, but the basic rhythm played during *bëkëtë* is indeed *baar mbaye*.

The procession slowly circles around a mortar and pestle, which the different women in the procession take turns pounding. The mortar is filled with millet. The procession continues until the millet is turned into flour. Occasionally one of the women breaks out to dance to the familiar *baar mbaye* rhythm, then returns to the procession. A few other women spectators may also dance. However, the focus is undoubtedly on the procession rather than the dancing.

Although I did not witness this at Ouly's *ngente*, Macheikh Mbaye told me that normally one of the women in the procession would hold a machete. The machete symbolizes the great ancestor Diagne Ndoye, who used to carry a machete when fighting in the battlefields. To perpetuate the tradition, people carry the machete, and some women even use another stick to beat the machete to accompany the drumming.

When the millet has been turned to flour (after about ten minutes or so), the procession stops and the mother and elder sister (who had been on all fours) sit down. Then the mistress of ceremonies (elderly woman griot) sings some praises, and money immediately flows from all family members to the woman griot. After this period of *woyang*, the drummers resume *baar mbaye*. The woman holding the baby takes it out of the basket and hands it to the designated other sister (who has string in her mouth). This sister sits facing the mother with the baby in her hands. She then holds out the baby as if to say, "Here is your child," and the mother outstretches her hands as if to say, "Give me my child," but the sister deceives her and does not give her the child. They repeat this gesture seven times.

In the meantime, another female griot (in Ouly's case, Maam Basin Thiam) has taken some of the millet and mixed it in a calabash with some *lait caillé* (sour milk).[25] Because the Ndoye/Mbaye family has spirits surrounding them, the millet is destined for those spirits—they are among us but we cannot see them—so some *lait caillé* is drunk, but some must be spat out for the spirits. Thus Maam Basin Thiam takes the mixture from the calabash, puts it in her mouth and spits it out everywhere (on the baby, the other women, the drummers—everybody, including me, an observer). Then the sister (who has the baby) drinks some and spits it onto the mother. Soon everybody is covered with the pasty white stuff, which is meant to be for the spirits. Before we know it, the ritual is over, and people are wiping themselves clean and soon are ready to prepare for the next event, the *sabar*.

According to Macheikh Mbaye, when people chant "*Bëkëtë bëkëtë*," others say, "*Rapp wu aay, yalla na la tegge doom*," which means, "Be protected from the evil spirits, evil tongue, evil eye [etc.]."

Of the different *rythmes* played in sabar, *baar mbaye* is the only *rythme* that appears to have a specific ritual function, as well as being a standard dance *rythme*. However, the ritual function is not altogether lost in the dance, since the drummers chant the same chant ("*Bëkëtë, bëkëtë, baar mbaye!*"), and the *rythme* seems to be a particular favorite among members of the Mbaye family (both to drum and to dance).

In *bëkëtë*, and in *ngente* in general, the sabar has its place in a traditional ritual context. As we have seen in other contexts, the sabar is associated with the female sphere (with the women coming in the afternoon to socialize and dance, while the men typically are around only during the morning). However, rather than just providing music for dancing, here the sabar also plays a key role in the ritual, helping to protect the child from harm. Through *ngente,* every child is brought into Senegalese society with the sound of sabars.

Muslim Holidays and *Ñaani Ndéwënël*

In Senegal, two of the most celebrated holidays in the Muslim calendar are *Korité* (the end of the fasting month of Ramadan, known in Arabic as *'Id al-Fitre*), and *Tabaski* (the day commemorating Abraham's faith, known in Arabic as *'Id al-Adha*). *Korité* marks the end of the fasting month of Ramadan and thus is the first day during which people can eat during daylight, and this is cause for much rejoicing. *Tabaski*, perhaps the most important Muslim holiday, marks the commemoration of Abraham's willingness to sacrifice his own son to God. On this day, thousands of sheep are slaughtered to commemorate Abraham. During both holidays, everybody wears their finest clothing and visits family and friends, asking each other for forgiveness and pardon. This is an important tradition, and both of these holidays (especially *Tabaski*) are widely anticipated (and prepared for, since one must have money to buy the new clothes and prepare the lavish meals to be eaten on those days).

However, these Muslim holidays hold another tradition for children and for *géwël* percussionists as well. That custom (*aada*) is *ñaani ndéwënël* (meaning 'to go ask for the monetary gift traditionally given to children and *géwël* at *Korité* and *Tabaski*).

Ñaani ndéwënël is an activity most explicitly linked to what *géwël* are known for: asking for money. Although this is an activity for all Senegalese children (griot or nongriot), who go door to door to ask for small change from their neighbors, many griots take this opportunity to do the same—to greet their friends and patrons with sabar drumming, and to receive money in turn.

Beginning in the late morning of either *Korité* or *Tabaski*, the drummers set out to make their rounds. Usually a small group, they go around from house to house, visiting select neighbors and other patrons throughout Dakar, to greet them, drum for them, wish them well, and, in return, receive monetary gifts. *Korité* is an especially happy occasion for griots because during the month of Ramadan they have not been drumming, so this is the first day that they can resume playing. (Often the night before is busily spent mounting new heads on the sabars so that they are ready to be played.)

I accompanied the Mbaye family percussionists on their *ñaani ndéwënël* excursions for *Korité* and *Tabaski* 1998. Because *ñaani ndéwënël* was essentially the same for both holidays, I will provide an ethnographic description of *Korité* on January 30, 1998.

In the Mbaye family, interestingly, the *ñaani ndéwënël* of 1998 was organized by two sons of Macheikh Mbaye, Moussa and Babacar Mbaye (twin brothers), who are not trained percussionists. (Both have taken on jobs in business.) Although they do not play well, they are able to play some basics, much to the amusement of their fellow drumming compatriots (who laugh at their lack of skill). Nonetheless, this does not seem to matter for *ñaani ndéwënël* because this is not an occasion for serious, high-level playing. Also, the art of praising and asking for money is equally important to the drumming in this custom, and both Babacar and Moussa are skilled in this area.

Around 9 a.m. on *Korité,* January 30, 1998, men dressed in their *grand boubous* started venturing out to pray in the mosques. The prayer was over well before 10 a.m., and the men returned home to eat their first daytime meal in over a month. Meanwhile, wives had been preparing the traditional breakfast of *laax* covered with *sow* (sweetened *lait caillé*). After breakfast was served, the women busily prepared the big meal of the day, usually chicken.[26]

Around 11 a.m., we set out to do *ñaani ndéwënël*. Everyone was in a jovial mood—the month of fasting was now over, and they could resume life as usual. Everybody was dressed in their finest clothing, and the drummers were of course happy to be able to play again after a month's rest.

The group was small: just Babacar and Moussa Mbaye, each on *cól*, and Lamine Touré and Moustapha Niasse on *mbëng-mbëng*. (It was necessary to keep the group small, especially when it came to transportation—so that we could all fit into one cab and not have to pay for two.)

We started out at a few houses in the HLM neighborhood. Generally, we would bring the drums to the outside courtyard and start playing. Sometimes Babacar would knock on the door or ring the doorbell first, but in general, that was not necessary because the sound of the four drums was enough to announce the *géwël's* arrival.

Within a minute or less, people would open the front door and either come out, stand in the doorway listening, or in a few cases even dance a bit. Often small children were the first to appear and were the most likely to dance. Some people even invited us in for a few minutes, in which case we would bring the drums inside and play indoors as well. Afterward, Babacar would shout some praises and ask for money, which he always received. Depending on the amount received, he might compliment their generosity and more drumming would ensue.

After visiting a few households in the immediate neighborhood, we hailed a cab and did rounds all over Dakar. Most of the people we visited were *turandos* (namesakes) of Babacar and Moussa, their bosses/employers and ex-bosses, and other *géer*. All households visited were of upper middle class families. The people also seemed prepared (since this is a yearly ritual). Although in some cases they seemed a bit embarrassed, they always immediately retreated to get some money and give it to the drummers. We were never refused, we were always treated with respect, and the people always seemed to enjoy the visit.

The drumming itself was fairly low-level. In general, they played *baar mbaye* and *Kaolack* and would only play for short periods of time (a few minutes) before stopping to let Babacar do his *woyang*. In some cases it took Babacar's *woyang* to get the head of the household to come to the doorway (if the door was first opened by small children). Babacar's praising/speech was as important as the drumming, as was the *géwël's* animated behavior in general. On occasion, Babacar or Moussa would even dance, and the general atmosphere was of mischief and fun. On this occasion, they acted with less restraint than they normally would in other situations. For *ñaani ndéwënël,* it seemed as if this was the quintessential opportunity for them to act as griots, and as a result, they felt the abandon to act in a loud, rowdy and playful way.

In about a four-hour span, we covered over a dozen houses, and, tired and hungry, we returned home for lunch. *Ñaani ndéwënël* was a success in every way: the drummers carried out the yearly tradition/custom (*aada*), had an opportunity to ask for pardon and to praise, and of course made a lot of money.

After lunch, the members of the Mbaye family would continue to visit their friends and relatives, but without their drums. This is a tradition for all Senegalese, whether griot or nongriot. Walking around in their finest clothes, everyone visited family and friends, especially those one had not seen in a long time. It was a time to ask for pardon from each other and to rekindle relationships.

Ñaani ndéwënël reaffirms the relationship between *géwël* and *géer*. Through this custom, the sabar drummers participate in a longtime tradition of *géwël* praise-singing and the solicitation of monetary gifts. Although the sabar is finding itself in increasingly modern contexts, such as *soirées sénégalaises* (to be explored below), its place in these Muslim celebrations reinforces the traditional role of Wolof *géwël.*

Sabar and Politics: The Political Meeting

Another context in which sabar drumming occurs is the political meeting. During every campaign season, politicians hire sabar drummers to play at their meetings. The sabar drumming is used to draw attention to the meeting and attract potential political supporters.

At political meetings, the sabar players play *animations* to attract attention. This may include any combination of *rythmes* and *bàkk*s; however, the drumming is not for dancing, but rather to introduce the politicians. At a political meeting, drummers will play as a politician arrives, then stop playing as he makes his speech, then resume playing as an interlude.

Special *bàkk*s are played in order to praise the political figures at hand. For example, a well-known *bàkk* that was created during Abdou Diouf's rule (1980–2000) is the catchy "*Abdou, avec Abdou, jusqu'à la mort*" (CD Track 26). This phrase translates as "Abdou, we are with Abdou until his death." Although this *bàkk* was created for Abdou Diouf, it is obviously versatile, and the name can be replaced by that of any other politician.

Politicians sometimes provide funds for a politically sponsored *tànnibéer* (not to be confused with the political meeting). In such a case, a politician will give money to a group of women, who will organize a *tànnibéer* in support of that particular political party. Sabar players perform at such *tànnibéer*s just as they would perform at any other *tànnibéer.*

According to Deborah Heath (1994, 93), political rallies and meetings in the Kaolack region in the early 1980s were often preceded by women dancing (to draw crowds and enliven those in attendance, as well as to demonstrate the hospitality and largess of the rallies' sponsors), sometimes with a *concours ventilateur* (*ventilateur* competition, such as that described in the sections on *tur*s and *soirées sénégalaises*). However, the dancing is said to be more restrained in these public, mixed-gender settings.

The link between sabar drumming and politics is more financial than political. Although some griots of the elder generation are linked to one or another of the political parties and have chosen to play only for the party they support, most of the younger griots will play for whoever hires them. As one *géwël* once put it, "It's not about which political party I support. I'm a drummer, and it's work. If someone hires me, I will go play for them." However, inasmuch as politics reflects the desires of the people, sabar becomes a part of this process. For example, in the recent monumental presidential elections on March 19, 2000, the victory of Abdoulaye Wade over incumbent Abdou Diouf was celebrated by *tànnibéer*s throughout the streets of Dakar in the days following the election results, reflecting the overwhelming optimism of the Senegalese people and their enthusiasm and hope for change.[27]

Reaching beyond national boundaries, sabar drums become a symbol of national pride and national identity when dignitaries from other countries come to visit. When Nelson Mandela visited Senegal in 1991, he was greeted by all the major *géwël* drum troupes, who composed new *bàkk*s especially for him (CD Track 27). One *bàkk*, the "Mandela" *bàkk*, remains popular more than a decade after Mandela's visit, thus memorializing this important event in Senegalese history.

At the turn of the twenty-first century, political leaders now serve as a sort of modern-day substitute for the traditional royalty and *géer*. As in the past, today's leaders need *géwël* support in order to succeed. Likewise, politics empower *géwël* by providing another venue for them to drum. By enlisting the support of *géwël*, and using sabar drums to attract attention at their political meetings, politicians reinforce the *géwël's* traditional role in a more modern context.

Traditional Senegalese Wrestling: The *Làmb*

In Senegal, traditional wrestling (*làmb*) remains the most popular national sport, even more popular than soccer. A mixture of sport, drumming, and many complicated mystical rituals, *làmb* is steeped in tradition. Although nowadays, top *lutteurs* (wrestlers, such as the current number one Mohammed Ndao "Tyson") are offered remarkably large cash prizes and are attributed heroic status in the daily newspapers (even more so than American boxers), Senegalese wrestling has its origins in the rural fields.[28] As Macheikh Mbaye explains,

> Wrestling comes from the Serer and the Lebou. I don't know about elsewhere, but here in Senegal, that's where it came from. Before colonisation, we didn't have masonry or other jobs; all our ancestors were doing was going to the fields, farming, and going to the sea. So when they were expecting a good harvest, everybody was happy. And to express that feeling, they would just get together at the meeting place [*penc*] to play and have fun. But they would do it at a certain time, particularly when there was a full moon, because at that time they didn't have electricity; they used to get together at night just to have those games. I'm telling you about history. So that was the very place and the very time all the youngsters in the village showed their strength and tried to challenge each other. That's where wrestling came from. And these ceremonies would go along with drumming, and the youngsters would wrestle just to have fun—nobody would get paid for that. . . . As time went on, it turned out to be what you see nowadays. (3/2/98)

One of the earliest written accounts of wrestling in the Senegambian region comes from Jean-Baptiste Gaby, in his 1689 *Relation de la Nigritie*. Thus we see that even in the seventeenth century, drumming was an integral part of the ceremony:

> On the afternoon of Frougar [a local holiday], five or six of their Guiriots come to the central square of the village, dragging on their left side their drums with a leather strap. They begin to sing and beat the drums in order to get everyone to come; and having assembled them, the leader of the band of Guiriots announces that Frougar will begin with a wrestling match, warning that only strong and robust men need present themselves, so that Frougar will be more enjoyable and entertaining. Then the symphony begins with seven or eight drums of different sizes, some large, some small. At the same time, men and boys who want to wrestle enter in the Frougar circle, naked to the belly button, stripped of clothing that might encumber them or be torn during the match. They dance in a slow manner, so that each can choose his equal, whom he takes by the head or embraces by the middle of the body, trying always to make him fall. When one of the two has beaten his man by throwing him to the ground, all the Guiriots, as well as his friends, congratulate him and sometimes give him some Couscous. (Halc 1998, 93)

Wrestling in the Dakar urban area has its genesis in the twentieth century. According to Macheikh Mbaye, in 1915–1920 his uncle Modou Ndiaye, also called Ndiaye Rabb, used to play for the famous wrestler Pate Diop in the theater El Malik, one of the first movie theaters built in Dakar by the French. A French woman by the name of Madame Vincent was the first to organize a wrestling match in this theater, where the most famous wrestlers fought. Macheikh Mbaye explains the history of the twentieth century's great wrestlers:

> The most famous wrestlers in that time were Saanoor, Medoun Xule [and others], and my [uncle] would attract people's attention, beating the drum, and at that time, everybody had to pay to get in. And the entrance fee was a *fiftin*—one franc. In that era, there was a very famous wrestler named Pate Diop; after him came Abdourahman Ndiaye Falang, Souley Ndoye, Babacar Thiaw, Talla Diagne, Ablaye Diop, Mbex Ndoye, Cheikh Mbaba (who lived in Mbour), Mbaye Gueye (who took after Falang), Isaa Fall, Modou from Thies, Araf Fall from Ndar, and after came Bosco Sow, Demba Thiaw, Modou Jaxate, Beekay Gueye no. 1, then after that generation came Robert, Mbaye Gueye, Mustapha Gueye, Manga, and so on. That is the actual genesis of wrestling in Dakar, according to history. (3/2/98)

Just as there are special *rythmes* for dancing, there are specific *rythmes* played at wrestling matches. The most important of these *rythmes* is *tuus*, which is played during the *lutteur*'s grand entry. *Tuus* is an ancient *rythme* that was originally played for anyone of importance and power (such as a *buur*, or king), though it quickly became a staple *rythme* to accompany the entry of a wrestler into the wrestling grounds (CD Track 28).[29]

Wrestlers have always been accompanied by their own special *bàkk*s.[30] For example, Mbaye Gueye and Mustapha Gueye have their own *bàkk* called *Ndia ja jinne*. The *bàkk* represents the saying: "*Jinne xam seen kër, te xamuloo këram, nja ja jinne,*" which means, "The spirits know where you live, but you don't know where they live." (3/5/98)

Macheikh Mbaye explains how the *lutteur* Falang used *tuus* and turned it into his own anthem:

> That's the way Falang would praise himself. He made it up by himself. That's his hymn. People had played that rhythm long before, but he turned it into his own hymn. He would go, "*Massambaye mberi ndaw, bey du raas, deemu bukki.* Which means, "A goat does not eat jujube around a hyena. You are goats, I am the hyena!" And if the goat picks up jujube in a hyena environment, he risks his life. And then the griot, Pappa Bunabas, would play the same thing on the drum. (3/5/98)

The most recent example of the close tie between sabar and wrestling is the invention of the *Tyson* rhythm. Although the rhythm has existed for some time (Serer percussionist Omar Thiam in Kaolack is widely credited with its creation), it was Bada Seck who popularized it in the mid 1990s when he turned it into the signature rhythm for the wrestler Mohammed Ndao (nicknamed "Tyson" after American boxing champ Mike Tyson).[31] As Tyson rose to become the number one wrestler in Senegal in the late 1990s, the *rythme* ascended in popularity as well, as a dance was created (mimicking the wrestler's movements). The *rythme* was newly dubbed *Tyson* and goes hand in hand with the *Tyson* dance, which mimics the stylized movements of the parading wrestler as he enters the arena (characterized by large, heavy steps, and swinging one's arms back and forth). The popularity of this *rythme* led to its being featured in a popular song in Bada Seck's 1997 release, *Génération Boul Falé*, as well as in another version by Alioune Mbaye Nder on his chart-topping cassette *Lenëen* (also released in 1997). The *Tyson rythme* and dance peaked in 1997, and by the summer of 1999 its popularity seemed to already be waning. However, in the year 2005, it still remains an important part of the wrestling repertory, as well as the general sabar repertory.

Tyson technically originated as a *bàkk* but has come to be treated as a *rythme*. *Tyson* is accompanied by *lëmbël* parts; however, the *Tyson rythme* transcribed below is prominently featured and played by the majority of the ensemble, and there is a specific dance that accompanies it as well. As such, it has come to function as a *rythme* all of its own. Nowadays, *Tyson* is not only played at Mohammed Ndao's *làmb*s, but at other wrestling matches as well, as it seems to have found a new place in the standard *làmb* repertory (CD Track 29; see Figure 6.2).

Wrestling is still steeped in tradition and mystical rituals. A wrestler is constantly surrounded by his entourage of young men, griots and religious advisors (marabouts), who carry out various rituals to aid his victory. Such rituals are difficult for an outsider to comprehend, and more research is needed in this area.

When Thio Mbaye and Group Rimbax arrived at the wrestling ground, as we stepped off the back of the van, we were to step onto the ground with our right feet only. As we carried the drums to the field, we had to be careful not to drop the drums or even put them down before we reached our particular playing spot. Finally, before sitting down, one of Balla Beye's entourage took salt from a calabash and sprinkled it all over the ground. At this point we were allowed to sit down.

The rituals continue throughout the event. The *lutteur* himself is always covered with *gris-gris*, with all sorts of leather amulets tied around his muscular body. In preparation for the *lutte*, various liquids (most often sour milk or some other white dairy product) are poured on his head. Again, sour milk carries ritual significance as it does in the *bëkëtë* ritual and at Muslim holiday celebrations. A deeper exploration of the meanings behind these rituals will prove a rich subject for future research.

Some of the rituals directly involve the sabar drums. Often some sort of magical powder is rubbed on the lead drum (which is always a *cól* in the context of

FIGURE 6.2. *Tyson*

*làmb*s). Also, when a *lutteur* enters the grounds (marching with his entourage in the stylized way), the first thing he does is approach the drummers. He then takes a rope that he is holding and wraps it around the lead drum (*cól,* also known as *làmb*—the same word as "wrestling") as if gaining power and spiritual energy from the drum itself.

These prematch ceremonies have been noted by earlier writers, with varying degrees of interest. In his ethnographic survey of the Wolof of Senegambia published in 1967, David Gamble writes about wrestling:

> Wrestling is the favourite sport of all the Senegal peoples. . . . To European eyes the wrestling is rather dull, for more time is devoted to preparing for the contests than the actual wrestling, and one needs to be brought up in the culture to appreciate its finer points. (Gamble 1967, 77)

Geoffrey Gorer provides a more appreciative account of these rituals, in his description of Senegalese wrestling matches in 1935:

> If a young man wishes to enter for the wrestling championship he will be accompanied everywhere by his griot who will look after his comfort and morals, help him with his *grigris*, act as his boaster in the arena, play the drum which will announce his entrance and collect the greater part of the money and gifts, which, should he be successful or popular, will be showered on him.
>
> The preliminaries to the wrestling are more entertaining than the actual fights. The fighters enter the arena in order of merit at about ten-minute intervals—there are several smaller fights as well as the championship, and the popular favourites make an appearance without the intention of fighting to gratify their fans—dressed in wrestling costume, a full dhoti-like loincloth in bright patterned materials, arranged so that a tail, sometimes in a different and contrasting material falls behind. Their bodies and arms are smothered in *grigris*. They are preceded by their griots with drums, and followed by a group of supporters and sparring partners dressed in the same fashion. The griots take up their position in a corner of the arena, playing for their patron regardless of the rival griots by them, shouting their patron's glory, occasionally turning somersaults and handsprings to make people laugh, and before the fight doing the necessary *gris-gris* with their patrons (this usually consists of praying to the objects, which must be hidden from the crowd, generally in a hat) and making spells to avert ill luck. Meanwhile the champions swagger round the ring . . . as they walk round the arena they chant the stories of their past victories (I am the man who threw Babakar Dy, I am the man who threw the champion of Joal . . .). (Gorer 1935, 49–50)

The ceremony surrounding the fights, including these rituals, is as much a part of the event as the fights themselves. There are often two or three matches of less experienced wrestlers that precede the main match. Although the entire event can take close to two hours, the actual wrestling matches usually last minutes or seconds.

The matches begin with the two wrestlers hunched over, facing one another, and pawing at each other in a stylized way. Suddenly, they attack each other, locking their bodies and arms together. This results in either one stepping out of bounds and having to start over again, or one flipping the other one over, ending the match. One *lutteur* usually goes down after the initial holding position is established.

Although the stadium often provides a drum troupe (hired by contract), individual wrestlers bring their own drumming troupe for their support. For example, in 1998, Thio Mbaye's sabar group supported *lutteur* Balla Beye no. 2. For each *lutte*, Thio Mbaye created a new *bàkk* for Balla Beye, which became the signature *bàkk* of the fight. Group Rimbax played a large repertory of *bàkk*s, since *bàkk*s, not dance *rythmes*, are featured in *luttes*. *Ya ñu moom* was also prominently featured, as it has religious significance and is generally used to bring good luck and protection.

Although there may be some women spectators, wrestling is primarily a male event. Interestingly, *rythmes* would be played at a dance event for women, whereas *bàkk*s are featured at wrestling matches. This suggests a clear gender division associating women with dance and men with wrestling.

Outdoor Entertainment: The *Simb*

Simb is the Wolof term for *faux lion,* or fake lion. At a *simb*, a *simbkat* wears *gris-gris* (mystical amulets) and thus becomes a lion, or rather, takes on the spirit of a lion. With his face painted red and black, with fake teeth, he has *gris-gris* tied all over him and patches of faux leopard-print fur tied around his arms and legs. Although nowadays *simbs* are seen mostly as a form of entertainment, stories of *simbs* from earlier times seemed to have more seriousness to them, with the *simbkats* seen as truly taking on the spirit of the lion and "becoming" a lion. One example is Sitapha Dieng, the famous *simb* in Kaolack and the *turando*/namesake of Sitapha "Thio" Mbaye. It is said that when Sitapha Dieng donned his *gris-gris*, he became so like a lion that his skin started to sprout lion's fur.

At the turn of the twenty-first century, *simbs* are less popular than they were fifty years ago. In the early 1950s, according to Macheikh Mbaye, *simbs* were extremely popular and considered more "genuine" than they are nowadays. In 1995, *simbs* experienced a sort of revival, and people organized them very frequently, but by 1997–98, they were less common. (During that time period, I only witness two *simbs*, both in February 1998.) Like any fad, *simbs* seem to go in and out of popularity, and there are periods when many are organized, and then periods where there are none for a long time.[32]

A *simb* takes place on the street as a *sabar* does and is accompanied by a sabar group. Unlike a *sabar* or *tànnibéer*, a *simb* requires tickets sold by the organizer (quite cheap, at 200 or 300 cfa typically). Anybody who buys a ticket is safe from the *simb*; but if the *simb* catches you and finds that you do not have a ticket, you can be forced to dance or do whatever else the *simb* makes you do.

Lamine Touré explains that this is what distinguishes a *simb* from a *sabar*:

> A *simb* is a spectacle. A *simb* is not a *sabar*. You must pay; you must buy a ticket to see a spectacle/show, even though it doesn't take place in a concert hall. We do it in the street because it's fun. At *simbs,* we play so that the lion will dance." (8/17/99)

Thus at a *simb*, the performance space consists of a blocked-off street, as at a sabar. The drummers play near one end, and spectators gather around to form a circle around the arena. There are some chairs set up, though the majority of the spectators are standing—so that they can more easily escape if need be!

There are always three *simbs* in total, two "lesser" *simbs* and then the main *simb*. The *simb* begins with the entry of one of the lesser *simbs*. As he enters, he is led into the circle with a sheet draped over his head so that the spectators cannot see him. Finally, he throws the sheet off, to the screams of the spectators. He then marches around the arena making scary movements and finally runs after different spectators. As he approaches some, people hold up their tickets, letting him know that they are not fair game. So generally, the *simb* goes after small children (who cannot afford to buy a ticket, but come to watch the event out of curiosity, despite knowing the danger of being caught). The *simb* sometimes chases children quite a ways down the road, and as he runs, children disperse in every direction, screaming loudly. As a result, the *simb* is a chaotic event, with people running all over the place and dust flying.

When a *simb* does catch a person, he has the power to make the person do whatever he wants them to do. Most often, the person, having been *attrapé* ('trapped') will be brought into the circle and forced to dance, and often will dance in a silly way to amuse the audience. Sometimes the *simbs* will dance with their captives. Some unlucky victims are forced to mimic more embarrassing and even lewd acts (for example, two young boys I witnessed were caught by a *simb* and forced to simulate sexual intercourse, much to the amusement of the spectators; afterward, the boys were rolled around in the dirt until they were covered with dirt, after which they were sent on their way [Kolobane *simb,* 4 February 1998]). However, one must note that although some dancing does take place, the *simb* is essentially not a dance event like a *sabar*; the drummers play for the lion to dance, but not for women. (In fact, *simbs* are attended mostly by men and young boys—few women are usually present.)

After the lesser *simbs* are each introduced, the final *simb* is let loose. The main *simb* is always the biggest and meanest looking of the three.

In addition to the three *simbs*, there is often an *animateur* (person with microphone, like a master of ceremonies), and also two or three *gainde-jigeens* (wives of the lions, played by male transvestites). These *gainde-jigeens* also sing, dance, and get lots of laughs.

There is also some ritual aspect to the *simb*. First of all, the *gris-gris* tied onto the *simbs* are (or at least once were) believed to really give the *simb* special powers, to instill the spirit of the lion within them. Other *gris-gris* are evident at the *simb*, such as pegs buried in the ground, or bonfires, or liquids poured in various places.

Similarly to the *sabar ngoon*, there are normally six to eight drummers playing *cól*s and *mbëng-mbëng*s. The drumming itself includes some *rythmes*, such as *baar mbaye* and *Tyson* (again, a wrestling *rythme*), but there exist other *rythmes* particular to *simbs*. The *rythmes* played at *simbs* are very similar to those played at *làmb*s (wrestling matches). *Simbkat*s are often played by *lutteurs*, who are the only ones who have the appropriate musculature to be a *simb*.[33] That is why often *rythmes* from *làmb*s have been introduced to *simbs*. For example, one of the most common *rythmes* played at *simbs* is *Fass*, a *rythme* played at *làmb*s associated with *lutteurs* from Fass, such as Tapha Gueye, though the *rythme* has existed long before.

The *rythmes* and *bàkk*s are not the only characteristics shared by *simb*s and wrestling matches. Both events are in the male domain, with few women present. Both are also "spectacle" events, meant to be watched, in contrast to the more socially interactive entertainment of a *tànnibéer*. Finally, there are ritual similarities between a *simb* and a *làmb* (wrestling match); just as the main match is preceded by two lesser matches, the main *simb* is preceded by two lesser *simb*s. Both *simbkat*s and *lutteurs* don a multitude of *gris-gris,* and perform numerous rituals as well.

Although the sabar drum plays an important role in traditional wrestling and *simb*s, its modern role has had perhaps the greatest impact on the perpetuation of *géwël* status. In the next two sections, we will discuss two such contexts: the first, a traditional sabar ensemble in a modern space; and the second, sabar in a completely modern context, the Senegalese popular music genre known as *mbalax*.

Traditional Dance in a Modern Space: The *Soirée Sénégalaise*

The *soirée sénégalaise* came into being upon the release of Thio Mbaye's solo cassette *Rimbax* in 1993. Due to the enormous success of this cassette, the proprietors of the popular Dakar nightclub called Sahel collaborated with Thio Mbaye and came up with the idea to hold a sort of *tànnibéer* inside the nightclub, with a cover charge at the door. With this, Thio Mbaye and his group Rimbax invented the *soirée sénégalaise*, which since 1993 has become a tradition in its own right and is a weekly event at most major nightclubs in Dakar.

Although sabars have long been played in nightclubs, up until this point, they had always been played in the context of popular music (mbalax) bands (to be explored in the following chapter). *The soirée sénégalaise* was the first time the entire sabar ensemble played in the nightclub setting, with women dancing as if at an outdoor *sabar*.

Soirée sénégalaises usually occur on a weekday night. At a *soirée sénégalaise*, women are encouraged to wear traditional Senegalese clothing (such as *boubous*) instead of the Western clubwear that is typically worn to nightclubs. Usually, if they dress in traditional clothing and enter the club by midnight, they can pay a reduced entry fee. Since traditional clothing is an integral part of *sabar* dance (with the effectiveness of the dance coming from the grabbing and lifting of the cloth), it is only fitting that traditional dress is encouraged.

From 10 p.m. to about 3 a.m., prerecorded music is played by a DJ, with a focus on the top mbalax hits. Without fail, the latest hits of Youssou N'Dour, Thione Seck, Omar Pène, and Alioune Mbaye Nder are heard. People dance to this music in the appropriate mbalax style (which involves fewer arm movements than *sabar* dancing, but lots of lower body movement, with hips gyrating and knees wiggling.) As some people remain on the dance floor, others sit and watch from the sidelines, sipping on (mostly nonalcoholic) drinks and chatting with friends.

Sometime after 3 a.m., the prerecorded music stops and a sabar group sets up on one side of the combination stage and dance floor. Usually the DJ becomes an MC and announces that the *sabar* is about to begin.

What is played during the *sabar* portion depends on the nightclub, the group performing, and whether there is an advertised competition in a specific dance. Many *soirées sénégalaises* I witnessed, animated by members of Group Rimbax, followed the natural order of a *tànnibéer* (with introductory *bàkk*s in the first ten to fifteen minutes, followed by the standard repertory of dance rhythms.) However, some *soirées sénégalaises* are advertised as, for example, a *lëmbël* competition, in which case most of the sabar playing will consist of *lëmbël*. Typically a *lëmbël* competition will have rewards for the best dancers (with both cash and large bags of rice the typical rewards).

With the women wearing traditional garb and the sabar drumming essentially the same as in a *sabar*, the most marked difference between a *soirée sénégalaise* and a *tànnibéer* is the modern setting. By being moved from an outdoor street corner to the floor of an air-conditioned nightclub, this *sabar* dance event has gone from being a public event available to everyone to an upper middle class event to which only people who can afford to pay the entry fee have access. The other large difference is that many men frequent nightclubs, whether it be men accompanying their girlfriends on a date, or just single men out for a drink or hoping to pick up a woman. In any case, whereas at a *tànnibéer* grown men are conspicuously absent, at a *soirée sénégalaise*, they are conspicuously present. In addition, rather than being in their neighborhood where they may be judged by others, the men are in a club where they can assume a certain anonymity; they thus do not have the same social pressures that they may have if watching a neighborhood *sabar*. Interestingly, despite the presence of men, women's *sabar* dancing at *soirées sénégalaises* does not appear to be restrained at all (and in the cases of *lëmbël* competitions, the dance can be extremely unrestrained and sexually explicit in nature).[34]

The *soirée sénégalaise* brings the traditional *sabar* or *tànnibéer* into a new, modern context. Instead of being out on a public street, free for everyone to attend, the *sabar* has moved into the nightclub, where one must pay a cover charge. In addition, what used to be a mostly women's sphere is now shared by men. Thus, in the example of the *soirée sénégalaise*, the sabar truly bridges the gap between male/female and traditional/modern contexts.

Although the *soirée sénégalaise* is a fairly recent phenomenon, the sabar drum itself has been an important part of the modern music scene since the 1970s. The role of sabar in mbalax will be explored in the next chapter.

7

The Pax You Play Is So Sweet

THE ROLE OF SABAR IN MBALAX

Yeah, you should *pax*
The *pax* you play is so sweet, so play it
Rimbax Papax
Yeah, the *pax* you play is sweet
—Thio Mbaye, "Rimbax"[1]

THIS CHAPTER EXAMINES the role of sabar in the popular music genre, mbalax, and looks at the rise of mbalax from its birth in the 1970s to its current status in the global music scene at the turn of the century.[2] As the rhythmic backbone of mbalax music, sabar has both tied mbalax to its traditional Wolof roots and propelled it into the international pop music scene, with singers such as Youssou N'Dour at the forefront. In an effort to better describe how sabar rhythms function in mbalax music, I will look at the importation of traditional Mbaye family *bàkk*s into popular songs.

Mbalax is a distinctive genre of percussion-based dance music that arose shortly after Senegal gained independence from France in 1960. Named for the accompaniment rhythm played on the sabar, which is prominently featured in this style of music, the term "mbalax" has since been used as an umbrella term for this genre of Senegalese popular music as a whole. Made famous by Senegalese singer Youssou N'Dour, mbalax came to full fruition in the 1970s through the 1980s, and continues to dominate modern Senegambian music in the twenty-first century.

A typical mbalax ensemble consists of lead vocal, sabar, electric guitars (rhythm and solo), bass guitar, kit drums, keyboards (one melodic, one rhythmic), optional horn section (trumpet and/or saxophone), backup vocals, and/or *tama* (talking drum). The roles of these instruments in a mbalax band is analogous to the roles of drums within a sabar ensemble, with the lead vocal as *nder* drum, the rhythm guitar as *mbëng-mbëng* drum, the keyboard as *talmbat* (bass drum accompaniment), and the bass guitar as *tulli* (solo bass drum). Thus, a mbalax ensemble, although consisting primarily of modern electric instruments, can be seen as a transformation of the traditional sabar ensemble.

Characteristics of a mbalax song include a strong rhythmic emphasis (provided by the sabar drums), repetitive chord progressions, fast, danceable tempos, syncopated guitar riffs, and a highly syncopated keyboard part. The vocal style is drawn from Wolof *géwël* vocal traditions, with lyrics covering a range of issues from praise songs for Muslim religious leaders to songs about everyday social pressures, relationships, and moral issues.[3] Mbalax music is first and foremost music to be danced to; it is most frequently performed live in Dakar nightclubs and disseminated via radio, televised video clips, and audio cassettes. Mbalax is a genre that appeals to all ages and socioeconomic groups within Senegal and thus plays a very important role in Senegalese culture.

The rhythmic foundation and primary identifiable feature of modern mbalax is the sabar.[4] As discussed in Chapter 5, in Wolof *géwël* percussionist parlance, *mbalax* literally means 'accompaniment'. Within a sabar ensemble, different drums play different roles, and *mbalax* refers to the accompaniment parts played by the *mbëng-mbëng*. However, the *mbalax* part varies rhythmically from one dance to another. One of the most popular dance rhythms is *Kaolack* (named after the region), and it is the *Kaolack* accompaniment part (*mbalax*) that is most prominently featured in the mbalax that we know of as the popular music genre, hence the name.

Kaolack is the rhythmic backbone to the overwhelming majority of mbalax songs. Its simple contour, full range of sounds, and flexibility in tempo have all contributed to its staying power. In recent years, other dance rhythms have found their way into the mbalax scene. *Lëmbël* is fast becoming a part of mbalax music, and more recently, *baar mbaye* has also been introduced. Nonetheless, *Kaolack*, or "mbalax," remains the most prominent and widespread of rhythms used in its namesake genre.

In addition to providing the rhythmic foundation for the music, sabars also serve as solo instruments, playing *bàkk*s that serve as "breaks" at key points in the music. In this way, the sabars function both as rhythmic accompaniment as well as solo instruments. There is also a close relationship between the sabar breaks and the dance, as dancers love to match the various *bàkk*s with dance steps that perfectly accentuate the drumming.

A typical mbalax band has four to six sabars played by one or two percussionists. Generally, one percussionist plays the *cól*, which keeps a bass beat, solos frequently, and plays *bàkk*s; the other percussionist primarily plays *mbalax* (*Kaolack*, or occasionally *lëmbël*) on the *mbëng-mbëng*, keeping the steady mbalax rhythm. This second percussionist also generally has two other sabar drums on either side of the *mbëng-mbëng*, which he can play simultaneously for a wider range of sounds.

Although one percussionist plays the *cól* and the other primarily mbalax, the two will join together to play *bàkk*s, which are prominently featured in the introduction, at the end of a chorus section, in between verses, or even as a special solo section.

The keyboard in mbalax plays a highly syncopated, percussive part referred to as *marimba* (imitating the marimba, which is similar to the West African *balafon*, a xylophone-like instrument). The "marimba" keyboard is likened rhythmically to the *talmbat* (accompanimental bass drum part) in a traditional sabar ensemble, and is especially prominent in "pure and hard" mbalax styles.[5]

Harmonically, mbalax music follows a cyclic form, with simple patterns of repeated chord progressions (often with just two to four different chords). This repetitive chord structure allows for greater opportunities for improvisation, both on the part of the lead vocalist and the instrumentalists. The chord progressions emphasize both major and minor modes, with common progressions such as I-IV-ii-V, iii-I-ii, or i-VI-i-VI.

The vocal style used in mbalax music has strong ties to traditional Wolof praise-singing and Islamic chant styles. Often in a high register, the vocal melodic lines tend to follow a Western diatonic scale, cascading in mostly conjunct motion, often with emphasis on repeated notes. In addition to singing, mbalax music sometimes contains *taasu*. The *taasu* is usually performed by a member of the band other than the lead vocalist, such as the percussionist or dancer or *animateur* (like the beloved Alla Seck).

Many mbalax singers are of *géwël* origin. Like *géwël* percussionists, *géwël* singers are born into their profession, exposed to singing and drumming at an early age, and learning from elder members of their families. The other instrumentalists in mbalax bands (keyboardists, guitarists, etc.) tend to be self-trained. Although some musicians attend the National Conservatory, few have formal training of any kind, and many simply learn by ear.

Mbalax: A Brief History

Historically, mbalax is very much a product of the post-Independence era in Senegal and in neighboring Gambia. By the end of World War II, Afro-Cuban dance band music came to dominate the Senegalese music scene, due in part to the wide dissemination of Afro-Cuban recordings. In 1933, His Master's Voice released numerous recordings of *sambas*, *boleros, rumba*, and *son* in its 'GV' series ('Grabado en Venezuela,' or 'pressed in Venezuela'). As the Senegalese elite turned to Latin and jazz styles, previous interest in European ballroom and orchestral music began to fade. The popularity of Latin music peaked in the postwar era, with classics such as Moises Simons' "Peanut Vendor" known to all. Although the 1960s saw the introduction of rock, soul, reggae, and disco (with French rocker Johnny Hallyday and James Brown as household names),

Afro-Cuban music, both imported and homegrown, continued to dominate the Senegalese music scene.

On August 3, 1960, Ibra Kassé brought together a group of musicians to perform at his Dakar club, the Miami, as part of Senegalese Independence celebrations. This group, the Star Band, became the first Senegalese dance band. In keeping with the Miami's reputation for featuring *pachanga*, the music of Orquesta Aragon and Johnny Pacheco, the Star Band played mostly Afro-Cuban hits, singing Spanish lyrics over the familiar mix of congas and brass. When the Star Band eventually broke up, the musicians regrouped into several new bands, including Star Band No. 1, Étoile 2000, and Étoile de Dakar (renamed Super Étoile de Dakar in 1981), which featured singer Youssou N'Dour.

In 1970, the Orchestre Baobab was formed to play at the newly opened Baobab Club. The band's singer Laye Mboup introduced traditional Wolof songs into the group's repertoire. Although the group's music remained mostly Afro-Cuban in style, this marked a major transition from Spanish to Wolof lyrics.

As singers turned to their native language of Wolof, the music also began to change. Traditional Wolof drums were introduced into the lineup and bands such as Étoile de Dakar and Super Diamono moved away from Spanish melodies toward a faster, more percussion-based dance music dubbed mbalax. Étoile de Dakar was one of the first to introduce the *tama* (small talking drum) into its lineup. In 1977, *géwël* sabar master Aziz Seck of Super Diamono [see Figure 4.4, family tree] was the first to introduce the sabar into popular music (*musique*), a trend that was quickly adopted by other bands. By the late 1970s and early 1980s, Youssou N'Dour had championed this transformation of traditional sabar parts to electric instruments. By this time, mbalax bands consisted of lead vocals, sabar, electric guitars, horns, kit drums, keyboards, and often a *tama* drum. The close relationship between dance and sabar carried on from its roots in traditional sabar ensembles. As mentioned before, the mbalax bands were traditional sabar ensembles adapted for modern instruments, with the guitars and keyboards transforming the percussion parts and creating a rhythmic, highly danceable mbalax sound.

Mbalax came to dominate Senegalese musical culture. It was a distinct popular music that the Senegalese people could call their own. With the incorporation of Wolof percussion and song texts reflecting traditional values and topical social issues such as Islam, polygamy, and unemployment, this music had a specifically Senegalese sound and meaning.

By the late 1970s, the Star Band and Orchestre Baobab had declined in popularity with the rise of younger groups such as Étoile de Dakar (featuring Youssou N'Dour) and Super Diamono. Whereas Youssou N'Dour's mbalax was very rhythmic and percussion-based, Super Diamono showed a greater influence of jazz, funk, and soul, calling their music "Afro-feeling." Mbalax reached new heights in the 1980s and 1990s, both in Senegal and abroad, as singers such as Youssou N'Dour branched out to the international market. In 1988, N'Dour took part in the Amnesty International Tour. Meanwhile Touré Kunda, a Senegalese fusion band based in Paris, enjoyed enormous popularity throughout Europe, the United States, and Japan. Its music included some Mandinka elements (using the kora and *balafon*), as well as a rhythm called *djambadong*, which strongly resembles a reggae beat, from the band's native Casamance region in southern Senegal. In the 1980s and 1990s, Ismael Lô, whose music ranged from mbalax to folk, gained a strong following in Europe and the United States, as did Baaba Maal, who drew on the music and dance of his native Fouta Toro region in northern Senegal. Cheikh Lô, a Mouride, whose music mixed Latin, jazz and mbalax components, was also successful at the international level. In the late 1990s, the young female singer Coumba Gawlo made her debut on the world music scene, achieving platinum sales in France with her album *Yo Male* (1998).

Throughout the 1990s, mbalax continued to thrive, although the decade saw the rise of many other genres including folk, neo-traditional, rap/hip-hop, jazz fusion, rock-mbalax and salsa-mbalax. For example, the African folk music of Les Frères Guissé reflected the band's Fouta origins with beautiful vocal harmonies accompanied by acoustic guitar and light percussion. Neotraditional music was performed by many groups fronted by female singers, many of whom had been members of the Ensemble Lyrique Traditionnel at the National Theater. Cheikh Tidjane Tall (formerly of Xalam, a fusion group active in the 1970s and 1980s) supported and served as producer for numerous female singers who later launched solo careers, including Kiné Lam, Dial Mbaye and Fatou Guewel.

At the turn of the century, *géwël* singer Fatou Guewel was at the forefront of the neo-traditional groups. With a band that included *xalam* (traditional plucked lute), a large percussion section (sabar and *tama*), a chorus of vocalists (often singing in traditional call-and-response format), electric bass and keyboards, the ratio of traditional to modern instruments was notably greater than in typical mbalax bands. While sometimes playing an mbalax groove, neo-traditional music tends to focus more on the *xalam* and have more traditional melodies. A devout Mouride, Fatou Guewel uses lyrics to reflect her religious devotion in the form of numerous praise-songs for Mouride leaders Cheikh Amadou Bamba and Cheikh Ibra Fall.

The most famous exponent of mbalax music is Youssou N'Dour, the long reigning "King of mbalax." With his band Super Étoile de Dakar, N'Dour has long been and still remains the most popular mbalax singer in the country and has become a national hero. In addition to his larger-than-life status in his home country, and his success as a business mogul, Youssou N'Dour was the first artist to bring mbalax to the international scene. His golden voice, which holds enormous power in the upper register and has an extremely wide range, has made N'Dour one of the leading vocalists from Africa. Despite his international success, he continues to be based in Senegal, regularly performing and releasing new cassettes containing a truer mbalax sound than the versions of his music released internationally, which tend to minimize the role of Senegalese percussion and provide a clearer backbeat. N'Dour has set up a nightclub (Thiossane), recording studio (Studio Xippi), and radio station (Sept FM) in Dakar.

Although mbalax is widely disseminated through cassette sales, radio, and television, the music is best experienced live in Dakar nightclubs. Throughout the city, live mbalax bands attract patrons from the upper-middle class on a regular basis. Youssou N'Dour owns the famous Thiossane nightclub, where he plays regularly. (Thione Seck and Assane Ndiaye also have standing engagements at the Kily and Sunset Sahel nightclubs, respectively.)

A soiree typically runs from after midnight to four o'clock in the morning, with bands playing two one-and-a-half-hour sets. People come exquisitely dressed, as is typical of the Senegalese (they are known for their exceptional care and fine taste in clothing). When the band begins playing, the dance floor immediately fills up and remains packed throughout the soiree.

The basic style of mbalax dance involves carefully nuanced pelvic gyrations and knee movements. Occasionally, when a dancer responds to a *bàkk* or other sabar solo, he/she will break out into the more traditional sabar dance style, with elegant jumps and flailing limb movements.

In addition to these basic moves, new mbalax dance crazes are constantly emerging, often with the rise of a particular song. Examples of such dances are the *ventilateur* ('electric fan', which describes the motion of buttocks swirling suggestively); *xaj bi* ('the dog', in which a dancer lifts his/her leg in imitation of a dog); *moulaye chigin* (which involves pelvic and knee movements that perfectly match the sabar breaks); and more recently, the *jelkati* (a dance in which the upper arms, bent at the elbows, move in parallel motion from left to right). Interestingly, all of these dance crazes are closely tied to sabar breaks, and some (such as *tawran tej*) are even named for the vocal mnemonics of the sabar rhythm they accompany.

The lyrics of mbalax songs are of tremendous import to the Senegalese public, addressing social, religious, familial, or moral issues. Common themes include the importance of respecting elders, respecting women and children, taking care of one's family, and having a strong work ethic. Some texts also address modern themes such as young lovers with disapproving parents, the complexities of polygamy, and the pressures on Senegalese immigrants living abroad.

As in the tradition of griot praise-singing, many mbalax songs praise important religious and/or historic figures such as Cheikh Amadou Bamba, the founder of the Mouride sect of Islam; the famous warrior Lat Dior; and king Alboury Ndiaye. Occasionally, singers praise wealthy patron friends in song as well, continuing the griot tradition. Mbalax is listened to and adored by most Senegambians, from young school children to the elderly; it is truly a genre that cuts across generations. Whereas other genres such as hip-hop only appeal to a particular age group, mbalax appeals to all ages. Mbalax stars such as Youssou N'Dour have become important cultural icons whose newest releases are broadcast on airwaves throughout the country. Music videos appear frequently on the national television station (RTS), and the careers and lives of mbalax stars are followed closely in the media.

In addition to being a national symbol, mbalax has been one of Senegal's most important commercial exports, competing with *soukous* (the popular Congolese musical style) as perhaps one of the best-known African music genres in the West. Ever since Youssou N'Dour entered the international scene through his participation in the Amnesty International tour and collaborations with Peter Gabriel and Paul Simon, mbalax artists have begun to release recordings as well as tour internationally. Artists who have had considerable international success, aside from Youssou N'Dour, include Baaba Maal, Ismael Lô, and Cheikh Lô.

As is the case for any artist trying to appeal to an international audience, mbalax musicians are faced with the problem of making their music more accessible to foreigners without compromising its integrity. Because the fast mbalax beat is said to be difficult to understand (and to dance to) by Westerners, mbalax bands often change their music rhythmically in order to emphasize beats one and three with the bass drum instead of with rim shots (which would give the music an emphasis on two and four instead); they also tend to simplify their texture (for example, having less syncopated marimba). They also sing more songs in French or English, rather than their native Wolof, which is only spoken in Senegal and the Gambia. Critics often say that Youssou N'Dour oversimplifies his music for international release. Regardless, mbalax musicians continue to make their mark on the international scene, with increasing numbers of young artists playing in important venues from Paris to New York.

Although mbalax has spread all over the world through recordings and live tours, mbalax remains a homegrown genre in that the vast majority of mbalax musicians are Senegalese. Some mbalax bands led by Senegalese immigrants exist in Europe and North America, but the most successful bands remain those from Senegal.[6]

Nder et le Setsima Group

While veterans such as Youssou N'Dour and Super Étoile, Thione Seck and Raam Daan, and Omar Pène and Super Diamono continued to perform regularly, the 1990s saw a proliferation of younger mbalax stars such as Alioune Mbaye Nder and the Setsima Group. Formerly of Lemzo Diamono, Nder began his solo career in 1995 and was considered an ambassador of the *génération boul falé* (the "I don't care" generation), a common Wolof expression that describes Senegalese youth who take "I don't care" to mean "I'll do it myself," and who try to make a difference by addressing social problems. (Forty-eight percent of Senegal's population are aged fourteen and under.) Nder's music is typical of the fresh mbalax sound, which features much sabar, strong marimba (on keyboards), and highly syncopated rhythm guitar riffs. Reaching out to his young audience, Nder sings about the importance of self-esteem, religious virtue, and respect for women.

Lamine Touré served as percussionist for Nder et le Setsima Group from 1997 to 2001. In the following section, we will look at how Touré makes use of family *bàkk*s in a hit mbalax song, "Lenëen."

From Family *Bàkk* to National Mbalax Hit: *Le Bàkk de Lenëen*

On October 1, 1997, Alioune Mbaye Nder et le Setsima Group released their new cassette, *Lenëen*. This cassette quickly hit the top of the charts, and the title song "Lenëen" remained the number one song for months. This popular song features a signature *bàkk* that comes in at the end of the chorus. In this section, I will trace the origins of the Lenëen *bàkk* and discuss some of the implications of its transformation into the popular music genre/scene.

The Lenëen *bàkk* was created by Thio Mbaye and Group Rimbax and remains a part of their sabar repertory. The *bàkk* was created collectively by the group but was originally inspired by the simple *rythme* of *Kaolack*. The *bàkk* is shown in Figure 7.1 (CD Track 30).[7]

Part of what makes this *bàkk* so interesting musically is that it begins with a rhythm exactly like Kaolack (*te tan pax gin*), only the timing is *contretemps* (that is, the strong beat is felt on **te** *tan pax gin*, instead of *te tan* **pax** *gin* as in *Kaolack*).

The part *ja pa ja gin gin ja jan pax gin* is a way of soloing that is characteristic of Thio's playing; thus the beginning of the *bàkk*, up to *ja pa ja gin gin ja jan pax gin* is attributed to Thio, whereas the answer/completion (*te tan pax,*

FIGURE 7.1. *Lenëen bàkk*

gin gin, te tan pax gin, rwa rwa rwan gin gin) is attributed to Lamine and the others in the sabar group.

The concept of call and response is indeed common when a *bàkk* is being created by more than one person. As one percussionist inspires another, *bàkk*s often begin with one person and then are completed by another.

The *bàkk* works well with "slow *mbalax*" (*Kaolack* played at a slow tempo). In discussing how he first came to play the *bàkk* with Setsima Group, Lamine Touré explained that the music of Setsima is very improvisatory in nature, and often new songs grow out of a section of an old song when the improvisatory explorations grow large enough to create a new song.

"Lenëen" grew out of the end of the song "Dërëm." While playing the end of "Dërëm," Lamine decided to introduce the above-mentioned *bàkk* because the tempo was right, and he felt it would go well. Nder (the lead singer) liked the *bàkk*, and, inspired by it, began inventing new lyrics to the song. According to Lamine Touré, it was the *bàkk* itself that led to the creation of a new song:

> When we went to the studio to record, the song "Lenëen" didn't even exist. . . . But later Nder began to sing about women. . . . Why was he inspired to create the lyrics about women? It was because of the *bàkk*—the *bàkk* completely changed the song. It forced him to think of new lyrics. If there is a lot of sentiment in the music, it's because of the sabar—it's the *bàkk* that brought it on . . . so, the *bàkk* was something I played in Thio's group, but when I listened to the music, it was the right tempo, so I thought of the *bàkk* and inserted it within. And it worked well. (8/17/99)

Although the *bàkk* only appears at the end of the chorus, its importance is evident. When the song is performed live, the audience can be seen moving to the *bàkk*, dancing in the livelier *sabar* style (as opposed to the more restrained mbalax, which has smaller limb movements). In general, in mbalax (the popular music genre), it is the *bàkk*s played on the sabars that inspire people to dance. The more sabars, the better, for the sabar is one of the main distinguishing characteristics of *mbalax* music.

When the song "Lenëen" came out, Thio Mbaye was very pleased to have their *bàkk* as part of this new hit song. By entering the popular music industry and being recorded, the *bàkk* had in a way become memorialized. Although the *bàkk* was now considered to be the creation of the percussionists of Setsima (that is, Lamine Touré and his cousin, Talla Seck), its association with their particular family was of paramount importance; that the whole Group Rimbax and Thio Mbaye originally created it did not matter. Now no other sabar group could steal it and claim it to be their own; this was clearly an Mbaye/Seck creation, and now that it had entered the realm of recorded popular music, it would remain this way forever.

Thio Mbaye, who has recorded with nearly every major artist in the country, regularly enjoys introducing *bàkk*s into the songs he records. A *bàkk* gains greater legitimacy once it has been recorded; it is as if nobody else can claim it, and it has been set in stone. Indeed, it has been officially copyrighted once it appears on a commercial recording.

Rythmes in Popular Music: Recent Innovations

As mentioned before, *Kaolack* is the *rythme* par excellence that defines *mbalax* music, providing the rhythmic backbone in over 90 percent of this genre. Its easy adaptability to fast and slow tempos and its simple contour that nonetheless explores the range of sounds produced on the sabar have certainly aided its staying power. In recent years, however, other *rythmes* have started to find their way into the popular music scene. *Lëmbël* is fast becoming a part of *mbalax* music (as in Alioune Mbaye Nder's "Pansement"), and most recently, *baar mbaye* has also been introduced (in the new ending of Alioune Mbaye Nder's "Sportif," performed live). Lamine Touré explains why he decided to introduce this *rythme* into the popular music scene:

> In Setsima's music, I was the one who introduced *baar mbaye*. I figured, "People love to dance sabar, and in sabar, they especially like *baar mbaye*, so if I introduce *baar mbaye* into *musique*, it will give it variety." When I did it, it worked really well and everybody loved it; when we played *baar mbaye*, everyone started dancing, and although there was the rest of the

> band accompanying, the musical foundation was *baar mbaye*. In *musique*, I'm starting to bring lots of sabar things into *musique*. There are some sabar *rythmes* in *musique*, but not many. The *rythmes* are *Kaolack* and a little bit of *lëmbël*. But *baar mbaye* now, and even *ceebu jën* will come someday. (8/12/99)

Despite *Kaolack's* prominence in Senegalese popular music, one can only speculate on why percussionists have only recently decided to experiment with other *rythmes*. One possibility is that *Kaolack* and *lëmbël*, the two *rythmes* used in popular music, are also the two *rythmes* that are typically played simultaneously with *bàkk*s. This "layerability" translates well to the popular music scene, where the sabar *rythme* may be overlaid with *bàkk*s, vocal melodies, as well as other instrumental textures.

Conclusion

Mbalax is the popular music genre par excellence of the Senegambian people. From its birth in the 1970s, mbalax has infused Latin dance music with Senegambian elements, from Wolof lyrics to sabar percussion. It has not only become a musical form but also a national symbol for Senegal, and it remains one of Senegal's most important exports. A dance music based rhythmically on the traditional sabar drum, mbalax is modern in its musical style, lyrical content, and national status. The sabar has thus played an important role in this popular music genre and afforded *géwël* drummers lucrative work options in a changing economy.

Conclusion

HAVING GAINED some understanding of the sabar's history, repertory, and performance contexts, we see that the sabar holds deep meaning not only to Wolof *géwël* but to Senegalese culture as a whole. In sum, sabar can be seen as a metaphor for the processes of Wolof life. Just as the family is of great importance in the broader context of Wolof society, the family is the center for the production and reproduction of sabar knowledge. The knowledge of sabar is passed down from one generation to another and kept strictly within the family. As urban-based families expand, with the arrival of relatives from rural areas seeking greater opportunities, family sabar groups are established and strongly maintained. In a rapidly changing society where family bonds might normally loosen, sabar brings *géwël* families together and becomes their primary marker of identity. Wolof *géwël* play sabar because it is their livelihood—and above all because it is "in their blood."

Through sabar, *géwël* families are able to negotiate between various spheres: male and female, private and public, and traditional and modern. The *géwël* lineage is traced through both the mother and the father. Although primarily men play the sabar, mostly women dance to it. The relationship between sabar drumming and dance, on a symbolic level, represents courtship and gender relations. Sabar drumming can take place at strictly female events (such as the *tur*) as well as mostly male events (such as wrestling matches and *simb*s).

The sabar also travels between both public and private events. A group of women may host a *tur* in the privacy of their own compound, using the opportunity to reinforce female camaraderie amongst close friends or relatives. On the other hand, a *tànnibéer* held in the street is open to everyone, a source of recreation for all to enjoy. In these contexts, sabar both cements close relationships and allows larger groups of people to come together. Sabar is about interpersonal relationships on both public and private levels.

For Muslim holidays, *géwël* use the sabar to perpetuate a long tradition of praising others in turn for monetary gifts. In this context, intercaste relations that date back over a thousand years are invoked. However, the importance of *géwël* in Wolof society is now being perpetuated and even augmented through modern venues. The *soirée sénégalaise* has brought the traditional sabar ensemble into a modern context, performance in nightclubs. More importantly, the role of sabar in *mbalax* music has thrust *géwël* drummers into the popular music scene, where they perform and record both in Senegal and on the international level. With the days of kings and nobles long gone, Wolof *géwël* have found new patrons: music lovers around the world who are willing to buy recordings and pay to see them perform.

On the most basic level, sabar is a celebration of life. As every Wolof child is brought into this world, he or she is accompanied by the sounds of sabar. Sabars were played to mark the transition from boyhood to manhood and are still present at the union between a man and a woman. Whether they are playing for young women to dance or for men to wrestle, Wolof *géwël* are an integral part of Senegalese culture. Indeed, the sabar is inseparable from all processes of Wolof life.

Many of the issues raised throughout this study will be the subject of future research and inquiry; it is understood that this is by no means a comprehensive study, and much remains to be learned about Wolof *géwël* and their sabar tradition. However, I hope that this book will at least provide readers with an introduction to this vast and interesting topic and be a first step toward understanding this wonderful musical tradition. The Mbaye family was kind enough to share their knowledge of sabar with me, and in writing this book, I hope to pass on some of this knowledge to others. As the sabar tradition becomes better known outside of Senegal, it is my hope that our *géwël* "family" will continue to expand to all those willing and interested to learn.

Notes

Introduction

1. For further reading, see Barry (1998), Curtin (1975), Klein (1993), and Rodney (1970).

2. For more information, see Crowder (1962).

3. The Wolof are also the dominant ethnic group in The Gambia.

4. Although French is still the official language of Senegal, there are six recognized national languages: Wolof (maternal language of about 40 percent of the population, though understood by 80 percent); Peul (maternal language of 17.5 percent); Serer (16.5 percent); Diola (8 percent); Mandinka (6 percent) and Soninke (6 percent). Source: Malherbe and Sall (1989, 22).

5. The Toucouleurs are Pulaar speakers (Fulbe) who live in the region of Futa Toro. Toucouleurs and Peuls (Fulbe from other areas) are often grouped together as *Haalpulaar'en*, or speakers of Pulaar (Clark and Phillips 1994, 269).

6. However, Claude Meillassoux (1991) argues that Mande oral traditions do not contain any explicit reference to Sundiata founding a state, contrary to popular belief.

7. For a more complete reading, the epic of Njaajaan Njaay can be found in Samba Diop (1997). The version is narrated by Sèq Ñan, transcribed and translated into English by Samba Diop. Njaajaan Njaay has also been the subject of popular song in Senegal, most notably by Youssou N'Dour (see *The Music In My Head*, Track 4, "Njaajan Njaay.")

8. From 1982–1989, Senegal and the Gambia formed a nominal federation. Although the two remain separate countries and political entities, because The Gambia is geographically surrounded by Senegal, the two countries are collectively referred to as Senegambia.

9. Just as Senegalese Wolof is mostly a creole of Wolof and French, Gambian Wolof is a creole of Wolof and English (due to the former British colonial presence).

10. Earliest attempts to write Wolof were in Arabic script around the eleventh century; during the colonial period, Wolof was transcribed using the Latin alphabet. In 1975, linguists at CLAD (Centre de linguistique appliquée de Dakar) attempted to standardize an official orthography, though many discrepancies remain (Malherbe 1989, 25).

11. The literacy rate (1995 est.) is only 33.1 percent.

12. See Villalón (1995) for further reading.
13. See Savishinsky (1994).
14. For further information, listen to Krémer (1989).
15. See McLaughlin (1997) for discussion of Islam and popular music in Senegal. For a more historical study, see Erlmann (1986) regarding the Islamic reform in the Early Sokoto Empire.
16. The applicability of the term "caste" to West African societies has been criticized, and will be discussed in detail in Chapter 3.
17. In this book, I will refer to the drum as sabar (without italics) and the event as *sabar* (italicized).
18. In this book, I will refer to the popular music genre as mbalax (without italics), and the drum accompaniment part as *mbalax* (italicized).

Chapter One

1. The Wolof term *tubaab* means 'white person', though it can also refer to black Americans, or Senegalese who emulate white European/American behavior and mannerisms.
2. The Ndiaye Rose family and the Faye ("Sing-Sing") family are two other major sabar families in Dakar.
3. Interestingly, Barbara Hoffman chose to be an "apprentice griot" among the Mande (2000). Joseph Hill also explicitly attempted to "become a griot" (Hill 1999). In theory, this is not possible, since being a griot is something into which one is born (unlike some other vocations, such as sorcery, into which one can be initiated following apprenticeship (see Stoller and Olkes 1987). Like Eric Charry (1992, 16), I was interested in making music like a Wolof griot and understanding how they understand music. However, rather than overstating my identity as an American scholar, I enjoyed my gradual acceptance (or "adoption") into the griot family with whom I was working through time spent at the household, as well as my increased involvement in family activities.
4. See Askew (2002, 194) for discussion of a similar practice at *taarab* performances in Tanzania.
5. Sticking a monetary bill between a *géwël*'s teeth is a common way of giving money because both their hands are occupied while drumming. Usually the drummer will leave the bill there for some time for all to see; eventually, when it is appropriate to take a break, he will then remove the money and put it in his pocket.
6. A *tànnibéer* is a sabar drum and dance event that takes place late at night.
7. For a discussion of the relationship between tipping and *taasu* (Wolof oral poetry), see McNee (2000).
8. In doing so, he reminded me that I was considered part of the family, and it was for this reason that he was willing to share his exclusive knowledge of *géwël* sabar traditions; however, I in turn must recognize the value of this information and show my appreciation.
9. See Stone and Stone (1981) for discussion of the merits of feedback and analysis made possible through videotaping.
10. My involvement with Setsima Group is further discussed in Dieng (1999) and Tang (2005a).

11. See Askew (2002), which discusses the author's experience as a *taarab* singer.

12. There is one other violinist, William Badji, who is well-known in Senegal; however, I have never had the opportunity to hear him play.

13. *Arigato* and *konnichiwa* mean respectively 'thank you' and 'hello' in Japanese.

14. Through consultation with friends, I have established that "hee-haw" is probably a bastardization of *ni hao*, which means 'how are you?' in Mandarin Chinese.

15. See Ebron (1997).

16. However, I should note that there were quite a few people who half-jokingly asked if I knew how to do kung-fu; apparently, Bruce Lee movies have reached a wide audience in Senegal.

17. See Kay Kaufman Shelemay on the "marginal male" (1991, 42) and Carol Babiracki on the "ungendered researcher" (1997, 123).

Chapter Two

1. From the song "Sabar Yi" from Bada Seck's 1997 cassette, *Génération Boul Falé* (Studio 2000, Senegal). Transcription and English translation from original Wolof by Patricia Tang.

2. In writings by Al-Bakri from 1068, "a drum is beaten" (Levtzion & Hopkins 1981, 87).

3. O. Dapper, *Description de l'Afrique* trans. from Flemish. Amsterdam: Wolfgang, Waesberge, Boom & van Someren. Repr. 1970, New York: Johnson Reprint Corp. 1686. Cited in Charry (1992, 325).

4. For further reading on African oral history, see Vansina (1965) and Bates, Mudimbe and O'Barr (1993).

5. See the life histories of Thio Mbaye and Lamine Touré in Chapter 4.

6. For a more detailed history of Kaabu, see Barry (1998).

7. "Tam-tam" is a generic name for "drum."

8. See Caschetta (1998) for more information on *tantango* and *bougarabou*.

9. Eastern Mande drums include the well-known *djembé* tradition, which is distinct from western Mande *tantango/saoruba*. See Charry (2000) for further reading on Mande drumming.

10. The term "*mbalax*" has several meanings. Most generally, it means "accompaniment," and it is this meaning that we will be using in the context of this discussion of the parts of the ensemble; however, it can also refer to a specific *rythme* (also known as *Kaolack*, to be explored in detail in Chapter 5), or to the genre of popular music that features this *rythme*.

11. In fact, anyone who is fortunate enough to witness the mounting of a sabar drumhead is considered very lucky and should put a coin on the head for good luck.

12. In the spring of 2000, some percussionists from the Faye (Sing-Sing) family living in New York came to Boston to play for a sabar dance workshop, and I lent them a few of my drums to use in the workshop. When one of the drummers saw my *cól* (named for Lendor Mbaye), he immediately reacted by talking about Lendor's recent death and expressing his sympathy.

13. Women's association gatherings are considered casual social events, in contrast to baptisms and weddings, which carry much more importance as life cycle celebrations.

14. The interaction between sabar drumming and dance will be further explored in Chapter 5.

15. Playing techniques will be explored in more depth in Chapter 5.

16. The frequency of tuning depends on the frequency of use. Drums that are used frequently are also more likely to rip altogether, thus making it necessary to mount a new skin entirely. If a sabar group is preparing for an important *tànnibéer,* they are likely to tune their drums beforehand to make sure the ensemble sounds its best.

17. *Tulli* and *talmbat* are the two parts played on the *cól.*

18. For an explanation of the terms here, see Chapter 5.

Chapter Three

1. From the song "Nguewel" from Bada Seck's 1997 cassette, *Génération Boul Falé* (Studio 2000, Senegal). Transcription and English translation from original Wolof by Patricia Tang.

2. From the Portuguese and Spanish word "casta," which was applied to Indian social organization as early as the mid-fifteenth century (Dumont 1970).

3. These categorizations are a summary of Abdoulaye-Bara Diop's work (1981).

4. However, this disdain is couched in general terms, not in reference to specific people.

5. Griots being better cooks is something that I even heard *géer* and people from other ethnic groups agree on; this is perhaps related to the *géwël's* traditional role in helping to cook for large parties at family ceremonies such as baptisms and weddings.

6. Indeed, Tal Tamari includes *gawlo* as a subcategory in both Tukulor and Fulani castes, separate from the Wolof ethnic group.

7. For example, the famous singer Youssou N'Dour has *gawlo* ancestry, but is often mistakenly referred to as a griot/*géwël.*

8. For example, when I attended the baptism of Talla Seck's son, Bahkane Seck, numerous *géwël* who took the microphone discussed the importance and unity of *askani-géwël*, or the griot lineage. (See also the opening quote of this chapter.)

9. Harold Gould (1987) has made similar observations on the interdependence of those at different rank levels in the Indian caste system.

10. The *xalam*, often mistakenly considered a *géwël* instrument, is in fact a *gawlo* instrument of Peul ethnic origin. Another percussion instrument, the *tama* (small talking drum), is played by *géwël* from the Waalo-Waalo area, but is likely of other ethnic origins, and holds neither the long history nor the prominence that the sabar holds in Senegalese culture. Since the sabar was the focus of my research, I will not be discussing *xalam* or *tama* at length. See Coolen (1979) for more information on the *xalam*.

Chapter Four

1. Note that "*bokk*" has no etymological relationship to the word "*bàkk*," despite similarity in sound.

2. See also Irvine (1978) for discussion regarding the importance of kinship and marital alliance in determining one's character and future behavior.

3. *Musique* is the general term for popular music in Senegal, as opposed to what is played by traditional sabar drumming ensembles.

4. It should be noted that although these three griot families are active in the traditional sabar scene, it is primarily the two latter families, the families of Mbaye Dièye Faye and Thio Mbaye, who dominate the popular music scene. Doudou Ndiaye Rose is well known internationally, touring worldwide with his family sabar troupe; however, his family members are not active in the mbalax scene.

5. "Jeri-Jeri" is a nickname (as Sing-Sing is for the Faye family) for a particular branch of the Mbaye family, most of whom carry the last name Seck. Both the Mbayes and the Secks trace their lineage back to a common ancestor, the famous *géwël*, Samba Maissa Seck. Thus, unless I specify otherwise, when I talk about the Mbaye family, I mean the extended Mbaye family, which includes the Seck and Mbaye branches. See family tree for clarification.

6. Although Moussa Traoré is not a griot by birth, he was raised by Mbaye Dièye Faye's family and is thus considered to be part of the Sing-Sing family. He is the one exception to the otherwise exclusive griot domination of sabar in mbalax bands.

7. Doudou Ndiaye Rose is the father of over forty children (the product of his polygynous marriages).

8. Although female *géwël* tend to become singers, *tassukats*, or dancers, many do know how to play sabar just from growing up in the sabar environment. However, the Rosettes became a sensation when they were touring, particularly on the Western concert stage, where female drummers are somewhat of a novelty.

9. Sing-Sing Rhythme also has offshoot groups of the same name led by brothers of Mbaye Dièye Faye, such as Cheikh Tairou Mbaye's Sing-Sing Rhythm in New York City.

10. For other literature on competition, see Gunderson and Barz (2000) and Ranger (1975).

11. Nowadays, some people lament that all griots automatically flock to support the winning party; after all, nobody wants to be associated with a losing party; also, the winning party is usually the most financially rewarding. As a result, griots will often play for whichever politician will give them more money to perform, regardless of whether the griot agrees with that particular political affiliation.

12. The role of sabar in traditional Senegalese wrestling will be explored in greater detail in Chapter 6.

13. This was mentioned in an interview with Macheikh Mbaye Jr. (7/25/98).

14. *Gris-gris*, or mystical amulets, are worn not only by *géwël* but also by nearly all Senegalese. Whereas a percussionist may wear a *gris-gris* to protect his hands, nonpercussionists may wear *gris-gris* to protect them more generally from the evil eye, evil tongue, etc. See Shelemay (1992) on the Ethiopian *dabtara* for another example of musician as person with mystical powers.

15. Tea (*attaya* in Wolof) is a postlunch social event. Lasting through the afternoon, teatime includes the brewing of very strong, sweet, frothed tea served in three rounds, the first round being the most bitter, and the last with mint added. While making tea, family and friends sit around and chat.

16. One should keep in mind, however, that I was associating primarily with musicians at musicians' homes, so the discussions might have been biased toward musical topics.

17. Slobin (1989, 78). This is from an "Interlude" in Slobin's book in which he introduces the life histories of three generations of immigrant hazzanim.

18. This was a conscious decision on my part, since I felt the interviews would feel less formal if I had already established a relationship with the people whom I was interviewing.

19. At this time, President Senghor had travelled to Mali and Guinea (under Sékou Touré's rule) and, seeing that each of these countries had formed a national ballet, he formed his own national ensemble upon his return.

20. The national theater (Théâtre Nationale Daniel Sorano) has been home to numerous government-sponsored ensembles, including the Ensemble Instrumental Traditionnel (now the Ensemble Lyrique Traditionnel), the ballet (Ballet La Linguère), and a drama troupe.

21. Macheikh Mbaye held an administrative job during his time at SOTRAC.

22. These percussionists were not blood relatives.

23. Pikine and Guediawaye are two large suburbs of Dakar.

24. Thio did become a part of the family through marital alliance, when he married one of Macheikh Mbaye's daughters, Maguette Seck. They have since divorced, but although Thio has his own home in a different neighborhood (HLM Grand Yoff), he still frequents the HLM 5 house and is very much a part of the family.

25. The following excerpt would be considered a "life story," which Jeff Titon considers a genre distinct from the "life history." The "life story" is a self-contained fiction, often longer and uninterrupted by questions (Titon 1980).

26. The *faux lion* or *simbkat* is literally a person who dresses up as and takes on the persona of a lion. The event, called a *simb*, is a performance put on for entertainment purposes and includes sabar drumming. For a more detailed explanation, see Chapter 6 on performance contexts.

27. Thio's mother's side is originally from Thies, and his father's side from Rufisque.

28. See family tree (Figure 4.4).

29. Lamine's parents divorced when he was young; after the divorce, he was raised by his mother and maternal relatives.

30. The mortars are made of wood and resemble the shape of the drum a bit more—a step up from the tomato can sabars he once knew.

31. Lendor and Karim are young brothers of Thio Mbaye, and thus Lamine's uncles, though they are closer in age to Lamine.

32. Omar Thiam is a well-known and well-respected Serer griot in the Kaolack region. (See Thiam 1997 for further listening.)

33. Lamine's elder brother, Alassane Djigo, was taken in by Macheikh Mbaye when he first arrived in Dakar, in much the same way that Thio Mbaye was.

34. Moustique, (in 1999) of the salsa-mbalax band Super Cayor.

35. "*Variétés*" refers to jazz and salsa standards, often played in restaurants.

36. Ballets were ensembles that combined music and dance, usually performing the traditional musics of various ethnic groups throughout Senegal. These ballets were first founded around Independence and nowadays tour internationally. Ballets may include sabar as well as *djembé* and drumming traditions of various origins. In contrast, traditional sabar groups play sabar only, perform for Wolof events, and are not mixed with other traditions. Mbalax bands are popular music bands that include sabar as part of their lineup.

37. The other percussionist in Nder's band and an uncle of Lamine's (see Figure 4.4, family tree).

38. Here it will be helpful to consult the family tree (Figure 4.4) to see how these people are related to one another.

39. This is true in Wolof culture in general, where respect for elders and age hierarchy are very important.

40. However, I did take formal lessons, as explained in Chapter 1.

41. Lendor Mbaye (1973–1999) died in November 1999.

42. Style and repertory will be further explored in Chapter 5.

43. *Soirées sénégalaises* will be described in greater detail in Chapter 6 (Performance Contexts).

Chapter Five

1. Diop (1992) and Thiam (1997). The author also plans to release a sabar field recording to complement the instructional CD that accompanies this book [forthcoming].

2. It is interesting to note that money-giving is something that occurs between drummers and among *géwël*, not just between *géer* (nobles) and *géwël*. This act may be seen by some as an encouragement for *géer* to give money, but from my observation, it is usually a genuine act of appreciation, and it boosts the morale of the drummers as a group.

3. Henceforth, *rythme* shall be distinguished from the English term *rhythm*, which will be used in the usual sense of the term.

4. This layperson's knowledge of sabar rhythms and dances is analogous to that of Americans familiar with ballroom dance, that is, being able to distinguish between, and dance to, tango, cha-cha, and waltz.

5. For example, *ceebu jën* is said by many to have existed for centuries. Unfortunately, this has not been documented.

6. However, this is a generalization, since some *bàkk*s that are very short do exist.

7. *Rythmes* such as *mbabas, niari gorong* and *yaaba composé* have faded from use; they will be discussed only briefly. Interestingly, the *rythmes mbabas* and *niari gorong* remain very much alive in the United States, taught at sabar dance classes in the New York area. These *rythmes* that are perpetuated in the diaspora are an indication of what was popular at the time the immigrants left Senegal, creating a sort of "snapshot" of a certain time period (such as the late 1980s).

8. *Musique* refers not to music in general, but rather popular music (that is, mbalax).

9. This is the typical order of sabar *rythmes* played at dance events between 1997 and 2005.

10. For context, this chart can be coordinated with the ethnographic description of a typical *tànnibéer* in Chapter 6.

11. For further discussion of this topic, see Shelemay (1998b) and Agawu (2003, 64–68).

12. I am very grateful to Michael Lewis for his invaluable assistance in editing the transcriptions as well as transferring them to Finale. Although we worked together on many of the examples, I take full responsibility for any errors that may exist in these musical transcriptions. I also note that as in any transcriptions, these transcriptions come

close to representing sabar rhythms, but are not always exact, as the expressive nuances that characterize sabar drumming are difficult to represent using Western notation.

13. The notehead shapes were chosen for their clarity and distinction. The author recognizes that in using these shapes, one cannot denote a note value with a duration greater than a dotted quarter note. However, articulation of the instrument does not allow for such longer duration, so this is not an issue.

14. It is likely that this *bàkk* predates Cheikh Amadou Bamba, and that the name "Bamba" was either inserted or substituted for something else.

15. This is in contrast to the other *rythmes*, which are played for a longer period of time.

16. Without exaggeration, if one listens to a sample of any number of mbalax songs by Youssou N'Dour or any other leading Senegalese mbalax band, one will undoubtedly pick out the constant "te tan pax, gin" of *mbalax*. The importance of sabar in mbalax music will be further explored in Chapter 6.

17. The *beeco* is a sort of undergarment worn by Senegalese women while dancing. It is a wrap that is worn underneath the traditional wrap. As women dance, they lift up their outer wraps, exposing this inner wrap (which is considered to be sexy, and often is made of brightly colored satin with netting/holes in it.) Nowadays, it is during the dance *lëmbël* that the women most boldly expose their *beeco* while dancing. Notably, the *beeco* also has more overt sexual connotations, as it is a tool that women use to seduce their partners in the bedroom. The *beeco*, along with *bin-bin* (beads) and *thiouraye* (incense), are essential tools in *mooku pocc*, the art of being a good wife. See Morales-Libove (2005).

18. Heath 1994 (see this article for a more detailed analysis of this text.)

19. Interview with Macheikh Mbaye, 3/5/98.

20. Interview with Macheikh Mbaye, 8/12/99.

21. *Niari gorong* is similar to *mbabas,* only the tempo is a bit slower.

22. *Sabar ngoon* is a *sabar* that takes place during the afternoon.

23. See Korom (1994) and Wolf (2000) for comparative studies of drum language in Trinidad and South Asia, respectively.

24. Samuella Faye's *tur*, Grand Yoff (2/22/98) animated by Group Rimbax with Karim Mbaye, *dirigeur*.

25. Interview with Massaer Daaro Mbaye, 7/3/98.

26. Interview with Macheikh Mbaye, 3/5/98.

27. The use of musical name tags is also a part of the Dagbamba *lunsi* tradition.

28. Although such lengthy rhythmic compositions are to my knowledge not common in West African drumming repertories, an example in Ewe drumming can be seen in a lead drum rhythm by Gideon Alorwoyie and C. K. Ganyo (see Locke 1979, 649–52).

29. Please note that this mnemonic transcription is copied from my drumming notebook as is. For rhythmic underlay, see text in musical transcription (Ex. 5j).

30. This *bàkk* took me nearly two months to learn. Lamine had told me that he thought it would be too difficult for me to learn, so I took this as a challenge. When he went on tour with Setsima Group for a month and a half, I decided to learn the *bàkk* as a surprise for him (during his absence, I studied with two of his cousins, Macheikh Mbaye Jr. and Mustapha Niass.) Upon his return, at my lesson, I played the *bàkk* all the way through for him. He could not believe it, and said that I must have been possessed by *rab* (spirit/devil).

31. Indeed, it is the combination of the *bàkk* and the underlying *rythmes* that creates the feeling of contretemps and makes the music more interesting.

32. Other, shorter *bàkk*s have been "stolen" and adapted by other families; however, there are no known attempts to "steal" the *bàkk de spectacle.*

33. *Jinné* means 'spirit' or 'supernatural being'.

34. *Feeling* is a Wolofized version of the English term and has adopted a slightly different meaning.

35. Interview with Lamine Touré 8/17/99.

Chapter Six

1. From the song "Papa Ndiaye Guewel" from Papa Ndiaye's 1997 cassette, *Papa Ndiaye Guewel* (Studio Xippi, Senegal). Transcription and English translation from original Wolof by Patricia Tang.

2. During Ramadan, the Muslim fasting month, no drumming occurs at all, not even in nightclubs, because most popular music bands do not perform during Ramadan.

3. The term *tànnibéer* originates from the Wolof term meaning "night talk." (Leymarie 1978, 198)

4. Interview with Massaer Daaro Mbaye, 7/3/98.

5. Just as most people keep their salaries private, so do *géwël*; so out of respect for my informants, I will not disclose the amount charged for a typical *tànnibéer,* as they requested. However, this amount does vary, depending on the size of the group and the popularity of the lead drummer (*dirigeur*).

6. However, in my experience, *tànnibéer*s are usually better served without microphones. The *tànnibéer*s I attended, which had microphones, tended to get sidetracked by microphone-happy *géwël* making lengthy speeches, thus interrupting the flow of the dancing.

7. Although it was my original intention to describe a truly "typical" sabar, I found this very difficult to do without using one particular example as a base model on which to elaborate.

8. Young *géwël* percussionists often have their first experience using real sabars through playing *saaji.*

9. See discussion and transcription of *ya ñu moom* in Chapter 5.

10. *Entrée* refers to a preparatory rhythm.

11. *Transfer* is a cue played by the lead drummer which signals movement from one *rythme* to the next.

12. See Heath (1994) and Morales-Libove (2005) for more details on women and sabar dancing.

13. See Qureshi (1995) for another example of the importance of giving money.

14. See Morales-Libove (2005) for a comprehensive study of gender, sexuality and dance at women's *tur*s.

15. The money from the *tur* is not specifically connected to the financing of the party; although the hostess is expected to hold a nice social gathering, she is not by any means expected to spend all her *tur* money on the occasion.

16. According to Lamine Touré, an ensemble of only a few drummers is needed for a *tur*, usually due to the fact that the event will take place at someone's house, which is not conducive to a large drum ensemble.

17. Deborah Heath has made similar observations (1994).

18. *Laaban* is discussed in Gueye (2004, 165–203).

19. In Dakar, circumcisions now take place at the hospital when the baby is quite young. However, in the neighboring regions and more rural areas, circumcisions are still performed in the more traditional way. From what I am told, sabar drumming is an integral part of these circumcision ceremonies; however, I have not been able to witness one firsthand. Likewise, the *laaban* (declaration of virginity) is less common nowadays in part due to the fact that few women are virgins on their wedding night. Modern thinking has made this declaration less important than it had been in the past, when a woman's virginity was important to family honor. In the past, the virginity would often be faked by putting chicken's blood on a sheet. According to Lamine Touré, only a small number of drummers (three or four) would come to play for a *laaban*; they would enter playing "*Tuus*," and then go to play indoors in the bedroom, usually just playing *rythmes* to accompany the women's *taasu* (oral poetry). Although Lamine has played at *laaban*s in the past, I did not witness him playing at any during my fieldwork (1997–98).

20. In a sense, the sabar group provides entertainment, something like a wedding band in the United States. However, on another level, their function as *géwël* and their presence at these life cycle ceremonies holds a more symbolic and traditional purpose that goes beyond just entertainment.

21. The father chooses the name, but a religious figure, an imam/marabout, then whispers the baby's name in its ear, thus naming the baby. Naming is an important part of Wolof culture, which has a tradition of *turando* (namesakes). Thus, every newborn baby will be named after a person of the older generation (often an aunt, uncle, or other close relative.)

22. *Laax* is a sweet porridge made of sour milk and pounded millet.

23. This section on *bëkëtë* is based on my observation of Oulymata Mbaye's *ngente* on November 30, 1997 (she is a granddaughter of Macheikh Mbaye—see family tree), as well as on an interview (3/5/98) with Macheikh Mbaye about the meaning of *bëkëtë*.

24. Another spiritual ceremony that includes sabar is *ndëpp*, the Lebou healing ceremony that has become more common among the Wolof in recent years.

25. The significance of *lait caillé* as a white liquid substance could be interpreted as symbolic of human bodily fluids such as breastmilk. Victor Turner (1967) has made similar observations regarding the symbolic significance of the milk tree in Ndembu ritual. John Blacking also discusses "white" ashes symbolic of semen in *domba*, a Venda premarital initiation dance (1973, 84). I am indebted to Kay Kaufman Shelemay for bringing this to my attention.

26. Chicken is more expensive than fish and thus is eaten more often on special occasions such as *Korité*. Naturally, sheep meat is eaten on *Tabaski*, the holiday for which sheep slaughter is part of the ritual.

27. Please note that I did not attend any political meetings during my field stay in Senegal, and the information is that relayed to me by my informants. It would have been exciting and interesting to be in Senegal in spring 2000, preceding the presidential elections.

28. This traditional wrestling event was called *mbappat*.

29. Interview with Lamine Toure, 8/17/99.

30. Although unsubstantiated, I will put forth the idea that wrestling could possibly be one of the origins of *bàkk*s, since the relationship between sabar and wrestling is so inextricable.

31. The reputation that Mike Tyson has in the United States (due to his rape conviction and biting Evander Holyfield's ear) has done little to tarnish his reputation among the Senegalese. Interestingly, Mohammed Ndao "Tyson" enters the wrestling grounds draped in an American flag.

32. Pap Ngom, who lives in Pikine, is one of the most famous *simbkat*s today in the Dakar area.

33. For example, the great *simbkat* of Kaolack, Sitapha Dieng, was formerly a wrestler.

34. From 2000 through 2005, I have witnessed a growing number of professional male dancers dancing *at soirée sénégalaises,* thus further breaking the traditional gender barriers of sabar.

Chapter Seven

1. From the song "Rimbax" from Thio Mbaye's 1993 cassette, *Rimbax* (Harry Son/Syllart, Senegal). Transcription and English translation from original Wolof by Patricia Tang.

2. I will use the unitalicized term "mbalax" to refer to the popular music genre, and the italicized version for the Wolof term for "accompaniment."

3. See McLaughlin (1997) for more on Islam and popular music in Senegal.

4. Although the small talking drum (*tama*) is usually heralded as the primary rhythmic feature of mbalax (see Durán 1989), it is in fact the sabar that serves as the rhythmic backbone of mbalax, whereas the *tama* is more of a solo instrument.

5. Keyboardist Moustapha Faye is credited with developing this signature Senegalese style of keyboard playing.

6. For reading and listening from Finnish mbalax to American mbalax, see Saarela (2002) and Touré (2005).

7. Listen to original mbalax song on Nder (1999).

Glossary of Terms

animateur: master of ceremonies.
animations: a showcase of *rythmes* and *bàkk*s played for show, not for dance. Usually takes place at the beginning of an event such as a *sabar* or political meeting.
ardin: the first *rythme* played at a sabar; this *rythme* is the only *rythme* not danced to.
balafon: West African xylophone.
bàkk: musical phrase. In general, longer than a *rythme*. *Bàkk*s can be derived from spoken word, or created as purely musical compositions.
baar mbaye: dance *rythme* originating from a ritual for protecting children.
batterie: ensemble, sabar drum ensemble.
bougarabou: goblet-shaped drum of the Jola people in the Casamance region of Senegal. Played by hand, usually in a set of three or four.
ceebu jën: dance *rythme* named for the Senegalese national dish of rice and fish.
cól: bass drum in sabar ensemble (closed-bottom). Also called *làmb* or *ndënd*.
dirigeur: leader (of a sabar ensemble).
djembé: single-headed goblet-shaped drum played with hands. Found in Senegal, Mali, Guinea, Burkina Faso, and Côte d'Ivoire.
farwu jar: dance *rythme*. Translates as "worthy boyfriend."
faux lion: see *simb*.
géer: uncasted, nobles (in the Wolof social system).
géwël: Wolof term for "griot."
gris-gris: mystical amulet worn for protection. Can also be in the form of a potion.
jaam: slaves (in the Wolof social system).
jali: Mande term for "griot."
jël: a preparatory rhythm that precedes *ardin*.
Kaolack: dance *rythme*. Named for the city and region from which it originates.
kasak: Wolof circumcision ceremony.
kora: twenty-one-stringed bridged harp-lute; played by Mande *jali*.
laax: sweet porridge made of sour milk and pounded millet.
lawbe: member of the woodworker's caste (those who carve the sabar from a tree).
lutte: wrestling match.
marabout: spiritual leader.
mbalax: literally means "accompaniment" in sabar vocabulary.

mbalax (without italics): genre of Senegalese popular music made famous by Youssou N'Dour; named after the sabar accompaniment part by the same name.
mbalax nder: an accompaniment part that is played on accompanying *nders*.
mbëng-mbëng: medium-sized sabar drum.
mbëng-mbëng ball: sabar drum slightly taller than an *mbëng-mbëng*.
mees: wide nylon ribbon, much like that found in camping gear.
musique: the Wolof term for "popular music" or *mbalax*.
ñaani ndéwënël: custom of asking for the monetary gift traditionally given to children and *géwël* at *Korité* and *Tabaski*
ndëc: another name for the *rythme* also known as *Kaolack* and *mbalax*.
nder: tallest drum in sabar ensemble. Most often used to lead ensemble.
ñeeño: endogamous casted groups (within Wolof social system).
ngéwël: "griotness" (the art of being griot).
ngente: baptism, naming ceremony.
pachanga: a style of Latin dance music that originated in Cuba in the 1960s.
rythme: dance rhythm. Usually a fairly short unit that is played repeatedly.
sabar (without italics): single-headed Wolof drum played by one hand and one stick; term refers to both the drum and dance traditions.
sabar: event at which the sabar (drum) is played.
saaji: warm-up period before a *sabar* or *tànnibéer* begins.
saoruba: set of three drums found in the Casamance region of Senegal. Smaller and skinnier than sabar drums.
simb: "fake lion" spectacle in which a person dresses up as and takes on the persona of a lion, dancing and chasing audience members, accompanied by sabar drumming and dance.
soirée: a late-night performance in a nightclub (usually beginning after midnight). This in contrast to a *concert*, which takes place in a concert hall and begins around 9 p.m.
soirée sénégalaise: Regular evening of prerecorded music at a nightclub, followed by a live sabar drum ensemble and usually a sabar dance competition (entry fee necessary).
soukous: genre of Congolese music characterized by intricate guitar melodies and dance rhythms.
taasu: Wolof oral poetry (spoken word, but often accompanied by sabar)
talmbat: closed-bottom sabar drum. Slightly smaller than a *cól*. Also refers to the part played on this instrument (to be distinguished from the *tulli* part).
tama: small double-headed talking drum; originally from the Waalo-Waalo region.
tambour-major: master drummer.
tànnibéer: a sabar (drum and dance event) that takes place late at night, usually beginning around 10 or 11 p.m.
tantango: a Mandinka three-drum ensemble.
tassukats: practitioners of tassu, a traditional verbal art form said to be a predecessor of rap.
tëggkat: percussionist/drummer (literally, "he who beats/hits").
Thiossane: literally "tradition" in Wolof. The name of one of Dakar's best-known nightclubs; owned by singer Youssou N'Dour.
tubaab: Wolof term for "white person;" but can also refer to black Americans, or Senegalese who emulate white European/American behavior and mannerisms.

tulli: a part played on the *cól*. Unlike the *talmbat*, which has a set accompaniment, the *tulli* part tends to include extensive improvisation.
tungune: shortest drum in sabar ensemble. Literally, "midget."
tur: women's association gathering.
xalam: Wolof plucked lute; played by the *gawlo.*
xiin: low-pitched cylindrical drum played by the Baye Falls (followers of Cheikh Ibra Fall).

References

Adam, Paul. 1914. "La Musique et Ballet au Senegal." *Société International de Musicologie* 10:6–9.

Adenaike, Carolyn Keyes, and Jan Vansina, eds. 1996. *In Pursuit of History: Fieldwork in Africa.* Portsmouth, NH: Heinemann.

Adjaye, Joseph K., and Adrianne R. Andrews, eds. 1997. *Language, Rhythm & Sound: Black Popular Cultures Into the Twenty-First Century.* Pittsburgh: University of Pittsburgh Press.

Agawu, V. Kofi. 1986. "'Gi Dunu,' 'Nyekpadudo,' and the Study of West African Rhythm." *Ethnomusicology* 30 (1): 64–83.

———. 1995. *African Rhythm: A Northern Ewe Perspective.* Cambridge: Cambridge University Press.

Agawu, Kofi. 2003. *Representing African Music: Postcolonial Notes, Queries, Positions.* New York: Routledge.

Akyeampong, Emmanuel. 1999. "Christianity, Modernity and the Weight of Tradition in the Life of Asantehene Agyeman Prempeh I, c.1888–1931." *Africa* 69 (2): 279–311.

Ames, David Wason. 1953. "Plural Marriage Among the Wolof in the Gambia." PhD diss., Northwestern University.

Anderson, Benedict. 1992. *Imagined Communities.* London: Verso.

Anderson, Ian. 1987. "Music of the Gambia." *Folk Roots* 46 (April): 28–30.

———. 1991. "A Modern Day Griot." *Folk Roots* 101 (November): 34–37.

Anderson, Lois Ann. 1984. "Multipart Relationships in Xylophone and Tuned-Drum Traditions in Buganda." In *Selected Reports in Ethnomusicology*, ed. J. H. Kwabena Nketia and Jacqueline Cogdel Djedje, 1 (V):121–32. Los Angeles: Institute of Ethnomusicology, University of California.

Aning, Ben A. 1982. "Tuning the Kora: A Case Study of the Norms of a Gambia Musician." *Journal of African Studies* 9 (3): 164–75.

Anyidoho, Kofi. 1983. "Oral Poetics and Traditions of Verbal Art in Africa." PhD diss., University of Texas at Austin.

Appadurai, Arjun, ed. 1986. *The Social Life of Things: Commodities in Cultural Perspective.* Cambridge: Cambridge University Press.

Appiah, Kwame Anthony. 1992. *In My Father's House: Africa in the Philosophy of Culture.* Oxford: Oxford University Press.

Arom, Simha. 1991. *African Polyphony and Polyrhythm.* Cambridge: Cambridge University Press.
Askew, Kelly M. 2002. *Performing the Nation: Swahili Music and Cultural Politics in Tanzania.* Chicago: University of Chicago Press.
Augis, Erin. 2002. "Dakar's Sunnite Women: The Politics of Person." PhD diss., University of Chicago.
Austen, Ralph. 1987. *African Economic History*. Portsmouth, NH: Heinemann.
Austerlitz, Paul. 1997. *Merengue: Dominican Music and Dominican Identity*. Philadelphia: Temple University Press.
Babiracki, Carol. 1997. "What's the Difference? Reflections on Gender and Research in Village India." In *Shadows in the Field,* ed. Gregory F. Barz and Timothy J. Cooley, 121–38. Oxford: Oxford University Press.
Balandier, Georges. 1948. "Femmes Possedées et Leurs Chants." *Présence Africaine* 5: 749–54.
Barber, Karin. 1991. *I Could Speak Until Tomorrow.* Washington, DC: Smithsonian Institution Press.
———, ed. 1997. *Readings in African Popular Culture*. Bloomington: Indiana University Press.
Barnes, Sandra. 1990. "Ritual, Power and Outside Knowledge." *Journal of Religion in Africa* 20 (3): 248–68.
Barry, Boubacar. 1985. *Le Royaume de Waalo*. Paris: Karthala.
———. 1998. *Senegambia and the Atlantic Slave Trade*. Trans. Ayi Kwei Armah (1988 orig.). Cambridge: Cambridge University Press.
Barz, Gregory. 2004. *Music in East Africa*. New York: Oxford University Press.
Barz, Gregory F., and Timothy J. Cooley, eds. 1997. *Shadows in the Field.* Oxford: Oxford University Press.
Bates, Robert H., V. Y. Mudimbe, and Jean O'Barr, eds. 1993. *Africa and the Disciplines.* Chicago: University of Chicago Press.
Baumann, Max Peter, ed. 1991. *Music in the Dialogue of Cultures: Traditional Music and Cultural Policy.* Wilhelmshaven: Florian Noetzel Verlag.
———. 2000. "The Local and the Global: Traditional Musical Instruments and Modernization." *The World of Music* 42 (3): 121–44.
Bebey, Francis. 1980. "La Musique Traditionelle au Senegal." *Balafon* 48:36–40.
———. 1983. "Le Monde ambigu des griots." *Balafon* 58:54–58.
Béhague, Gerard, ed. 1984. *Performance Practice: Ethnomusicological Perspectives*. Westport, CT: Greenwood Press.
Behrman, Lucy. 1969. "The Islamization of the Wolof by the End of the Nineteenth Century." In *Western African History*, ed. Daniel F. McCall, Norman R. Bennett, and Jeffrey Butler, 102–31. New York: Frederick A. Praeger.
———. 1970. *Muslim Brotherhoods and Politics in Senegal.* Cambridge, MA: Harvard University Press.
Bender, Wolfgang, ed. 1989. *Perspectives on African Music.* Bayreuth African Studies Series, vol. 9. Bayreuth: D. Gräbner.
———. 1991. *Sweet Mother: Modern African Music.* Chicago: University of Chicago Press.
Berenger-Feraud, L. J. B. 1879. *Les Peuplades de la Sénégambie*. Paris: Ernest Leroux.
———. 1882. "Etude sur les Griots des Peuplades de la Senegambie." *Revue d'Ethnographie* (Paris) 5:266–79.

Berliner, Paul. 1981. *The Soul of Mbira.* Chicago: University of Chicago Press.
———. 1994. *Thinking in Jazz: The Infinite Art of Improvisation.* Chicago: University of Chicago Press.
Blacking, John. 1973. *How Musical Is Man?* Seattle: University of Washington Press.
———. 1986. "Identifying Processes of Musical Change." *The World of Music* 28 (1): 3–14.
———. 1995. "The Study of Musical Change." In *Music, Culture and Experience: Selected Papers of John Blacking*, ed. Reginald Byron, 148–73. Chicago: University of Chicago Press.
Boahen, A. Adu. 1987. *African Perspectives on Colonialism.* Baltimore: Johns Hopkins University Press.
Bourdieu, Pierre. 1994. *Language and Symbolic Power.* Cambridge, MA: Harvard University Press.
Brinner, Benjamin. 1995. *Knowing Music, Making Music: Javanese Gamelan and the Theory of Musical Competence and Interaction.* Chicago: University of Chicago Press.
Broughton, Simon et al., eds. 1994. *World Music: The Rough Guide.* London: Rough Guides.
Burnim, Mellonee. 1985. "Culture Bearer and Tradition Bearer: An Ethnomusicologist's Research on Gospel Music." *Ethnomusicology* 29 (3): 432–47.
Carrington, J. F. 1976. "Talking Drums of Africa." (Orig. pub. 1949.) In *Speech Surrogates: Drum and Whistle Systems, Part II,* ed. Thomas A. Sebeok and Donna J. Umiker-Sebeok, 591–68. Paris: Mouton.
Caschetta, Todd. 1998. "A Case Study in Syncretism and Meaning in Contemporary Mandinka Tantango and Jola Bugarabu Performance." Paper presented at Society for Ethnomusicology Meeting, Bloomington, Indiana, October 23.
Castaldi, Francesca. 2006. *Choreographies of African Identities: Negritude, Dance, and the National Ballet of Senegal.* Champaign: University of Illinois Press.
Catchpole, Brian, and I. A. Akinjogbin. n.d. *A History of West Africa in Maps and Diagrams.* London: Collins Educational.
Cathcart, Jenny. 1989. *Hey You! A Portrait of Youssou N'Dour.* Witney: Fine Line Books.
———. 1994. "Our Culture: Senegambian Stars are Here to Stay." In *World Music: The Rough Guide*, ed. Simon Broughton et al., 263–74. London: Rough Guides.
———. 2001. "Mbalax." *Songlines.* Winter: 32–39.
Charles, Eunice A. 1977. *Precolonial Senegal: The Jolof Kingdom, 1800–1890.* Brookline, MA: African Studies Center, Boston University.
Charry, Eric. 1992. Musical Thought, History and Practice Among the Mande of West Africa." PhD diss., Princeton University.
———. 1996. "A Guide to the Jembe." *Percussive Notes* 34 (2): 66–72/
———. 2000a. *Mande Music.* Chicago: University of Chicago Press.
———. 2000b. "Music and Islam in Sub-Saharan Africa." In *The History of Islam in Africa,* ed. Nehemia Levtzion and Randall L. Pouwels. Athens: Ohio University Press, 545–73.
———. 2001. "Senegal." In *New Grove Dictionary of Music and Musicians, 2nd ed.*, vol. 23, 74–78. London: Macmillan.
Charters, Samuel. 1982. *The Roots of the Blues: An African Search.* New York: Perigee Books.
Chernoff, John Miller. 1979. *African Rhythm and African Sensibility.* Chicago: University of Chicago Press.

Coles, Catherine, and Beverly Mack, eds. 1991. *Hausa Women in the Twentieth Century.* Madison: University of Wisconsin Press.

Collins, John. 1992. *West African Pop Roots.* Philadelphia: Temple University Press.

Comaroff, Jean, and John Comaroff, eds. 1993. *Modernity and its Malcontents: Ritual and Power in Postcolonial Africa.* Chicago: University of Chicago Press.

Connerton, Paul. 1989. *How Societies Remember.* Cambridge: Cambridge University Press.

Conrad, David C., and Barbara E. Frank, eds. 1995. *Status and Identity in West Africa.* Bloomington: Indiana University Press.

Coolen, Michael T. 1979. "Xalamkats: the Xalam Tradition of the Senegambia." PhD diss., University of Washington.

———. 1982. "The Fodet: A Senegambian Origin for the Blues?" *The Black Perspective in Music* 10 (1): 69–84.

———. 1983. "The Wolof Xalam Tradition of the Senegambia." *Ethnomusicology* 27 (3): 477–98.

———. 1984. "Senegambian Archetypes for the American Folk Banjo." *Western Folklore* 43 (2): 117–32.

———. 1991. "Senegambian Influences on Afro-American Musical Culture." *Black Music Research Journal* 11 (1): 1–18.

Cooper, Barbara M. 1997. *Marriage in Maradi: Gender and Culture in a Hausa Society in Niger, 1900–1989.* Portsmouth, NH: Heinemann.

Coplan, David. 1982. "The Urbanisation of African Music: Some Theoretical Observations." *Popular Music* 2:112–29.

———. 1991. "Ethnomusicology and the Meaning of Tradition." In *Ethnomusicology and Modern Music History*, ed. Stephen Blum et al., 35–48. Urbana: University of Illinois Press.

———. 1994. *In the Time of Cannibals: The Word Music of South Africa's Basotho Migrants.* Chicago: University of Chicago Press.

Creevey, Lucy E. 1968. "The Islamization of the Wolof by the End of the Nineteenth Century." In *West African History,* ed. Daniel F. McCall, Norman R. Bennet, and Jeffrey Butler. New York: Praeger.

———. 1985. "Muslim Brotherhoods and Politics in Senegal in 1985." *Journal of Modern African Studies* 23 (4): 715–21.

———. 1991. "The Impact of Islam on Women in Senegal." *Journal of Developing Areas* 25 (3): 347–69.

Crichton, Kimberly. 1967. "The Changing Role of the Marabout in Wolof Society." Senior thesis, Harvard University.

Crowder, Michael. 1962. *Senegal: A Study of French Assimilation Policy.* London: Oxford University Press.

Cullman, B. 1990. "World Music's Hope; Can West Africa's Youssou N'Dour Pass the Global Test?" *Rolling Stone* 15 (591): 21.

Curtin, Philip D. 1975. *Economic Change in Precolonial Africa: Senegambia in the Era of the Slave Trade.* Madison: University of Wisconsin Press.

Dagan, Esther A., ed. 1993. *Drums: The Heartbeat of Africa.* Montreal: Galerie Amrad African Art Publications.

Danielson, Virginia. 1991. "Shaping Tradition in Arabic Song: The Career and Repertory of Umm Kulthuum." PhD diss., University of Illinois at Urbana-Champaign.

———. 1997. *The Voice of Egypt.* Chicago: University of Chicago Press.

Diallo, Yaya, and Mitchell Hall. 1989. *The Healing Drum: African Wisdom Teachings.* Vermont: Destiny Books.
Diawara, Mamadou. 1996. "Le griot mande à l'heure de la globalization." *Cahiers d'Etudes africaines*, 144 (XXXVI-4): 591–612.
Diawara, Manthia. 1998. *In Search of Africa.* Cambridge: Harvard University Press.
Dieng, Meadow, and Modou Dieng. 1999. "Patricia Tang et le Setsima Groupe: un violon pour le Mbalax." *Orange Light* (Sept.–Oct.): 31.
Diop, Abdoulaye-Bara. 1981. *La Société Wolof: Tradition et Changement: les systèmes d'inégalité et de domination.* Paris: Karthala.
———. 1985. *La famille Wolof: Tradition et Changement.* Paris: Karthala.
Diop, Samba. 1995. *The Oral History and Literature of the Wolof People of Waalo, Northern Senegal: The Master of the Word (Griot) in the Wolof Tradition.* Lewiston, NY: E. Mellen Press.
———. 1997. "The Epic of Njaajaan Njaay." Narrated by Sèq Ñan, transcribed and trans. Samba Diop. In *Oral Epics from Africa*, ed. John William Johnson, Thomas A. Hale, and Stephen Belcher, 201–210. Bloomington: Indiana University Press.
Diouf, Jean Leopold. 1991. *J'apprends le wolof = Damay jang wolof.* Paris: Karthala.
Diouf, Mamodou. 1996. "Urban Youth and Senegalese Politics: Dakar 1988–1994." *Public Culture* 8 (2): 225–249.
DjeDje, Jacqueline Cogdell, ed. 1992. *African Musicology: Current Trends Vol. II.* Los Angeles: University of California Los Angeles.
Doubleday, Veronica. 1988. *Three Women of Herat.* Austin: University of Texas Press.
Drame, Adama, and Arlette Senn-Borloz. 1992. *Jeliya: être griot et musicien aujourd'hui.* Paris: L'Harmattan.
Drewal, Margaret Thompson. 1992. *Yoruba Ritual: Performers, Play, Agency.* Bloomington: Indiana University Press.
Dumont, Louis. 1966 [1970]. *Homo Hierarchicus: The Caste System and Its Implications.* Chicago: University of Chicago Press.
Durán, Lucy. 1981. "A Preliminary Study of the Wolof Xalam (with a List of Recordings at the BIRS)." *Recorded Sound* 79: 29–50.
———. 1989. "Key to N'Dour: Roots of the Senegalese Star." *Popular Music* 8 (3): 275–84.
———. 2001. "Baobab Bounce Back." *Folk Roots* 23:5:221 (November): 20–21, 23, 25, 27.
Ebron, Paulla. 1993. "Negotiating the Meaning of Africa: Mandinka Praisesingers in Transnational Context." PhD diss., University of Massachusetts.
———. 1997. "Traffic in Men." In *Gendered Encounters,* ed Maria Grosz-Ngaté and Omari H. Kokole, 223–44. New York: Routledge.
———. 2002. *Performing Africa.* Princeton: Princeton University Press.
Erlmann, Veit. 1986. *Music and the Islamic Reform in the Early Sokoto Empire.* Stuttgart: Steiner Verlag.
———. 1996. *Nightsong.* Chicago: University of Chicago Press.
Erni, Corinne. 1998. "Rhythms of Changes: From the Sabar to the Mbalax." *Black Renaissance* 2 (1): 35
Ewens, Graeme. 1991. *Africa O-Ye! A Celebration of African Music.* Middlesex: Guinness Publishing, 1991.
Eyre, Banning. 1993. "Sweet Sounds of Senegal Belie a Troubled Reality." *Billboard* 105 (19): 1–2.

———. 2000. *In Griot Time: An American Guitarist in Mali.* Philadelphia: Temple University Press.

Fabian, Johannes. 1990. *Power and Performance: Ethnographic Explorations through Proverbial Wisdom and Theater in Shaba, Zaïre.* Madison: University of Wisconsin Press.

Fage, John D. 1987. "Compiling a Guide to the Original Sources for Pre-Colonial Western Africa Published in European Languages." *Paideuma* 33:207–30.

Fal, Arame, Rosine Santos, and Jean Léonce Doneux. 1990. *Dictionnaire wolof-français.* Paris: Karthala.

Feld, Steven. 1990. *Sound and Sentiment.* 2nd ed. Philadelphia: University of Pennsylvania Press.

Fernandez, James W., ed. 1991. *Beyond Metaphor.* Stanford, CA: Stanford University Press.

Fosu-Mensah, Kwabena, Lucy Duran, and Chris Stapleton. 1987. "On Music in Contemporary West Africa." *African Affairs* 86 (343): 227–40.

Friedson, Steven. 1996. *Dancing Prophets: Musical Experience in Tumbuka Healing.* Chicago: University of Chicago Press.

Furniss, Graham, and Liz Gunner, eds. 1995. *Power, Marginality and African Oral Literature.* Cambridge: Cambridge University Press.

Gaby, Jean-Baptiste. 1689. *Relation de la Nigritie.* Paris: E. Couterot.

Gamble, David P. 1967. *The Wolof of Senegambia* (with notes on the Lebu and the Serer). London: International African Institute.

Geertz, Clifford. 1973. *The Interpretation of Cultures.* New York: Basic Books.

Gellar, Sheldon. 1995. *Senegal: An African Nation Between Islam and the West.* 2nd ed. Boulder, CO: Westview Press.

Gilroy, Paul. 1993. *The Black Atlantic: Modernity and Double Consciousness.* Cambridge, MA: Harvard University Press.

Gorer, Geoffrey. 1935. *Africa Dances.* London: John Lehmann.

Gould, Harold A. 1987. *The Hindu Caste System.* Delhi: Chanakya Publications.

Graham, Ronnie. 1988. *Stern's Guide to Contemporary African Music.* London: Zwan.

———. 1992. *The World of African Music: Stern's Guide to the World of Contemporary African Music.* Vol. 2. London: Pluto Press.

Gravrand, Henry. 1983. *Cosaan: La Civilisation Serer.* Paris: Les Nouvelles Éditions Africaines.

Gueye, Marame. 2004. "Wolof Wedding Songs: Women Negotiating Voice and Space through Verbal Art." PhD diss., State University of New York at Binghamton.

Guilbault, Jocelyne. 1993. *Zouk: World Music in the West Indies.* Chicago: University of Chicago Press.

Gunderson, Frank, and Gregory Barz, eds. 2000. *Mashindano! Competitive Music Performance in East Africa.* Dar Es Salaam: Mkuki Na Nyota Publishers.

Gyekye, Kwame. 1997. *Tradition and Modernity.* New York: Oxford University Press.

Hagedorn, Katherine J. 2001. *Divine Utterances: The Performance of Afro-Cuban Santería.* Washington, DC: Smithsonian Institution Press.

Hale, Thomas A. 1990. *Scribe, Griot, and Novelist: Narrative Interpreters of the Songhay Empire.* Gainesville: University of Florida Press.

———. 1998. *Griots and Griottes.* Bloomington: Indiana University Press.

Haley, Alex. 1976. *Roots.* New York: Doubleday.

Heath, Deborah. 1988. "The Politics of Signifying Practice in Kaolack, Senegal: Hegemony and the Dialectic of Autonomy and Domination." PhD diss., Johns Hopkins University.

———. 1990. "Spatial Politics and Verbal Performance in Urban Senegal." *Ethnology* 29 (3): 209–23.

———. 1994. "The Politics of Appropriateness and Appropriation: Recontextualizing Women's Dance in Senegal." *American Ethnologist* 21 (1): 88–103.

Herbert, Eugenia W. 1993. *Iron, Gender and Power: Rituals of Transformation in African Societies*. Bloomington: Indiana University Press.

Héricé, M. 1847. *Mémoire presenté à M. le Ministre de la Marine et des colonies, relativement à quelques améliorations à porter à la colonie du Sénégal.* Paris: Plon.

Herson, Benjamin. 2000. "Fat Beats, Dope Rhymes and Thug Lives: Youth, Politics and Hip-Hop in Dakar." Undergraduate thesis, Hampshire College.

Hill, Joseph B. 1999. "People of Word, Song, and Money: The Evolution of Senegalese Griots and Their Art." Undergraduate thesis, Brigham Young University.

Hobsbawm, Eric, and Terence Ranger, eds. 1992. *The Invention of Tradition*. Cambridge: Cambridge University Press.

Hoffman, Barbara G. 1995. "Power, Structure, and Mande *jeliw*." In *Status and Identity in West Africa: Nyamakalaw of Mande*, ed. David C. Conrad and Barbara E. Frank, 36–45. Bloomington: Indiana University Press.

———. 2000. *Griots at War: Conflict, Conciliation, and Caste in Mande.* Bloomington: Indiana University Press.

Innes, Gordon, ed. and trans. 1976. *Kaabu and Fuladu: Historical Narratives of the Gambia Mandinka.* London: SOAS, University of London.

Irvine, Judith. 1978. "When is Genealogy History? Wolof Genealogies in Comparative Perspective." *American Ethnologist* 5 (4): 651–74.

Irvine, Judith T., and J. David Sapir. 1976. "Musical Style and Social Change among the Kujamaat Diola." *Ethnomusicology* 20 (1): 67–86.

Jackson, Irene V., ed. 1985. *More Than Drumming.* Westport, CT: Greenwood Press.

Jatta, Sidia. 1983. "Born Musicians: Traditional Music from The Gambia." In *Repercussions: A Celebration of African-American Music*, ed. Geoffrey Haydon and Dennis Marks, 14–29. London: Century Publishing.

Jessup, Lynne. 1981. "Musical Instruments of The Gambia." *Gambia Museum Bulletin* (Banjul) 1:39–42.

Johnson, John William, Thomas A. Hale, and Stephen Belcher, eds. 1997. *Oral Epics from Africa.* Bloomington: Indiana University Press

Joseph, George. 1979. "The Wolof Oral Praise Song for Semu Coro Wende." *Research in African Literatures* 10:145–178.

Kartomi, Margaret, and Stephen Blum, eds. 1994. *Music-Cultures in Contact: Convergences and Collisions*. Basel, Switzerland: Gordon and Breach.

Kaschula, Russell H., ed. 2001. *African Oral Literature: Functions in Contemporary Contexts.* Claremont, South Africa: New Africa Books.

Keil, Charles. 1979. *Tiv Song*. Chicago: University of Chicago Press.

Kisliuk, Michelle. 1998. *Seize the Dance! BaAka Musical Life and the Ethnography of Performance.* New York: Oxford University Press.

Klein, Martin A. 1968. *Islam and Imperialism in Senegal.* Stanford, CA: Stanford University Press.

———, ed. 1993. *Breaking the Chains: Slavery, Bondage, and Emancipation in Modern Africa and Asia*. Madison: University of Wisconsin Press.

Knight, Roderic. 1973. "Mandinka Jaliya: Professional Music of the Gambia." PhD diss., University of California, Los Angeles. 2 vols.

———. 1974. "Mandinka Drumming." *African Arts* 7 (4): 24–35.

———. 1975. "The Jali, Professional Musician of West Africa." *The World of Music* 17 (2): 8–13.

———. 1980. "Gambia." In *The New Grove Dictionary of Music and Musicians,* vol. 7, 139–42. London: Macmillan.

———. 1982. "Manding/Fula Relations as Reflected in the Manding Song Repertoire." *African Music* 6 (2):37–47.

———. 1984a. "Music in Africa: the Manding Contexts." In *Performance Practice: Ethnomusicological Perspectives*, ed. Gerard Béhague, 53–90. Westport, CT: Greenwood Press.

———. 1984b. "The Style of Mandinka Music: A Study in Extracting Theory from Practice." *Selected Reports in Ethnomusicology* 5:2–66.

———. 1991. "Music Out of Africa: Mande Jaliya in Paris." *The World of Music* 33 (1): 52–69.

Koetting, James. 1970. "Analysis and Notation of West African Drum Ensemble Music." *Selected Reports in Ethnomusicology*, ed. J. H. Kwabena Nketia and Jacqueline Cogdel Djedje, 1 (3):115–146. Los Angeles: Institute of Ethnomusicology, University of California.

———. 1985. "Assessing Meter in Kasena Jongo." *Sonus* 5 (2): 11–19.

Konte, Lamine. 1986. "The Griot: Singer and Chronicler of African Life." *UNESCO Courier* (April): 21–26.

Korom, Frank J. 1994. "The Transformation of Language to Rhythm: The Hosay Drums of Trinidad." *The World of Music* 36(3): 68–85.

Koskoff, Ellen, ed. 1987. *Women and Music in Cross-Cultural Perspective*. Westport, CT: Greenwood Press.

Kubik, Gerhard. 1986. "Stability and Change in African Musical Traditions." *The World of Music* 28 (1): 44–69.

———. 1987. *Malawian Music: A Framework for Analysis.* Zomba: University of Malawi.

Kwamena-Poh, M., J. Tosh, R. Waller, and M. Tidy. 1982. *African History in Maps*. Essex: Longman.

La Courbe, Michel Jajolet de. 1913. *Premier voyage du Sieur de La Courbe fait à la Coste d'Afrique en 1685.* Ed. Pierre Cultru. Paris: Champion.

Lamiral, M. 1789. *L'Afrique et le Peuple Afriquain.* Paris: Dessenne.

Le Maire, Jacques Joseph. 1695. *Les Voyages du Sieur Le Maire aux Isles Canaries, Cap-Verd, Senegal, et Gambie*. Paris: Jacques Collombat.

Levtzion, N., and J. F. P. Hopkins, eds. 1981. *Corpus of Early Arabic Sources for West African History.* Cambridge: Cambridge University Press.

Leymarie, Isabelle. 1978. "The Role and Functions of the Griots Among the Wolof of Senegal." PhD diss., Columbia University.

———. 1999. *Les Griots Wolof du Sénégal.* Paris: Maisonneuve et Larose.

Leymarie-Ortiz, Isabelle. 1979. "The Griots of Senegal and Change." *Africa* (Rome) 3 (September): 183–97.

Linares, Olga F. 1992. *Power, Prayer and Production: The Jola of Casamance, Senegal.* Cambridge: Cambridge University Press.

Lobeck, Katharina. 2004. "A Little Egypt." *Folk Roots* 26:1:253 (July): 30–31, 33.

Locke, David. 1979. "The Music of Atsiagbeko." PhD diss., Wesleyan University.

———. 1982. "Principles of Offbeat Timing and Cross-Rhythm in Southern Eve Drumming." *Ethnomusicology* 26 (2): 217–46.

———. 1983. "Atsiagbeko: The Polyrhythmic Texture." *Sonus* 4 (1): 16–38.

———. 1987. *Drum Gahu.* Crown Point, IN: White Cliffs Media Company.

———. 1990. *Drum Damba: Talking Drum Lessons.* Crown Point, IN: White Cliffs Media Company.

———. 1992. *Kpegisu: A War Drum of the Ewe.* Tempe, AZ: White Cliffs Media Company.

Lord, Albert Bates. 2000. *The Singer of Tales.* 2nd ed. Ed. Stephen Mitchell and Gregory Nagy. Cambridge, MA: Harvard University Press.

Lortat-Jacob, B., ed. 1987. *l'Improvisation dans les musiques de tradition orale.* Paris: Societe d'Etudes Linguistiques et Anthropologiques de France.

Magel, Emil A. 1984. *Folktales from the Gambia: Wolof Fictional Narratives.* Trans. and annotated by Magel. Washington, DC: Three Continents Press.

Maiga, Mohamed. 1980. "Le Griot, Memoire du Temps Present." *Jeune Afrique* (Paris) 25 (June): 66–68.

Makward, Edris. 1990. "Two Griots of Contemporary Senegambia." In *The Oral Performance in Africa,* ed. Isidore Okpewho, 23–41. Ibadan: Spectrum Books.

Malherbe, Michel, and Cheikh Sall. 1989. *Parlons Wolof: langue et culture.* Paris: L'Harmattan.

Manchuelle, François. 1997. *Willing Migrants: Soninke Labor Diasporas, 1848–1960.* Athens: Ohio University Press.

Mangin, Timothy R. 2004. "Notes on Jazz in Senegal." In *Uptown Conversation: The New Jazz Studies,* ed. R. O'Meally, Brent Hayes Edwards, and Sarah Jasmine Griffin, 224–48. New York: Columbia University Press.

Manning, Patrick. 1988. *Francophone Sub-Saharan Africa 1880–1985.* Cambridge: Cambridge University Press.

———. 1990. *Slavery and African Life.* Cambridge: Cambridge University Press.

Manuel, Peter. 1993. *Cassette Culture: Popular Music and Technology in North India.* Chicago: University of Chicago Press.

Mark, Peter. 1985. *A Cultural, Economic, and Religious History of the Basse Casamance Since 1500.* Stuttgart: Franz Steiner Verlag.

Mauny, Raymond. 1955. "Baobab-Cimetières à Griots." *Notes Africaines de l'IFAN* 67 (July): 72–75.

"Mbalax." 1989. In *The Penguin Encyclopedia of Popular Music,* ed. Donald Clarke, 784. New York: Viking.

McCall, Daniel F., Norman R. Bennett, and Jeffrey Butler, eds. 1969. *Western African History.* New York: Frederick A. Praeger.

McLaughlin, Fiona. 1995. "Haalpulaar Identity as a Response to Wolofization." *African Languages and Cultures* 8 (2): 153–68.

———. 1997. "Islam and Popular Music in Senegal: The Emergence of a 'New Tradition.'" *Africa: Journal of the International African Institute* 67 (4): 560–81.

———. 2001. "Dakar Wolof and the Configuration of an Urban Identity." *Journal of African Cultural Studies* 14 (2): 153–72.

McLeod, Norma. 1964. "The Status of Musical Specialists in Madagascar." *Ethnomusicology* 8 (3): 278–89.
McNaughton, Patrick R. 1988. *The Mande Blacksmiths: Knowledge, Power, and Art in West Africa.* Bloomington: Indiana University Press.
McNee, Lisa. 1996. "Selfish Gifts: Senegalese Women's Autobiographical Discourses." PhD diss., Indiana University.
———. 2000. *Selfish Gifts: Senegalese Women's Autobiographical Discourses.* Albany: State University Press.
Meillassoux, Claude. 1986 [1991]. *The Anthropology of Slavery*. Trans. Alide Dasnois. London: Athlone Press.
Meintjes, Louise. 2003. *Sound of Africa! Making Music Zulu in a South African Studio.* Durham: Duke University Press.
———. 2004. "Shoot the Sergeant, Shatter the Mountain: The Production of Masculinity in Zulu Ngoma Song and Dance in Post-Apartheid South Africa." *Ethnomusicology Forum* 13 (2): 173–201.
Mirza, Sarah, and Margaret Strobel, eds. and trans. 1989. *Three Swahili Women: Life Histories from Mombasa, Kenya.* Bloomington: Indiana University Press.
Mitchell, Tony. 1996. *Popular Music and Local Identity*. London: Leicester University Press.
Moloney, C. A. 1889. "On the Melodies of the Wolof, Mandingo, Ewe, Yoruba, and Hausa People of West Africa." *Journal of the Manchester Geographical Society* 5 (7–9): 227–98.
Monson, Ingrid. 1996. *Saying Something: Jazz Improvisation and Interaction*. Chicago: University of Chicago Press.
———, ed. 2000. *The African Diaspora: A Musical Perspective.* New York: Routledge.
Monteil, Vincent. 1980. *L'Islam Noir: une religion à la conquête de l'Afrique.* Paris: Éditions du Seuil.
Moore, Sally Falk. 1994. *Anthropology and Africa: Changing Perspectives on a Changing Scene.* Charlottesville: University Press of Virginia.
Morales-Libove, Jessica. 2005. "Dancing a Fine Line: Gender, Sexuality and Morality at Women's *Tours* in Dakar, Senegal." PhD diss., Rutgers, State University of New Jersey.
Mudimbe, V. Y. 1988. *The Invention of Africa: Gnosis, Philosophy, and the Order of Knowledge*. Bloomington: Indiana University Press.
Munro, Pamela. 1997. *Ay baati Wolof: a Wolof Dictionary.* Rev. ed. Los Angeles: Department of Linguistics, University of California Los Angeles.
Mustafa, Hudita Nura. 1997. "Practicing Beauty: Crisis, Value and the Challenge of Self-Mastery in Dakar, 1970–1994." PhD diss., Harvard University.
———. 2001a. "Oumou Sy: The African Place, Dakar, Senegal." *Nka: Journal of Contemporary Art* (Fall/Winter): 44–46.
———. 2001b. "Ruins and Spectacles: Fashion and City Life in Contemporary Senegal." *Nka: Journal of Contemporary Art* (Fall/Winter): 47–53.
Nettl, Bruno, ed. 1978. *Eight Urban Musical Cultures: Tradition and Change.* Urbana: University of Illinois Press.
Nettl, Bruno, and Philip V. Bohlman, eds. 1991. *Comparative Musicology and Anthropology of Music.* Chicago: University of Chicago Press.
Neuman, Daniel M. 1990. *The Life of Music in North India: The Organization of an Artistic Tradition.* Chicago: University of Chicago Press.

Niane, Djibril T. 1979. *Sundiata: An Epic of Old Mali.* London: Longman.

Nikiprowetzky, Tolia. 1963. "The Griots of Senegal and Their Instruments." *Journal of the International Folk Music Council* 15:79–82.

———. 1967. *Trois Aspects de la Musique Africaine: Mauritanie, Senegal, Niger.* Paris: Office de Cooperation Radiophonique.

———. 1980. "Senegal." In *The New Grove Dictionary of Music and Musicians,* vol. 17, 127–29. London: Macmillan.

Nketia, J. H. Kwabena. 1963a. *Drumming in Akan Communities of Ghana.* London: Thomas Nelson and Sons Ltd.

———. 1963b. *African Music in Ghana.* Chicago: Northwestern University Press.

———. 1974. *The Music of Africa.* New York: W. W. Norton.

———. 1976a. "Drumming In Akan Communities." In *Speech Surrogates: Drum and Whistle Systems, Part II,* ed. Thomas A. Sebeok and Donna J. Umiker-Sebeok, 772–805. Paris: Mouton.

———. 1976b. "Surrogate Languages of Africa." In *Speech Surrogates: Drum and Whistle Systems, Part II,* ed. Thomas A. Sebeok and Donna J. Umiker-Sebeok, 825–64. Paris: Mouton.

Nourrit, Chantal, and Bill Pruitt. 1979. *Musique Traditionelle de l'Afrique noire: discographie. No. 4: Senegal et Gambia.* Paris: Radio-France Internationale.

Novicki, Margaret A. 1990. "A conversation with Baaba Maal [interview]." *Africa Report* 35 (4): 70.

Nussbaum, Loren V. 1970. *Dakar Wolof: A Basic Course.* Washington, DC: Center for Applied Linguistics.

O'Brien, Donal B. Cruise. 1971. *The Mourides of Senegal: The Political and Economic Organization of an Islamic Brotherhood.* Oxford: Clarendon Press.

Okpewho, Isidore. 1975. *The Epic in Africa: Towards a Poetics of the Oral Performance.* New York: Columbia University Press.

———. 1992. *African Oral Literature.* Bloomington: Indiana University Press.

Olatunji, Babatunde. 2005. *The Beat of My Drum: An Autobiography.* Philadelphia: Temple University Press.

Ong, Walter. 1977. "African Talking Drums and Oral Noetics." In *Interfaces of the Word: Studies in the Evolution of Consciousness and Culture,* 92–120. Ithaca, NY: Cornell University Press.

Ottenberg, Simon. 1996. *Seeing With Music: The Lives of Three Blind African Musicians.* Seattle: University of Washington Press.

Panzacchi, Cornelia. 1990. *Griot: seine Darstellung in der frankophonen westafrikanischen Literatur.* Rheinfelden (Switzerland): Schauble Verlag.

———. 1994. "Livelihoods of Traditional Griots in Modern Senegal." *Africa* 64 (2): 190–210.

———. 1996. *Mbalax Mi: Musikszene Senegal.* Wuppertal: Hammer.

Phillips, L. G. Colvin, and Andrew Clark. 1994. *Historical Dictionary of Senegal.* 2nd ed. Metuchen, NJ: Scarecrow Press.

Polak, Rainer. 2000. "A Musical Instrument Travels Around the World: *Jenbe* Playing in Bamako, West Africa, and Beyond." *The World of Music* 42 (3): 7–46.

Potekhina, G. 1966. "Les Griots Mandings et la Tradition Historique Orale." In *Essays on African Culture*, ed. M. A. Korostovstev, 62–71. Moscow: Nauka.

Prince, Rob. 1990. "There's a Griot Going On! [Interview with Kasse Mady Diabate.]" *Folk Roots* 81:23.

———. 1991. "Baaba Maal talks to Rob Prince about the importance of traditional music." *Folk Roots* 95:34–37.

Qureshi, Regula. 1995. *Sufi Music of India and Pakistan: Sound, Context, and Meaning in Qawwali.* Chicago: University of Chicago Press.

Ranger, T. O. 1975. *Dance and Society in Eastern Africa 1890–1970.* Berkeley: University of California Press.

Rattray, R. S. 1976. "The Drum Language of West Africa." In *Speech Surrogates: Drum and Whistle Systems, Part I,* ed. Thomas A. Sebeok and Donna J. Umiker-Sebeok, 366–389. Paris: Mouton.

Reed, Daniel B. 2003. *Dan Ge Performance: Masks and Music in Contemporary Côte d'Ivoire.* Bloomington: Indiana University Press.

Reyes Schramm, Adelaida. 1979. "Ethnic Music, the Urban Area, and Ethnomusicology." *Sociologus* 29:1–21.

Rice, Tim. 1994. *May It Fill Your Soul: Experiencing Bulgarian Music.* Chicago: University of Chicago Press.

Robinson, David. 2004. *Muslim Societies in African History.* Cambridge: Cambridge University Press.

Rodney, Walter. 1970. *A History of the Upper Guinea Coast 1545–1800.* Oxford: Clarendon Press.

Romero, Patricia W., ed. 1988. *Life Histories of African Women.* London: Ashfield Press.

Rouget, Gilbert. 1955/56. "La Musique du Senegal, de Casamance, et de Guinee." *Présence Africaine* 5:108.

Rule, Sheila. 1992. "An African Superstar [Youssou N'Dour] Sings Out to the World." *New York Times* 141, 5 September 1992.

Saarela, Mikko. 2002. Trans. Spencer Allman. "African Music in Finland." *FMQ* (March): 13–19.

Sakata, Hiromi Lorraine. 1983. *Music in the Mind: The Concepts of Music and Musician in Afghanistan.* Kent, OH: Kent State University Press.

Samb, Amar. 1975. "Folklore Wolof du Senegal." *Bulletin de l'IFAN*, Serie B, 37 (4): 817–48.

Sanjek, Roger, ed. 1990. *Fieldnotes: The Makings of Anthropology.* Ithaca: Cornell University Press.

Savishinsky, Neil J. 1994. "The Baye Faal of Senegambia: Muslim Rastas in the Promised Land?" *Africa* 64 (2): 211–20.

Schacter, Daniel L. 1996. *Searching for Memory.* New York: Basic Books.

Schimmel, Annemarie. 1989. *Islamic Names.* Edinburgh: Edinburgh University Press.

Schissel, Howard. 1989. "Coloring History: Senegalese Glass Painting." *Africa Report* 34 (2): 69.

Schulz, Dorothea E. 1997. "Praise Without Enchantment: Griots, Broadcast Media, and the Politics of Tradition in Mali." *Africa Today* 44 (4): 443–64.

———. 1998. "Morals of Praise: Broadcast Media and the Commoditization of Jeli Praise Performances in Mali." *Research in Economic Anthropology* 19:117–32.

———. 1999. "Pricey Publicity, Refutable Reputations: *Jeliw* and the Economics of Honour in Mali." *Paideuma* 45:275–92.

———. 2001a. "Music Videos and the Effeminate Vices of Urban Culture in Mali." *Africa* 71 (3): 345–71.

———. 2001b. *Perpetuating the Politics of Praise: Jeli Singers, Radios, and Political Mediation in Mali.* Köln: Köppe Verlag.

———. 2002. "The World is Made by Talk: Female Fans, Popular Music, and New Forms of Public Sociality in Urban Mali." *Cahiers d'Etudes Africaines* 168 (XLII-4): 797–829.

Sebeok, Thomas A., and Donna Jean Umiker-Sebeok, eds. 1976. *Speech Surrogates: Drum and Whistle Systems, Part I & II.* Paris: Mouton.

Seeger, Anthony. 1987. *Why Suya Sing.* Cambridge: Cambridge University Press.

Segalen, Martine. 1986. *Historical Anthropology of the Family.* Cambridge: Cambridge University Press.

Senghor, Léopold Sédar. 1979. *Élégies Majeures.* Paris: Éditions du Seuil.

Shelemay, Kay Kaufman. 1991. *A Song of Longing.* Urbana: University of Illinois Press.

———. 1992. "The Musician and the Transmission of Religious Tradition: The Multiple Roles of the Ethiopian Dabtara." *Journal of Religion in Africa* 22 (3): 242–60.

———. 1996a. "Crossing Boundaries in Music and Musical Scholarship: A Perspective from Ethnomusicology." *Musical Quarterly* 80 (1): 13–30.

———. 1996b. "The Ethnomusicologist and the Transmission of Tradition." *The Journal of Musicology* 14 (1): 35–51.

———. 1998a. *Let Jasmine Rain Down.* Chicago: University of Chicago Press.

———. 1998b. "Notation and Oral Tradition." In *The Garland Encyclopedia of World Music: Africa,* ed. Ruth M. Stone, 1:146–63. New York: Garland Publishing.

Shostak, Marjorie. 1983. *Nisa: The Life and Words of a !Kung Woman.* New York: Vintage Books.

Slobin, Mark. 1989. *Chosen Voices: The Story of the American Cantorate.* Urbana: University of Illinois Press.

Smith, Mary F. 1981. *Baba of Karo: A Woman of the Muslim Hausa.* New Haven: Yale University Press.

Spradley, James P. 1980. *Participant Observation.* Fort Worth: Harcourt Brace Jovanovich College Publishers.

Stapleton, Chris, and Chris May. 1990. *African Rock: The Pop Music of a Continent.* New York: Dutton.

Stewart, Gary. 1992. *Breakout: Profiles in African Rhythm.* Chicago: University of Chicago Press.

Stokes, Martin, ed. 1994. *Ethnicity, Identity and Music: the Musical Construction of Place.* Oxford: Berg.

Stoller, Paul. 1989. *The Taste of Ethnographic Things: The Senses in Anthropology.* Philadelphia: University of Pennsylvania Press.

Stoller, Paul, and Cheryl Olkes. 1987. *In Sorcery's Shadow.* Chicago: University of Chicago Press.

Stone, Ruth M. 1982. *Let the Inside Be Sweet: The Interpretation of Music Event Among the Kpelle of Liberia.* Bloomington: Indiana University Press.

———. 1986. "Commentary: The Value of Local Ideas in Understanding West African Rhythm." *Ethnomusicology* 30 (1): 54–57.

———, ed. 1998. *The Garland Encyclopedia of World Music.* Vol. 1: Africa. New York: Garland Publishing.

Stone, Ruth M. 2005. *Music in West Africa.* New York: Oxford University Press.

Stone, Ruth M., and Verlon L. Stone. 1981. "Event, Feedback and Analysis: Research Media in the Study of Music Events." *Ethnomusicology* 25 (2): 215–25.

Sugnet, Charles. 1997. "I Sing All the Space: A Conversation with Baaba Maal." *Transition* 74:184–98.

———. 2000. "Eyes Open: Reading Dakar Social Stresses Through Music Videos." *Orange Light* (January): 26–28.

Sunkett, Mark. 1995. *Mandiani Drum and Dance.* Tempe, AZ: White Cliffs Media.

Swigart, Leigh. 1992a. "Women and Language Choice in Dakar: a Case of Unconscious Innovation." *Women and Language* 15 (1): 11–21.

———. 1992b. "Practice and Perception: Language Use and Attitudes in Dakar." PhD diss., University of Washington.

———. 1994. "Cultural Creolization and Language Use in Post-Colonial Africa: The Case of Senegal." *Africa,* 64 (2): 175–89.

Tamari, Tal. 1991. "The Development of Caste Systems in West Africa." *Journal of African History* 32:221–50.

———. 1995. "Linguistic Evidence for the History of West African 'Castes.'" In *Status and Identity in West Africa: Nyamakalaw of Mande*, ed. David C. Conrad and Barbara E. Frank, 61–85. Bloomington: Indiana University Press.

Tang, Patricia J. 2005a. "Negotiating Performance in Senegalese Popular Music: Sound, Image, and the Ethnomusicologist as Exoticized 'Other.'" *Journal of Popular Music Studies* 17 (3):275–300.

———. 2005b. "Senegal." In *The Continuum Encyclopedia of Popular Music of the World, Vol. 6: Africa and Middle East*, ed. John Shepherd et al. London: Continuum International Publishing Group.

Tedlock, Dennis. 1977. "Toward an Oral Poetics." *New Literary History* 8 (3): 507–19.

Télémaque, Hamet Sow. 1916. "Folklore: Origine des griots." *Bulletin de l'Association de l'Enseignement de l'Afrique Occidentale Française* 25 (June): 277.

Thompson, Robert F. 1974. *African Art in Motion: Icon and Act.* Los Angeles: University of California Press.

Thompson, Robert L. 1993. "Mandinka Drum Patterns in the Gambia." In *Drums: The Heartbeat of Africa,* ed. Esther A. Dagan, 82–83. Montreal: Galerie Amrad African Art Publications.

Titon, Jeff Todd. 1980. "The Life Story." *Journal of American Folklore* 93 (369): 276–92.

Topouzis, Daphne. 1988. "Voices from West Africa: Youssou N'Dour and Salif Keita." *Africa Report* 33 (5): 66–70.

———. 1990. "Baaba Maal: a Peulh Troubador." *Africa Report* 35 (4): 67–70.

Turino, Thomas. 1993. *Moving Away from Silence.* Chicago: University of Chicago Press.

Turner, Victor. 1967. *The Forest of Symbols: Aspects of Ndembu Ritual.* Ithaca: Cornell University Press.

———. 1974. *Dramas, Fields, and Metaphors: Symbolic Action in Human Society.* Ithaca: Cornell University Press.

———. 1986. *The Anthropology of Performance.* New York: PAJ Publications.

Underwood, Tamara. 1988. *Femmes wolof: pouvoirs et savoirs-faire.* Dakar: ENDA Tiers-Monde.

Van Maanen, John. 1988. *Tales of the Field: On Writing Ethnography.* Chicago: University of Chicago Press.

Vander, Judith. 1988. *Songprints: The Musical Experience of Five Shoshone Women.* Urbana: University of Illinois Press.

Vansina, Jan. 1961 [1965]. *Oral Tradition*. Trans. H. M. Wright. Chicago: Aldine Publishing Company.

Velez, Maria Teresa. 1998. *Drumming for the Gods*. Philadelphia: Temple University Press.

Villalón, Leonardo A. 1994. "Sufi Rituals as Rallies: Religious Ceremonies in the Politics of Senegalese State-Society Relations." *Comparative Politics* 26 (4): 415–37.

———. 1995. *Islamic Society and State Power in Senegal*. Cambridge: Cambridge University Press.

———. 1999. "Generational Changes, Political Stagnation, and the Evolving Dynamics of Religion and Politics in Senegal." *Africa Today* 46 (3/4): 129–48.

von Rosen, Franziska. 1998. "Music, Visual Art, Stories: Conversations with a Community of Micmac Artists." PhD diss., Brown University.

Wade, Bonnie. 1984. *Khyal: Creativity within North India's Classical Music Tradition*. Cambridge: Cambridge University Press.

Waterman, Christopher. 1990. *Jùjú: A Social History and Ethnography of an African Popular Music*. Chicago: University of Chicago Press.

Webster, J. B., and A. A. Boahen, with M. Tidy. 1980. *The Revolutionary Years: West Africa since 1800*. Essex: Longman.

Welburn, Ron. 1986. "Toward Theory and Method with the Jazz Oral History Project." *Black Music Research Journal* 6:79–95.

Williamson, Nigel. 2000. "Youssou N'Dour: A Universal African." *Songlines* (Winter 1999/Spring 2000): 24–26.

Wolf, Richard K. 2000. "Embodiment and Ambivalence: Emotion in South Asian Muharram Drumming." *Yearbook for Traditional Music* 32:81–116.

Wright, Bonnie L. 1989. "The Power of Articulation." In *Creativity of Power*, ed. W. Arens and Ivan Carp, 39–57. Washington, DC: Smithsonian Institution Press.

Zemp, Hugo. 1966. "La legende des griots Malinke." *Cahiers d'etudes africaines* 6 (24): 611–42.

———. 1971. *Musique Dan*. Paris: Mouton.

Discography

Ames, David, notes and recording. 1955. *Wolof Music of Senegal and The Gambia.* Folkways FE 4462.

Charters, Samuel, notes and recording. 1975. *The Griots: Ministers of the Spoken Word.* Folkways FE 4178.

Diop, Mapathé. 1992. *Sabar Wolof: Dance Drumming of Senegal.* Village Pulse VPU-1003.

Double Concentré. 1996. Dakar Sound 006 and 007.

Etoile de Dakar. 1994. *Xalis.* Popular African Music ADC 303. Recorded in 1987.

Faye, Mbaye Dieye et Sing Sing Rythms. 1995. *Oupoukay.* Saprom. Cassette.

———. 1996. *Tink's Daye Bondé Biir Thiossane.* Jololi. Cassette.

Gawlo, Coumba. 1998. *Yo Male.* BMG France/RCA 74321579732.

Guewel, Fatou, and Groupe Sopey Noreyni. 1998. *Fatou.* Stern's Africa 1078.

Krémer, Gérard, recording. 1989. *Messe et Chants au Monastère de Keur Moussa, Sénégal.* Arion ARN 64095.

Kunda, Touré. 1999. *Légende.* Sony U10132.

Lam, Kiné. 1996. *Praise.* Shanachie 64062.

Lemzo Diamono. 1997. *Marimbalax.* Stern's Africa 1076. Original recordings released in 1992–1995.

Lô, Cheikh. 1996. *Né la thiass.* World Circuit/Nonesuch 79471–2.

Lô, Cheikh N'Digël. 2000. *Bambay Gueej.* World Circuit WCD 0057.

Lô, Ismael. n.d. *Natt.* Syllart 38740–2.

Maal, Baaba. 1994. *Firin' in Fouta.* Mango 162–539 944–2.

Mbaye, Cheikh Taïrou. 2003. *Mame Bouna.* Mame Bouna Productions.

Mbaye, Thio. 1993. *Rimbax.* Harry Son/Syllart. Cassette.

———. n.d. *Rimbax.* Syllart 38122–2.

———. 2000. *Ndaabi.* Studio 2000. Cassette.

The Music In My Head [various]. 1998. Stern's Africa STCD 1081.

Nder, Alioune Mbaye et le Setsima Group. 1996. *Aduna.* PCS 2000. Cassette.

———. 1997. *Lenëen.* PCS 2000. Cassette.

———. 1998. *Aladji.* Studio 2000. Cassette.

Nder et le Setsima Group. 1999. *Pansement.* Studio 2000. Cassette.

———. 1999. *Nder et le Setsima Group.* Africa Fête Diffusion AFD 002.

———. 2000. *S. T. Super Thiof.* Studio 2000. Cassette.

Ndiaye Guewel, Papa. 1997. *Papa Ndiaye Guewel.* Studio Xippi. Cassette.
———. 2000. *AOI.* Studio 2000. Cassette.
Ndiaye Rose, Doudou. 1994. *Djabote.* Real World Carol 2340–2.
Ndiaye Rose, Ibrahima. 2003. *Delo Njukël Doudou N'Diaye Rose.* Studio Jalucine.
N'Dour, Youssou. 1986. *Nelson Mandela.* Polygram 831 294–2.
———. 1990. *Set.* Virgin V2–86195.
———. 1994. *The Guide (Wommat).* Sony OK 53828.
———. 2000. *Joko.* Sony COL 489718–2.
———. 2002. *Nothing's in Vain.* Nonesuch 79654–2.
Orchestre Baobab. 1993. *Bamba.* Stern's Africa 3003.
———. 1998. *N'Wolof.* Dakar Sound 2003620. 1970–71 original release.
———. 2002. *Specialist in All Styles.* World Circuit/Nonesuch 79685–2.
Pène, Omar and Super Diamono. 1993. *Fari.* Stern's Africa STCD 1051.
Positive Black Soul. 1996. *Salaam.* Mango/Island/PolyGram 162–531 029–2.
Safford, Kimberly, recordings. n.d. *Songs From Senegal.* Lyrichord LLST 7381.
Sapir, J. David, notes and recordings. 1965. *The Music of the Diola-Fogny of the Casamance, Senegal.* Folkways FE 4323.
Seck, Bada. 1997. *Génération Boul Falé.* Studio 2000. Cassette. Senegal.
———. 1998. *Saloum Saloum.* Studio 2000. Cassette.
Seck, Bakane et les Jeri-Jeri. 1999. *Nawett.* Studio 2000. Cassette.
Seck, Thione. 1997. *Daaly.* Stern's Africa 1081.
Streets of Dakar: Generation Boul Falé. 1999. Stern's STCD 1084.
Tama Walo: Keepers of the Talking Drum. 1998. Village Pulse VPU-1008.
Thiam, Omar and Jam Bugum. 1997. *Sabar: the Soul of Sénégal.* Produced by Mark Sunkett. White Cliffs Media WCM 9915.
Touré, Lamine and Group Saloum. 2005. *Lamine Touré & Group Saloum.* Nomadic Wax.
Zanetti, Vincent, notes and recordings. 1997. *Le Saoruba de Casamance.* VDE CD-926.

Interviews

3/2/98	Macheikh Mbaye. March 2, 1998. Mbaye residence, HLM5, Dakar.
3/5/98	Macheikh Mbaye. March 5, 1998. Mbaye residence, HLM5, Dakar.
4/28/98	Lamine Touré. April 28, 1998. Monaco Plage, Dakar.
4/29/98	Lamine Touré. April 29, 1998. Tang apartment, Dakar.
5/8/98	Mari Sow. May 8, 1998. Sow residence, Kaolack.
5/23/98	Thio Mbaye. May 23, 1998. Mbaye residence, HLM Gr. Yoff, Dakar.
7/2/98	Mari Sow. July 2, 1998. Sow residence, Kaolack.
7/3/98	Massaer Daaro Mbaye. July 3, 1998. Mbaye residence, Kaolack.
7/25/98	Macheikh Mbaye Jr. July 25, 1998. Mbaye residence, HLM5, Dakar.
8/16/98	Karim Mbaye. August 16, 1998. Mbaye residence, HLM Gr. Yoff, Dakar.
8/5/99	Lamine Touré. August 5, 1999. Tang apartment, Dakar.
8/12/99	Lamine Touré. August 12, 1999. Tang apartment, Dakar.
8/12/99	Macheikh Mbaye. August 12, 1999. Mbaye residence, HLM5, Dakar.
8/17/99	Lamine Touré. August 17, 1999. Tang apartment, Dakar.

Index

Patricia Tang is Associate Professor of Music at the Massachusetts Institute of Technology. She is a scholar and performer of Senegalese music.